LIVING & WORKING

in Kuala Lumpur

LYNN WITHAM

TIMES BOOKS INTERNATIONAL
Singapore • Kuala Lumpur

In the same series

Argentina	France	Malaysia	Sweden
Australia	Germany	Mauritius	Switzerland
Bolivia	Greece	Mexico	Syria
Borneo	Hong Kong	Morocco	Taiwan
Britain	Hungary	Myanmar	Thailand
Burma	India	Nepal	Turkey
California	Indonesia	Netherlands	UAE
Canada	Iran	Norway	Ukraine
Chile	Ireland	Pakistan	USA
China	Israel	Philippines	USA–The South
Cuba	Italy	Singapore	Venezuela
Czech Republic	Japan	South Africa	Vietnam
Denmark	Korea	Spain	
Egypt	Laos	Sri Lanka	

Living & Working Abroad: Barcelona	A Globe-Trotter's Guide
Living & Working Abroad: Chicago	A Parent's Guide
Living & Working Abroad: Havana	A Student's Guide
Living & Working Abroad: Jakarta	A Traveller's Medical Guide
Living & Working in Kuala Lumpur	A Wife's Guide
Living & Working Abroad: London	Living & Working Abroad
Living & Working Abroad: New York	Working Holidays Abroad
Living & Working Abroad: Paris	
Living & Working Abroad: Rome	

Illustrations by TRIGG

© 2001 Times Media Private Limited

Published by Times Books International
an imprint of Times Media Private Limited
Times Centre, 1 New Industrial Road
Singapore 536196
Tel: (65) 2848844 Fax: (65) 2854871
e-mail: te@tpl.com.sg
Online bookstore: http://www.timesone.com.sg/te

Times Subang
Lot 46, Subang Hi-Tech Industrial Park
Batu Tiga, 40000 Shah Alam
Selangor Darul Ehsan, Malaysia
Tel & Fax: (603) 7363517
e-mail: cchong@tpg.com.my

Printed in Singapore

ISBN 981 232 102 0

CONTENTS

ACKNOWLEDGEMENTS

One of the great pleasures in preparing this book has been meeting the numerous Malaysians and expatriates from 23 countries who so generously gave of their time and energy. Although it is impossible to list all your names here, I am grateful to each and every one of you. My sincere appreciation to the following people for their most valuable contributions and support: Kenneth and Anne Witham, Jaina Ibrahim, Osman bin Hj. Awang, Siti Eshah Hj. Ishak, Asma Abdullah, Dr. A. Baskaran, Henry Bong, Margot and William Carrington, Christine Cheong, Catherine Cook, William Doelger, Mohammad Fallah, Johnathan Griffiths, Alexis Johnson, Kay Jones, Kayvon Karbasioun, T.P. Lim, Shova Loh, Doris Loo, Hojat Moradi, Ulli Muenker, Mahin Nafez, Harun Noordin, Linda Normandeau, Candace Palermo, Violet Phoon, C.K. Puah, George Renwick, Faridah Samsudin, Mohammad Sarlak, Ann Tan, Tan Aun Gim, Alice Thayer, Calvin Yip, and B.D. Zuni.

I also wish to express my gratitude to the people in the following organisations who contributed information and support for the book: Tourism Malaysia, Malaysia Airlines, Sapura Computer Service Centre, Diversitec CSC, Renaissance New World Hotel, MIDA, Automobile Association of Malaysia, Citibank, Bank Negara, JED Realty, Hoon Chin Soon Research, American Embassy, Australian High Commission, British High Commission, American Association of Malaysia, Association of British Women in Malaysia, Association Français de Malaysia, Canadian Women's Association, Canadian Association, Deutsche Women in Kuala Lumpur, Japan Club of Kuala Lumpur, Malaysian Australian New Zealand Association, Scandinavian Society Malaysia, and Russian Cultural Centre.

For contribution of photographs for this book, special thanks to Pucuk Rebung Malaysian Heritage and Style, Snap-ni Snap-tu Studio, Jaina Ibrahim and T.P. Lim. Photographs contributed courtesy of Pucuk Rebung Malaysian Heritage and Style (Suria KLCC, Level 3, Lot 305; Tel: 03-382-0769) were taken by Puah Chin Kok. Photographs contributed courtesy of Snap-ni Snap-tu Studio were taken by Puah Chin Kok and Tan Ee Long (Tel: 603-406-4028; E-mail: puahck@yahoo.com). (These photographs are the sole property of the contributing organisations and photographers and should not be reproduced in any format without their express written permission.)

INTRODUCTION

Selamat datang ke Kuala Lumpur (Welcome to Kuala Lumpur). This capital city of Malaysia is not well known outside Southeast Asia as it is relatively new, relatively small, and seldom in the international news. These are just a few of the factors that contribute to making the city a safe and pleasant place to visit and to live in.

Compared to many capital cities of the world, Kuala Lumpur, commonly referred to as K.L. to its residents, has a short history. It was founded as a shanty town in 1857 when tin mines were established nearby, and gained its status as the capital of Malaysia when the country became independent one hundred years later. The city and surrounding territory in the State of Selangor now serve as the commercial and administrative hub of the country, and are home to more than 4 million people, 1.5 million of whom live in the city itself. Residents are a multi-cultural mix of Malays and other *Bumiputra* (indigenous groups), Chinese, Indians, Eurasians, and foreign workers. This diversity creates a vibrant mixture of sights, sounds, aromas, activities, foods and festivals.

K.L. is a study in contrasts: Islamic mosques, Buddhist temples, Hindu temples, and Christian churches; old colonial shop houses, sleek modern skyscrapers, and the tallest building in the world; polite, reserved, ritualised social interaction and aggressive driving habits; traditional Malay, Indian and Chinese clothes and modern international designer fashions; subtle sounds of the traditional *gamelan* orchestra, localised versions of Arab, Indian and Chinese music, and not-so-subtle sounds of Western rock; tasty hawkers' stalls serving local favourites, Western outlets serving fast foods, and world-class restaurants serving international gourmet cuisine. It is these contrasts that give K.L. its character.

This book is designed to assist you in finding your way and feeling at home in this city of contrasts. Whether you are a visitor or a resident, it can serve as an orientation prior to your arrival and as a reference during your stay. Although the primary focus of the book is Kuala Lumpur, much of the information is applicable to other areas of the country. Every effort has been made to ascertain that the information in this book is accurate. Our apologies if a reference to a bookstore takes you to a coffee shop in this rapidly changing city. Enjoy your stay!

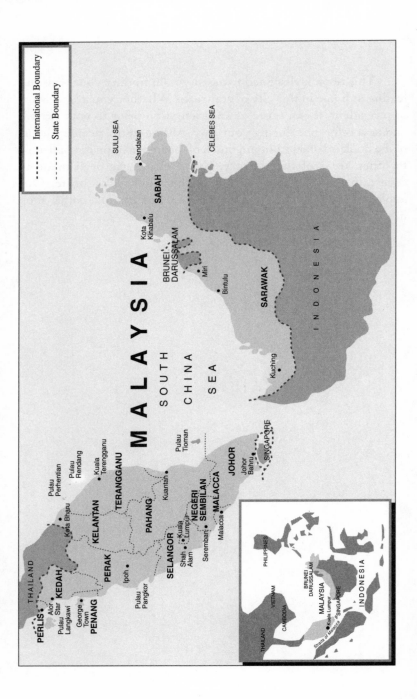

CHAPTER ONE

UNDERSTANDING THE COUNTRY

A GLIMPSE OF HISTORY

The history of Malaysia and the growth of Kuala Lumpur are strongly influenced by the migration of people, the flow of international trade and the spread of religions. Some historical highlights are outlined below. Books such as *Crossroads: A Popular History of Malaysia and Singapore*, by Jim Baker, give a more in-depth look at the history of the country and the city.

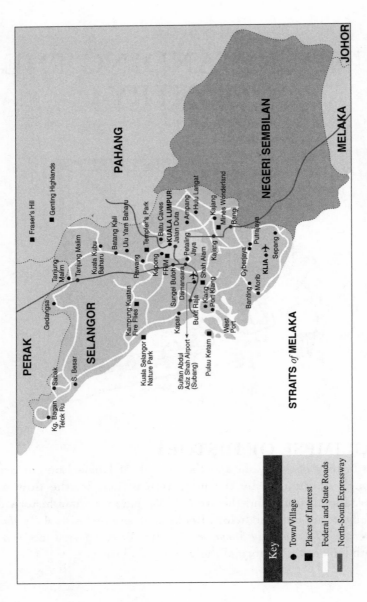

Map of Selangor

Early History

Kuala Lumpur is located in the Klang River Valley near the west coast of Peninsular Malaysia. Archaeological evidence shows that the Klang Valley has been a site of human habitation since Neolithic times, 3,000 to 1,500 years ago. Little is known about the earliest inhabitants of the valley. Among the numerous theories regarding their origins are that they were descendants of people who had migrated to the Malay Peninsula from the Hoabinh area of Indochina or from the southern Chinese province of Yunnan.

Through the centuries, the west coast of the Peninsula, bordered by the Straits of Melaka, attracted traders from far and wide, and their presence influenced the development of the area. In the first century B.C., Indian traders established communities on the west coast and introduced Hinduism. In the early fifteenth century A.D., Arab traders visited the west coast port of Melaka and introduced Islam. The religion spread across the Peninsula after Parameswara (Iskandar Shah), the Sumatran prince who had established the port kingdom in 1403, and other regional leaders converted to Islam.

By the turn of the century, several European countries began vying for control of the lucrative spice trade in Southeast Asia and focused their attention on the strategically located Straits of Melaka and its prospering port. In 1511, the Portuguese captured the port of Melaka. In 1641, the port fell to the Dutch.

It was during this time that the Klang Valley began to grow in importance due to the fertile soil and the valuable tin deposits that were being discovered there. Transport of agricultural produce and tin posed little problem as the Klang River emptied into the Straits of Melaka. The small Klang port became a primary outpost of Melaka and both the Portuguese and the Dutch made unsuccessful attempts to wrest control of the tin trade from the local sultan.

11

British Control

Seeking greater influence in Southeast Asia and needing a safe harbour for its ships, in 1786 the British East India Company secured rights to Penang Island and in 1800 gained control of Province Wellesley, the mainland territory adjacent to the island. In 1819, Sir Stamford Raffles purchased the island of Singapore from the Sultan of Johor. Trading posts were subsequently established in both locations and began to lure trade away from the port at Melaka. By 1824, the British convinced the Dutch to relinquish control of the port. Two years later, the British formed a colony, called the Straits Settlements, composed of Singapore, Melaka, Penang Island and Province Wellesley.

The British saw the benefits of investing in the Straits Settlements and in the inland territories belonging to the local sultans. When world demand for tin soared, they opened more tin mines in two of those territories, Selangor and Perak, leading to the growth of several small towns. Due to a shortage of labourers, the British imported large numbers of Chinese to work in the expanding tin industry. In 1857, a group of Chinese tin miners, supported by Raja Abdullah, the ruler of Klang, discovered rich new tin deposits in Selangor and established a small shanty town known as Kuala Lumpur (which literally means "muddy estuary") along the confluence of the Klang and Gombak Rivers. As miners, merchants and Malay princes vied for their piece of the wealth, the town became a thriving commercial centre for the tin trade. Soon the strong influence of the tin mine chiefs upset the local balance of power, and in 1860 civil war broke out between Chinese tin miners and local noblemen. The British Army intervened in 1874 and forced the local sultan to accept a British Resident Advisor. In 1880, the British shifted their administrative centre from Klang to Kuala Lumpur.

British influence in the area continued to grow, and in 1896, the British sent advisors to the Malay states of Selangor, Pahang,

Perak and Negeri Sembilan and formed a federation known as the Federated Malay States. Bustling Kuala Lumpur was chosen as the capital. In 1909, four more states (Perlis, Kedah, Kelantan and Terengganu) came under British control, followed by Johor in 1914. These became known as the Unfederated Malay States.

Social Changes

Between 1911 and 1931 large numbers of Chinese workers were imported to support the growing tin industry and an influx of Indian labourers followed the establishment of the rubber industry in 1910 and the palm oil industry in 1917. The immigrants differed from ethnic Malays in language, culture, religion and appearance. Most of the early immigrants entered Malaya without their families and with the intention of returning home after they had earned a good sum of money.

In the 1920s, as a reaction to domination by foreign powers and to the presence of large numbers of alien Chinese and Indians, a movement which became both anti-colonial and nationalistic in nature spread among the Malays. Fearing they would soon be outnumbered by immigrants, the Malays formed state-based associations designed to protect their rights.

Independence

By the 1930s, many Chinese and Indians began to regard Malaya as their permanent home and loyalties to their homelands diminished. This was particularly true for Chinese in the Straits Settlements, many of whom had been born in Malaya and who had gained a strong foothold in commerce as small shopkeepers, retail traders and middlemen in trade between the Malays and foreigners. The Chinese and the Indians proposed the idea of making Malaya an independent country belonging to all its resident races. Both groups formed political associations and organised campaigns for citizenship and equal rights.

The movement was temporarily interrupted between 1941 and 1945 when Japan occupied Malaya and Singapore. After the war ended, control of the area returned to the British, and Malays, Indians and Chinese each formed political parties. In 1948, the British formed the Federation of Malaya, consisting of all Malayan states headed by a British High Commissioner; the capital was Kuala Lumpur. In 1955, in a move to consolidate influence against the British and push for independence, the Alliance Party, combining the Malay, Indian and Chinese political parties, was formed. Independence from the United Kingdom was granted on August 31, 1957.

The New Nation

The new Federation chose to become a member of the British Commonwealth. On July 9, 1963, the eleven Malay states joined with Singapore to form the Federation of Malaysia. Later that year, the North Borneo states of Sabah and Sarawak voted to join the Federation. Tunku Abdul Rahman became the first Prime Minister. Singapore withdrew from the Federation on August 9, 1965, to become an independent republic within the Commonwealth. Kuala Lumpur remained the capital of the Federation and also the capital of the State of Selangor. On February 1, 1974, the Sultan of Selangor ceded the territory of Kuala Lumpur to the Federal Government and moved the capital of the State of Selangor to Shah Alam, a suburb of Kuala Lumpur.

After independence, the government faced the challenge of governing a multi-cultural population. In 1969, racial tensions erupted in bloody riots after elections and a state of emergency lasting until 1971 was declared. A Department of National Unity was established to formulate a national ideology. Islam was designated the official religion; Malay culture was chosen to form the base of a new national culture; Malay rulers were allowed to remain national symbols of sovereignty; and the Malay language was selected to be the official national language and to replace English as the language of business and the medium of instruction in the schools. Because these new guidelines were potentially controversial, in 1971 a Constitutional Amendment made seditious the questioning or public debate of sensitive issues regarding the national language, the rights of citizenship, the sovereignty of the monarchy and the special position of Malays and other *Bumiputra* (indigenous peoples). This amendment is still in effect.

Government Policies

In 1971, the Government implemented the twenty-year New Economic Policy (NEP) designed to eradicate poverty regardless of race by raising income levels, to eliminate the identification of race with economic function, and to restructure the society so as to reduce the economic imbalance that existed among the racial groups. The NEP gave qualified Malays and other *Bumiputra* (whose per capita income and standard of living had remained below that of the Chinese) special privileges intended to raise their economic standing. In 1991, the NEP was replaced by the National Development Policy (NDP), which is essentially a continuation of the NEP.

A Vision for the Future

To usher in the last decade of the century, in 1991 the Government announced Vision 2020 (*Wawasan 2020*), a goal for the country to reach developed-nation status by the year 2020. Achievement of this goal would require the country to double its income every ten years and to sustain a minimum of 7% growth. Vision 2020 has become a motivating factor and source of pride for the people of Malaysia, and they are adopting a "can do" (*"Malaysia boleh!"*) attitude toward it.

GOVERNMENT

Heads of Government and State

Malaysia is governed by a parliamentary democracy with a constitutional monarchy. The Head of Government is the Prime Minister (known as *Perdana Menteri* in Malay) who presides over the Cabinet and is the leader of the political party or coalition that wins the most seats in Parliament. The country's first Prime Minister, Tunku Abdul Rahman, was followed by Tun Abdul Razak in 1970 and by Tun Hussein Onn in 1976. The present Prime Minister, Dato' Seri Dr. Mahathir Mohamad, took office in 1981.

The Head of State is the Yang di-Pertuan Agong, often referred to as the King. He performs a variety of constitutional duties and is the leader of Islam in his own state and in the states of Penang, Melaka, Sabah and the Federal Territory. The eleventh and present King, (Seri Paduka Baginda Yang di-Pertuan Agong XI) who took office in 1999, is Sultan Salahuddin Abdul Aziz Shah, the Sultan of Selangor.

The Monarchy

Malaysia's monarchy is unique in that it is an elected monarchy. When the Federation of Malaya was established in 1957, nine of the Federation's eleven states had their own ruling Sultan. Selection of one Sultan as permanent Head of State would have created power struggles among the others. The solution chosen was to elect one ruler every five years to hold the office of King or Yang di-Pertuan Agong (One Who Is Chief Among The Most Prominent). The King acts on the advice of the Parliament to appoint Governors as heads of Penang, Melaka, Sabah and Sarawak, the four states that do not have hereditary rulers.

The Cabinet and Parliament

Cabinet Ministers are appointed by the King, on the advice of the Prime Minister, from among ruling party members of the Parliament. The bicameral Parliament consists of a Senate (*Dewan Negara*) and a House of Representatives (*Dewan Rayakat*). The Senate has 70 members, referred to as Senators, who serve terms of up to six years. Two from each state are selected by the state legislatures and the remainder are appointed by the King. The House of Representatives is allowed a total of 193 members, one for each constituency. (These numbers increase periodically as the population increases and the electoral boundaries of Malaysian states are redefined.) Referred to as MPs, members of the House are selected in general elections held at least every five years. Each state government consists of a Cabinet and a one-chamber Legislature. The right to vote is granted to all citizens aged twenty-one or over who are judged to be of sound mind.

POLITICAL PARTIES

The Malaysian Government comprises representatives elected from political parties that are members of the ruling coalition, as well as from parties that are not members. Loyalty to the country's 36 registered political parties is based primarily on racial identification rather than on class identification.

The ruling coalition is the Barisan Nasional or National Front, a multi-racial coalition made up at present of fourteen political parties. Barisan Nasional evolved from the Alliance Party which took control at the time of Independence in 1957. The largest political party in the coalition is the United Malays National Organisation (UMNO), pronounced "Am-no") which represents the majority of Malays, especially those who are urban, educated and relatively affluent. UMNO's most influential coalition partners in the National Front are the Malaysian Chinese Association (MCA) and the Malaysian Indian Congress (MIC). Other parties

17

that joined the coalition during the 1970s are the Gerakan, a party strong in Penang and predominantly supported by urban Chinese; the Sarawak-based SUPP, which espouses a multi-racial philosophy despite its predominantly Chinese membership; and SNAP, a multi-racial party controlled predominantly by the Iban, Sarawak's largest indigenous community.

The major opposition parties to the Barisan National coalition are the Democratic Action Party (DAP), the Parti Islam Sa Malaya (or Pan Malaysian Islamic Party) known as PAS, and the newer Parti Keadilan Negara (KeAdilan). PAS and KeAdilan are now direct rivals for the UMNO Malay vote. These opposition parties have an electoral hold in both Peninsular and East Malaysia.

THE LEGAL SYSTEM

The Malaysian legal system is modelled on English common law, but has been modified to take into account certain civil laws and Islamic laws (known as *syariah*). Malaysian states, especially those with large Muslim populations, have established active *Syariah* courts that have jurisdiction over Muslim residents. The Malaysian Supreme Court, comparable to the United States Supreme Court, has exclusive jurisdiction in constitutional matters, in civil and criminal cases, and in disputes between the states or between the states and the Federal Government. The High Court of Peninsular Malaysia and the High Court of Sabah and Sarawak fall under the jurisdiction of the Supreme Court. In Malaysia, litigation is used to resolve civil disputes much less frequently than in many countries in the West.

CHAPTER TWO

EXPLORING THE CITY

THE FEDERAL TERRITORY OF KUALA LUMPUR

Malaysia's capital city and surrounding areas offer much to entertain visitors and residents. Books that give a comprehensive overview of the sites are the *Guide to Kuala Lumpur and the Klang Valley* and the *Visitors' Guide to Malaysia*. For information about current events such as concerts, nightlife, exhibitions and conferences, consult **Tourism Malaysia** (Tel: 03-441-1295) and the tourist publications such as *Day & Night, Kuala Lumpur Now!* and *Vision Kuala Lumpur*. Also check the **K.L. Homepage** on the Internet (www.mnet.com.my/klonline/www/klomain.htm).

RAIL-BASED TRANSPORT NETWORK IN THE KLANG VALLEY

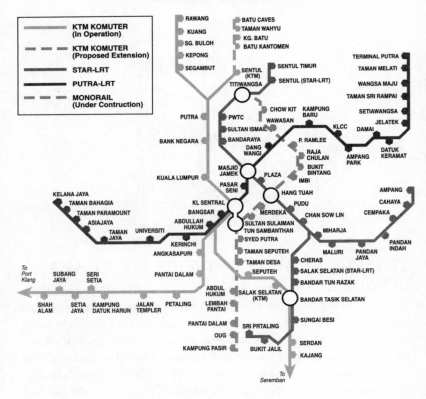

Transit Map of K.L. and Klang Valley, courtesy of "The Star", Malaysia.

The Geographical Landscape

The Federal Territory of Kuala Lumpur (known in Malay as *Wilayah Persekutuan*) is located in the Klang River Valley in the Malaysian State of Selangor, and is about one hour from Port Klang, the country's largest port. The city proper covers an area of 244 square kilometres (94 square miles).

The climate in Kuala Lumpur, as in the rest of Malaysia, is tropical and monsoonal. Temperatures range from 33°C (91°F) or higher during the afternoon and occasionally drop to a refreshing 23°C (70°F) in the early morning. Humidity averages 80%. There are no distinct seasons, only periods of more rain and less rain. Wind systems originating in the Indian Ocean and South China Sea bring monsoons to the K.L. area from November to December. Sudden downpours called *sumatras* and short-lived thunderstorms, often accompanied by raging winds and followed by rapid clearing and bright sunshine, are common in Kuala Lumpur in March, April and October. While scattered flooding plagues parts of K.L. and other areas during heavy rains, the country remains untouched by major disturbances such as earthquakes or tidal waves.

The Architectural Landscape

Literally translated, Kuala Lumpur means "muddy estuary," a label the city has long outgrown. K.L., as it is commonly known to residents, is a bustling, prosperous and modern city. It now serves as the country's centre of commerce, industry, administration and communications, and is rapidly becoming a leading business and convention city in the fast-developing Pacific Basin. On the outskirts of this modern city stand reminders of an earlier era—the immense tin mines, rubber plantations and oil palm estates that form the backbone of the nation's economy. In recent years, many of the verdant rubber plantations have been cleared to make way for housing, commercial centres and highways. Noting that the city is built on the site of former tin mines, local residents sometimes express concern about the stability of the ever-increasing number of high-rise buildings.

Kuala Lumpur boasts an unpredictable mixture of architectural styles including half-timbered Tudor, turreted Moorish, glassy Western and sleek modern Islamic, as well as intricately carved Malay, and ornate multi-coloured Chinese and southern Indian. To ride through K.L. is to suddenly realise you have entered unfamiliar territory.

Historical Landmarks

Some of the city's most striking landmarks were constructed at the turn of the century under the direction of the British Resident Sir Frank Swettenham. The **Sultan Abdul Samad Building** on Jalan Raja was built between 1894 and 1897 in a style inspired by British Edwardian and Northern Indian Mughal architecture. Formerly known as the State Secretariat, it is one of the most photographed buildings in the country. The clock tower is a city landmark and when the Japanese occupied the country in 1942 during World War II, they purposely advanced the clock by two hours to correspond with Tokyo time. Among the other impressive buildings are the **Railway Station** and the adjacent **Railway Administration Headquarters** on Jalan Hishamuddin. Constructed in 1911 in Moorish design, they feature a fascinating combination of domes, spires, towers and elaborate decoration.

Just across the *padang*, or cricket field, sits the stately **Royal Selangor Club**. It was built in 1884 and is said to have been fondly nicknamed the "Spotted Dog" after the large dalmatian dogs who stood guard at the club whenever the wife of one of the British founders went inside. With its black half-timbering, the building is a fine example of Tudor-style architecture. During the colonial era, the club was the favoured recreational spot for the British elite. Today it is still an exclusive club, and a popular place for rugby and cricket matches and lengthy discussions of business and politics. Another distinctive landmark is the **National Palace** (*Istana Negara*), located on a hill near the Railway Station. Constructed in 1928 by a local millionaire, it is the official residence of the ruling King, the Yang di-Pertuan Agong, and the Queen, the Raja Permaisuri Agong.

Photo by Lynn Witham

Kuala Lumpur ~ The Past and the Present

Modern Landmarks

Notable modern additions to the city's architectural landscape are the Dayabumi Complex, the Putra World Trade Centre, the K.L. Tower and the Petronas Twin Towers. Part of a project to create a self-sufficient city within a city, the **Dayabumi Complex** houses the Main General Post Office and the Kuala Lumpur Commodity and Stock Exchanges (KLSE), as well as commercial outlets and

23

Photo by Lynn Witham

Petronas Twin Towers

private and government offices. The **Putra World Trade Centre**, located just across the street from a large shopping complex, **The Mall**, houses offices, convention and exhibition facilities, the luxurious Pan Pacific Hotel and the head office of Tourism Malaysia. The **Menara Kuala Lumpur** (K.L. Tower) on Bukit Nanas is the third tallest tower in the world and a good vantage point from which to view the surrounding area. At 451.9 metres, the impressive **Petronas Twin Towers** for a time has the distinction of being the tallest building in the world. The towers are part of the prestigious City Centre complex which also includes the shopping mall known as **Suria KLCC**, the Philharmonic Concert Hall, and a beautiful lake garden. When you visit the complex, you might enjoy relaxing at one of the cafés along the lake and then taking a walk through the park, savouring the natural and man-made beauty of your surroundings.

Museums and Galleries

To gain insight into Malaysia's culture and history, you can visit several museums. The **National Museum** (*Muzium Negara*) on Jalan Damansara is a Malay-style building with high sloping roofs and enormous mosaic murals. It features well-designed exhibits of traditional Malaysian arts, crafts, birds, mammals and weapons, as well as displays of the country's major economic activities. Exhibitions of a Melakan Chinese house, a Malay *kampung* (village) and an aboriginal village provide insight into daily life in the country. The **National Museum of History** on Jalan Raja showcases the richness of the historical heritage of the various races in Malaysia. The **Islamic Arts Museum** on Jalan Lembah Perdana has exhibits of Islamic art from Malaysia and many other areas of the world.

Museums and galleries also offer examples of Malaysia's varied arts and crafts. The **National Art Gallery** on Jalan Hishamuddin houses collections of Malaysian artists and periodically shows foreign works. The **Crafts Museum,** located in the Komplex Budaya Kraf on Jalan Raja Chulan, features changing exhibits of local and regional crafts. The **Textile Museum** in the Sultan Abdul Samad Building on Jalan Raja displays Malaysian-made textiles from throughout the country. Finally, the **Pucuk Rebung Malaysia Heritage and Style** shop and gallery in Suria KLCC offers a closer look at Malaysia's heritage of arts and crafts.

Places of Worship

The variety of places of worship scattered throughout Kuala Lumpur is testimony to the multi-cultural and multi-religious composition of the city's population. The most important religious site for the city's Muslims is the **National Mosque** (*Masjid Negara*), a modern Islamic-style structure with a cool marble interior and a carpeted main hall that can accommodate 8,000 worshippers. Completed in 1965, the mosque is surrounded by reflecting pools, sparkling fountains and vast manicured lawns, and is dominated by a dome representing a star with eighteen points symbolizing the country's thirteen states and the Five Pillars of Islam. The faithful are called to prayer five times a day from a minaret that towers above the mosque. Non-Muslim visitors are welcome except during prayer times and on Fridays.

The Chinese community is served by many temples. The oldest, **See Yeah,** located off Jalan Bandar, is dedicated to the patron saint of tin miners, Sen Ta. One of the most ornate, **Chan See Chu Yuen**, on Jalan Petaling Jaya, is used for religious ceremonies and meetings of Chinese community members. Constructed in 1906 in typical Chinese fashion, it is decorated with wooden carvings in the interior and glazed ceramic sculptures on the facade.

An important religious gathering place for Malaysia's Hindu community is the impressive limestone formation, known as the **Batu Caves**, located in Selangor, just outside the city. During the Hindu festival of Thaipusam in late January or early February, devotees carry *kavadi* (large decorated steel arches) up the 272 steps to the cave entrance. In addition to sparkling stalagmites, the cave contains a Hindu temple dedicated to Lord Subramaniam and an Art Museum displaying elaborately carved and painted statues of prominent figures in Hindu mythology. The **Sri Mahahariamman** temple, one of the largest and most ornate temples in the country, was built in 1873 and is decorated with Spanish and Italian gold, ceramic tiles and precious stones.

Relaxation Spots

The most popular relaxation spots for urban dwellers are the beautiful **Park at KLCC** (Petronas Twin Towers) and the **Lake Gardens** (Taman Tasik Perdana) off Jalan Parlimen. The latter is a lush 160-acre park where people go for an enjoyable picnic, a refreshing run, a leisurely stroll or a relaxing boat ride. Located within the gardens are the modern white **Parliament House** (an eighteen-storey structure built in 1962 to house the Senate and House of Representatives), the **War Memorial** (a bronze sculpture honouring those who died in Malaysia's twelve-year struggle against communist insurgents) and the **National Planetarium.**

Sports Venues

Focal points of the city's sporting events are the **Selangor Turf Club**, the site of heated weekend race course betting, and the **National Sports Complex** at Bukit Komenwel near Cheras. The latter was built for the Commonwealth Games in 1998 and is part of a sports township with residences, schools, shopping complexes, a hotel, exhibition halls, entertainment centres and a training centre for all kinds of sports.

Commercial Hubs

Among the busiest of commercial sections in the city, and one of the oldest, is **Chinatown**, located in the area bordered by Jalan Sultan, Jalan Bandar and Jalan Petaling. Here you can buy fruit, flowers, herbs, gold, casual clothes, "genuine copy" designer bags and watches, ceremonial joss sticks, colourful caged birds and a myriad of other items. Along the side streets you can sample tasty Chinese snacks and have your fortune told. At night Jalan Petaling is closed to traffic and the whole street becomes a lively market. Within walking distance is the **Central Market**. Built on the former site of a wet market, it is now a popular place to shop for regional crafts.

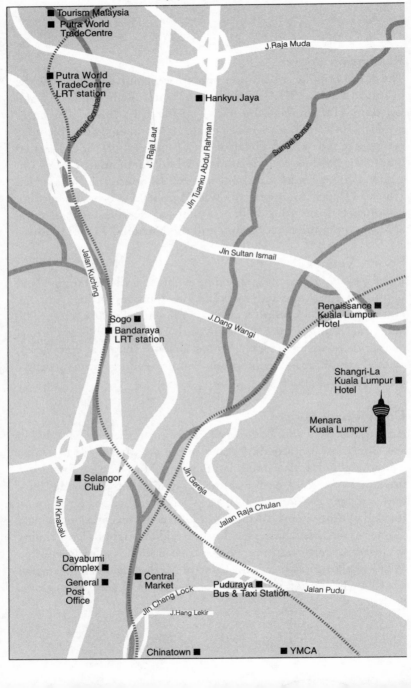

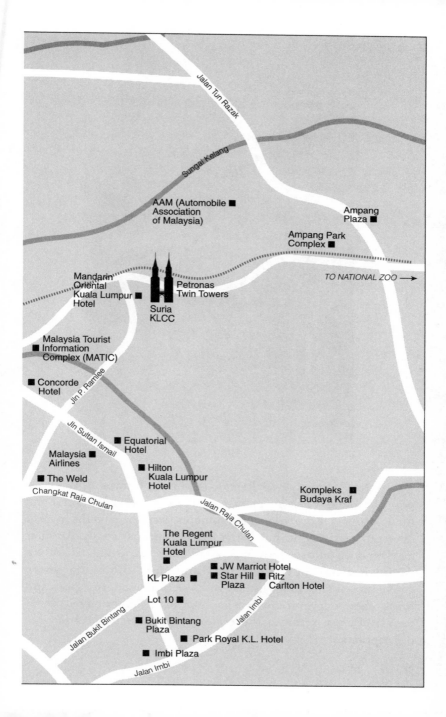

Photo by Lynn Witham

Chinatown

Intrepid shoppers will enjoy exploring **Kampung Bahru**, a popular Malay open-air market selling clothes, handicrafts and food products. Located just ten minutes from the city, the market operates every night, but is the liveliest on Saturdays. Another market, open only on Saturday nights, takes place on Jalan Tunku Abdul Rahman in front of the Globe Silk Store. For more conventional shopping, there are numerous modern "glass and brass" shopping centres which have sprung up in the city in recent years. (Please refer to the chapter on *Making Purchases* for descriptions.)

Meeting Spots

In addition to Suria KLCC mentioned above, another popular meeting spot for expatriates, tourists and Malaysians is the area known as the **Golden Triangle** near the corner of Jalan Bukit Bintang and Jalan Sultan Ismail. It is the site of several hotels, department stores, shopping complexes and two streets lined with outdoor cafés. A future meeting spot will be **KL Sentral** complex in Brickfields, adjacent to the Lake Gardens. Scheduled for completion by the year 2007, this business and commercial district will include offices, hotels, service apartments, condominiums, retail outlets, sports and cultural facilities, as well as the new KL Sentral Railway Station.

PROMINENT TOWNS

Becoming geographically oriented to K.L. and its suburbs can take some time. Listed below are the towns that you will hear and read about most frequently and descriptions of towns in which the largest numbers of expatriates live.

North: Batu Caves, Gombak, Rawang
Far Northeast: Fraser's Hill, Genting Highlands
East: Ampang, Ulu Klang, Ukay Heights
South: Kajang, Country Heights, Bangi
Far South: Putrajaya, Cyberjaya
Southwest: Petaling Jaya, Bandar, Sungai Way, Subang Jaya
Far Southwest: Shah Alam, Port Klang
West: Bangsar, Taman Tun Dr Ismail, Damansara
Northwest: Bandar Utama, Kepong, Mont Kiara

Ampang and Ulu Klang

Located to the east of K.L., Ampang and Ulu Klang (also Hulu Kelang) is a rapidly growing, up-market, green area, with luxury condos and large houses. It is the site of many embassies, international schools (including the International School of Kuala Lumpur) and the National Zoo and Aquarium.

Petaling Jaya and Bangsar

Located about ten kilometres southwest of K.L., Petaling Jaya is the largest satellite town in Malaysia. Commonly known as P.J., the town has a population of approximately 300,000 and serves as a pleasant residential community for many people who work in Kuala Lumpur. It is divided into 25 planned sections, the most well known being **Damansara Utama** (a centre for shops, restaurants and nightclubs), **Bandar Utama** (site of the large One Utama shopping mall), and **Section 2** (SS2) (site of a lively *pasar malam* (night market). Petaling Jaya has ample cinemas, shopping centres, recreation parks (including the popular **Sunway Lagoon**) and medical facilities, and has become an industrial centre and the site of nearly 200 factories.

Between P.J. and K.L. lies **Bangsar**, an up-scale residential community popular among middle-class Malaysians and expatriates alike. It features luxury bungalows, condos and townhouses surrounded by lush greenery, and lively venues for shopping, eating and dancing. The centres of the action are the Telawi area in Bangsar Baru, the Bangsar Shopping Centre, and the Saturday night market. Even if you don't live here, you'll enjoy periodic visits.

Shah Alam

Shah Alam, the capital of Selangor, is a satellite city located about thirty kilometres west of K.L. Founded in 1963 as an industrial zone, Shah Alam now comprises about 10,000 acres and is built on the site of former rubber and palm oil estates. Shah Alam's plan to attract capital-intensive industries that have minimal pollution and are research and development oriented has been successful, and these industries now employ over 50,000 people. The city plan follows the "Neighbourhood Concept," whereby every section is a unit comprised of homes, a commercial centre, community centre, school, mosque, recreation area and other public amenities. The town is served by the KTM train and will soon have LRT/Monorail service.

Attractions in the town include the **Shah Alam Lake Gardens**, a pleasant place for picnics and boat rides, and the **Wet-World Water Theme Park**, with a 222-metre-long watercoaster. The **Shah Alam Museum** houses folk arts and crafts and has an aviary open to the public. The **Sultan Salahuddin Abdul Aziz Shah Mosque**, known as the "Blue Mosque," is the largest in the country and can accommodate 24,000 people. Located on the

Photo by Lynn Witham

The "Blue Mosque" in Shah Alam

outskirts of town is the **Malaysia Agricultural Park** which features orchid, cactus, bamboo, mushroom and ornamental gardens, a fishing lake, and hiking trails. Visitors can rent bicycles and camp or rent chalets for overnight stays.

Putrajaya and Cyberjaya

Putrajaya is a new satellite garden city that is being constructed in Selangor, about 25 kilometres south of K.L. The Federal Government is in the process of transferring its administrative functions (except for the foreign affairs and trade ministries) to Putrajaya in order to relieve the strain on K.L.'s infrastructure and to allow it to continue growth as a commercial hub.

Adjacent to Putrajaya is Cyberjaya, a carefully planned showcase city that the Government hopes will serve as a model for the country's use of advanced technology. Multi-national high tech companies and leading local multimedia companies are being

Photo by Lynn Witham

Bangunan Perdana Putra (Prime Minister's Department), Putrajaya

encouraged to locate there to undertake remote manufacturing as well as to introduce high value-added IT goods and services. Cyberjaya is a dedicated "intelligent" city housing an information technology university. It will serve as the centre of the new **Multimedia Super Corridor** (MSC), a 15-by-50-kilometre corridor between the K.L. City Centre and the new K.L. International Airport (KLIA) in Sepang. One of Malaysia's dreams is to develop the MSC into the information technology hub for the country and perhaps eventually for Southeast Asia.

34

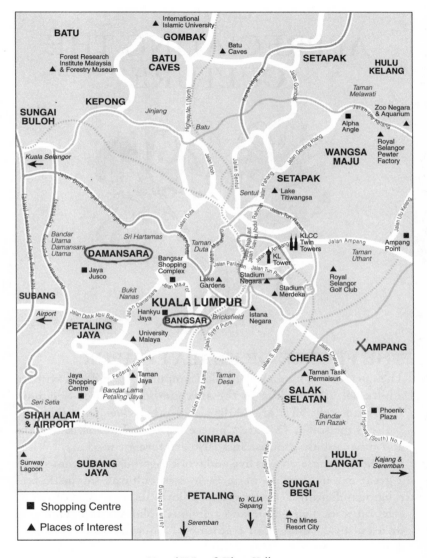

Map of K.L. and Klang Valley

APPRECIATING THE CULTURE

THE PEOPLE OF KUALA LUMPUR

The current population of Kuala Lumpur is 1.5 million, with an additional 2.86 million in the surrounding State of Selangor. Approximately 36% are Malays and other *Bumiputra* (literally "sons of the soil"), 42% are Chinese, 12% are Indians, Eurasians and other ethnic groups, and 10% are foreign workers. While members of these groups live and work together harmoniously, to a great extent they maintain their own cultural, linguistic and religious identities. Each group follows its own way of dress, celebrates its own ethnic and religious holidays, and retains its own cultural values and traditions. This diversity creates a dynamic mixture of sights, sounds and aromas in the city.

MALAYS

While Malays and other *Bumiputra* form just over one-third of the population in K.L., they account for approximately 58% of the country's total population. They are believed to be descendants of people who migrated to the Peninsula from Southern China around 300 B.C. Virtually all are, to various extents, followers of the Sunnite branch of Islam that was introduced to the Malayan Peninsula and several islands of Indonesia by Indian traders some 600 years ago. Malays follow a strong tradition of *budi*, a code of behaviour that promotes respect and obedience towards parents and elders.

During colonial days, most Malays lived in rural areas and engaged in fishing, subsistence agriculture, rice cultivation and rubber production, while an educated elite held administrative positions in the Government. Since independence, Malays have gained greater access to education and have migrated to urban areas. They now fill the majority of positions in the public sector, and with the help of Government incentives are becoming more active in the private sector. They are involved in business at all levels and are becoming well represented in all the professions. Their average income still lags behind that of the Chinese, and the economic disparity between the two groups is of continuing concern to the Malaysian Government.

Malay Celebrations

Malays and other Muslims follow the **lunar calendar** which is based on twelve lunar months totalling 354 days. No compensation is made for the eleven days lost annually, so festivals move forward from year to year. The two most important festivals are **Hari Raya Puasa** (*Aidil Fitri*), marking the end of the fasting month of Ramadhan, and **Hari Raya Haji** (*Aidil Adha*), commemorating the end of the pilgrimage to Mecca. The **Birthday of the Prophet Muhammad** (*Maulud Nabi*) is also cause for yearly celebration.

In addition, family celebrations are held to honour engagement, marriage, childbirth, circumcision of boys and piercing of the ear lobes of girls. Most celebrations are accompanied by feasts (*kenduri*) and Islamic prayers (*doa*).

Malay Dress

For daily dress, Malay men wear either Western clothes, the traditional *baju Melayu* (loose trousers and a cotton shirt), or what is locally referred to as a lounge suit (matching trousers and short-sleeved shirt). On ceremonial occasions, men often wear a loose shirt (*baju*), long trousers with a sarong wrapped around the waist and a hat called a *songkok*. The *songkok* may be worn indoors and during meals, and is often worn to work, especially on Friday, the Muslim holy day.

Photo by Jaina Ibrahim

Malays in Religious Attire

Photo by Jaina Ibrahim

Malay Ladies, Jalan Mesjid India

Malay women wear either Western clothes or Malay clothes as daily dress. The latter consist of a loose-fitting, long-sleeved tunic and a matching floor-length skirt (*baju kurung*), or a tight-fitting blouse and a sarong (*baju kebaya*). For ceremonial dress, women normally wear the *baju kurung*. Some religiously conservative women and older girls wear a white, black (or other solid colour) head covering (*mini-telekung*) to hide their hair from view; some simply wear a scarf (*tudung*).

Malay Names

Most Malays do not have family surnames that are passed on through the generations. Instead, children use their father's name connected to their given name with the Arabic word *bin* meaning "son of," or *binti* meaning "daughter of". The son of Ahmad bin

39

Osman, for example, could be Awang bin Ahmad, and his son could be Muhammad bin Awang. The daughter of Ahmad bin Osman could be Siti binti Ahmad. Sometimes the words *bin* and *binti* are omitted.

Ahmad bin Osman would be addressed by friends as Ahmad, by acquaintances as Encik Ahmad, and by foreigners as Encik Ahmad or Mr. Ahmad. His unmarried daughter, Siti binti Ahmad, would be addressed by friends as Siti, by acquaintances as Cik Siti, and by foreigners as Cik Siti, or Miss or Ms. Siti.

Malay women usually retain their maiden names after they marry. If Siti binti Ahmad is married to Hassan bin Abdul, Malays will call her Puan Siti or Puan Siti Ahmad and foreigners may call her the same or Mrs. Siti, Mrs. Siti Ahmad or Mrs. Siti Hassan Abdul.

Malay Muslims may attach certain titles to their names. *Syed* is both a male name and a title that signifies direct blood descent from the Prophet Muhammad; *Sharifah* is the female equivalent. Men who have made the pilgrimage to Mecca are accorded the title *Haji*, and women the title *Hajah*. A variety of honorary titles may be affixed to Malay and other Malaysian names. Many of these are discussed in the section on Religious and Official Titles in the chapter on *Joining the Workforce*.

The Malay Language
The national language of Malaysia and the mother tongue of the Malays is Malay or *Bahasa Malaysia*. The language is similar to the Indonesian language and together the two languages have about 100 million speakers. Malay contains many words of Sanskrit, Arabic and Persian origin. Modern Malay is written using two distinct writing systems: Rumi (romanised script, like English) and Jawi (Arabic script with some letters added).

Traditional Malay literature was influenced by Hindu epics and Javanese adventure tales, and later by romantic folk tales from Persia and Muslim India. The most important original work, *Sejarah Melayu (Malay Annals)*, described life in early 16th century Melaka. Modern Malay literature includes proverbs, *pantun* (rhyming couplet), folk tales and fairy tales that have been passed orally through several generations.

Photo courtesy of Pucuk Rebung

Batik on silk from HRH the Raja Perumpuan of Kelantan's Batik Atelier, contemporary, Malay, Kelantan.

CHINESE

About 42% of the population of K.L. and 24% of the total population of Malaysia is Chinese in origin. Malaysian Chinese can trace their heritage to several different provinces in China; the largest provincial groups are Cantonese, Hokkien, Hakka and Teochew. Most speak one or more Chinese dialects; those educated in Chinese schools also speak and write Mandarin.

The majority of Chinese practise a religion that is a combination of beliefs and rituals derived not only from Buddhism, but from the traditional Chinese philosophical systems of Taoism and Confucianism. Many different forms of Buddhism are practised in Malaysia. A small number of Malaysian Chinese have converted to Islam or Christianity.

Since Independence, some Malaysian Chinese who had the financial means have emigrated either temporarily or permanently to other countries in search of better job opportunities and a more cosmopolitan lifestyle. As the economy in Malaysia has grown, some people have returned.

A unique group of Chinese are the **Baba Chinese**, descendants of the earliest male immigrants who migrated from the villages of Fukien province in China and married the daughters of Buginese and Minangkabau traders who had migrated from Indonesia to the Malay Peninsula. The Baba, who lived primarily in Melaka (Malacca), adopted many local customs and developed

Photo courtesy of Pucuk Rebung

Kamcheng, polychromed ware of famille rose type, commissioned by wealthy Peranakans

a dialect that was a mixture of Hokkien, Buginese, Minangkabau and Malay. During the period of British Rule, some Baba children attended English-medium schools and adopted Christianity. The culture of the people became known as Peranakan. (When you visit Melaka, be sure to tour the Baba Nyonya Heritage House.)

Chinese Celebrations

In addition to celebrating religious occasions, Chinese celebrate family and ethnic festivals. Festival dates follow the **lunar calendar** and vary from year to year. The festival in which all Chinese participate is **Chinese New Year**, which marks the beginning of the lunar year. Festivities last for fifteen days and require advance preparations such as cleaning the home, hanging red banners, and paying all debts. In the fourth lunar month, on the occasion of **Cheng Beng** (Qing Ming), Chinese clean and repair the graves of their ancestors and leave offerings to appease the local God of the Soil.

The seventh lunar month is the **Month of the Hungry Ghosts**, during which many Chinese believe that the souls of their deceased ancestors are freed to roam the world of the living. People recite special prayers and make offerings of food and paper clothing in an effort to keep the souls happy and to prevent them from interfering with the lives of the living. On the fifteenth day of the eighth lunar month, Chinese celebrate a harvest festival known as the **Moon Cake Festival**.

Chinese Dress

Most Chinese men wear Western-style attire; batik shirts are also popular. Many Chinese women wear Western-style dress; some wear Malay-style, long-sleeved tunics and long skirts (*baju kurung*); some wear the traditional Chinese jacket and trousers (*samfoo*). On ceremonial occasions, women sometimes wear the *cheongsam*, a short-sleeved, close-fitting, floor-length dress with a high collar

43

and a slit up one side of the skirt. For everyday dress they may wear a shorter version of the *cheongsam*.

Chinese Names

When Chinese write their names, the order is usually surname first, followed by the middle name and the given name. Some Chinese men prefer to be called by their surname. Thus, Tan Chong Khoon is called Mr. Tan by acquaintances and Chong Khoon, C.K. or Tan by friends and business associates.

A Chinese woman may keep her maiden name after she marries or may use her husband's name. Thus, Leong Yoke Chu, the wife of Tan Chong Khoon, could be called Madam Leong or Mrs. Tan. Her friends will call her Yoke Chu.

Some Chinese, especially Christian Chinese, have English given names, and write their surname after their given name.

INDIANS

Approximately 7% of the population of Kuala Lumpur, 17% of the population of Selangor, and 7% of the total population is Indian in ethnic origin. Most Malaysian Indians are descendants of Indians, Sri Lankans and Pakistanis who came to Malaysia at the turn of the twentieth century to work as civil servants in the British colonial government, or as labourers on the rubber plantations or in the Public Works Department. Today, Indians work in business, agriculture and Government service, and are well represented in law and medicine.

The majority of Malaysian Indians speak Tamil; others speak Urdu, Hindi, Telegu, Punjabi, Sinhalese, Gujerati or Malayalam. Some have grown up speaking English at home and have been educated in English.

Most Malaysian Indians follow the Hindu religion, but about 20% are Sikhs, Muslims or Christians; for many Indians, religious teachings are mixed with folk customs and beliefs. In recent years, Malaysia's Indians, particularly the South Indian Hindus, have become active in a revival of their artistic and religious heritage. A special group of Indians are the Sikhs, who follow a religion that is a sixteenth century schism of Hinduism combined with some Islamic beliefs. There are about 40,000 Sikhs in Malaysia, most in the Klang Valley.

Indian Celebrations

Hindus follow a **lunar calendar** that is modified by the addition of a month every three years so that it will correspond to the solar calendar. Hindus and other Indians in Malaysia celebrate several festivals and days commemorating religious events. Among the most important are **Hindu New Year, Deepavali, Thaiponggol** and **Thaipusam**.

Hindus celebrate their new year by cleaning and decorating their homes, preparing traditional foods for family and friends, and saying special prayers. **Deepavali** is a spectacular festival of lights signifying the triumph of light over darkness or wisdom over ignorance, in commemoration of the slaying of the mean king, Naragasura. On the morning of Deepavali, people light candles and lay cakes and fruits on banana leaves. **Thaiponggol** marks the beginning of the rice paddy harvest and is an auspicious month for weddings.

Thaipusam commemorates the victory of Lord Subramaniam over demons and symbolises the triumph of good over evil. Devotees who wish to do penance carry offerings to the temples on *kavaði*, semi-circular steel arches with metal spikes that pierce their skin. The largest Thaipusam celebrations are held at the Batu Caves in K.L., where devotees climb 272 steps to reach the Temple Cave. This is a celebration worth seeing at least once!

Indian Ladies at a Thaipusam Ceremony, Batu Caves

Indian Dress

On ceremonial occasions, men wear traditional Indian dress consisting of the *dhoti*, a short white sarong, and a *vesti* or *kurta*, a thin white cotton shirt. At other times they wear traditional dress or Western clothes. The daily and ceremonial dress of many Indian women is a colourful *sari* with a short tight blouse called a *choli*. Some women choose to wear Western clothes, for all but special occasions.

Indian Names

Indian family names are passed on for only one generation. A father's given name becomes the surname of his sons and daughters. Therefore, the son of a man whose given name is Gopal, might be named Chandra son of Gopal. People will address him as Chandra or Mr. Chandra. He will write his name as G. Chandra, except on certain official documents where he will write "Chandra s/o Gopal" to show that he is the son of Gopal. His children will be sons and daughters of Chandra and will use the initial C. before their given names.

Similarly, the daughter of Mr. Gopal might be named Devi daughter of Gopal. She will be addressed as Devi or Selvi Devi (Miss Devi). She will write her name as G. Devi or Devi d/o Gopal. After marriage she will use her husband's initial in place of her father's initial. Therefore, if she marries a man named Samy, she will write her name as S. Devi and be addressed as Thirumati Devi (Mrs. Devi).

For convenience, long Indian names are sometimes shortened in conversation. Christian Indians place their given name before their father's name.

Photo by Lynn Witham

Indian Ladies Enjoying a Chat

OTHER ETHNIC GROUPS

Residents of K.L. also include members of a variety of other races and ethnic groups. Some were born in the city; others have migrated there for education or work. Many are Eurasians, descendants of intermarriages between the local people and Europeans, primarily British Portuguese and Dutch. Others are members of East Malaysian ethnic groups such as the Iban (Sea Dayak), Melayu (Malays), Bidayuh (Land Dayak) or Melanau from Sarawak, and the Kadazan, Bajau, Murut, Melayu (Malays) from Sabah.

Photo courtesy of Pucuk Rebung

Contemporary acrylic painting of the old grand Iban warrior by Malaysian artist, Tan Wei Kheng, 1998.

THE CHANGING SOCIETY

The population of K.L. is made up not only of the Malays, Chinese, Indians, Eurasians, and other groups mentioned above. In recent years, due to the country's rapid industrial development and need for labour, the Government has issued work permits to large numbers of foreign workers, primarily from Indonesia, Bangladesh, the Philippines, Thailand, India, Pakistan, Sri Lanka and Myanmar. The majority are employed in K.L. and Selangor in the agrarian, manufacturing, construction and service sectors. In addition, large numbers of illegal workers who have managed to enter the country have migrated to K.L. to find work.

On the other end of the economic spectrum are the foreign teachers, professors, business people and diplomats who live and work in K.L. The largest groups are Americans, Japanese, Germans, British, Australians, Dutch, Canadians and Singaporeans, with smaller numbers from the EU countries, Eastern Europe, Russia, the Middle East and other parts of the world. Finally, there are the substantial numbers of tourists who visit the city to sample all that it has to offer. This cultural diversity is just one of the factors that makes K.L. an interesting place in which to live.

Chapter Four

INTERACTING WITH THE PEOPLE

CUSTOMS AND COURTESIES

One characteristic shared by Malaysians of all ethnic groups is the desire to maintain proper and harmonious interpersonal relationships through the use of long-accepted customs and courtesies. Although Malaysians will not expect you to know or follow these customs and courtesies, you will earn their respect if you do. For additional information on customs and courtesies, please see the sections on Business Etiquette and Business Communication in the chapter *Joining the Workforce*.

MEETING AND GREETING

In Malaysia, the rituals involved in meeting and greeting others are an important part of showing respect and of building relationships.

- In Kuala Lumpur, the most common greeting in business and social situations is a gentle **handshake**. Business people usually shake hands again on departure. As not all Malaysians feel comfortable shaking hands with people of the opposite gender, it is probably best for a foreigner to offer his or her hand to a Malaysian of the opposite gender only if the Malaysian offers his or her hand first.

- Malays often greet each other with the *salam*, a gesture made by lightly touching the other person's hands with two palms, and then bringing your hands towards your heart.

- Sometimes, instead of using a handshake or the *salam*, Malaysians simply place their right hand over their heart while nodding.

- The Malay conversational equivalent to the English "How are you?" is *Apa khabar?* (What news?), to which the response is usually *Khabar baik* (Good news, meaning "All is well".)

- Muslims often greet each other with the Arabic phrase *A'salaamu-alaikum* (Peace be with you), to which the response is *Wa'alaikum-u'salaam* (And with you be peace).

- When friends or acquaintances pass by each other in hallways, elevators and similar situations, they may inquire, "Have you taken your lunch/dinner yet?" Occasionally, people will ask, "Where are you going?", to which the response can be specific or simply, "Nowhere special" or "For a stroll".

MAKING SOCIAL VISITS

Malaysians follow certain customs when making social visits and when receiving visitors.

- Written **invitations** often include the time, date, location, suggested attire, and who is invited. Invitations are often extended and accepted or declined at the last minute.

- To be polite, when making informal social arrangements, Malaysians may not say directly what is most convenient for

51

them. If one person **hesitates**, that is a cue to the other to suggest an alternative time or place.

- Some Malaysians are habitually on **time** for appointments and social engagements. Others operate on *"janji Melayu"* (the Malay promise) and arrive when they arrive.
- Upon entering a home, guests remove their **shoes**.
- When guests are served **beverages**, they do not drink until the host invites them to do so.
- During the Muslim **fasting** month of Ramadhan (the dates of which vary yearly), non-Muslims do not "flaunt" their food or drink in the presence of Muslim friends or colleagues.
- Guests usually ask permission before **smoking** or using the **toilet**. Incidentally, there are two types of toilets in Malaysia: the Western-style commode on which one sits and the Eastern-style ceramic bowl in the floor over which one squats while facing the door. Most floor toilets have a water hose for personal hygiene. Toilet paper is not always present, so you'll need to carry your own supply of tissues. Toilet paper should not be put into floor toilets and some commode toilets as it can block the plumbing. While toilets in most homes are kept clean and in good working order, the same cannot be said of many public toilets, even though usually there is a charge for usage.
- Guests also ask permission before taking **pictures** at a home or at a religious ceremony or cultural festival.
- If hosts have pets, they usually keep the **pets** away from the guests, as some Malaysians, for religious and cultural reasons, prefer to avoid contact with animals.
- Malaysian Muslims generally observe early **evening prayers** *(sembahyang magrib)* between 7:15p.m. and 8:15p.m. Consequently, they prefer not to receive phone calls or visitors during this time, and find it most convenient to attend social functions that end before, or begin after, this time. (For a list of daily prayer times, consult the front page of the *New Straits Times* newspaper.)

MATTERS OF THE BODY AND THE HEART

Ways of showing respect and of showing certain emotions may be different in Malaysia than in your country.

- To show **respect**, Malaysians hand and receive objects (such as documents, gifts and sometimes money) with both hands.
- To **beckon** someone, the palm of the hand is turned down and the fingers are waved toward the palm.
- The "**thumbs up**" sign means "good show" or "everything is okay".
- To indicate **direction** (or to refer to a person standing nearby), Malaysians do not point with the forefinger. Instead they use the whole hand or fold the fingers of the right hand under and use the thumb.
- The gesture of slapping a fist against an open hand is **obscene**, as is the gesture of making a fist with the thumb placed between the index finger and second finger.
- At all times, Malays are careful to avoid having the soles of their **feet** face other people.
- In the presence of **royalty** it is considered improper to cross one's legs while sitting in a chair.
- A **smile** or **giggle** may hide a "loss of face" when one feels shy, nervous or embarrassed, and may cover sadness when one gives or receives distressing news.
- In some situations, Malaysians are rather informal about **queuing up**. It is not uncommon for people to "jump the queue" and such behaviour meets with little overt response from other Malaysians.
- Men and older people may **enter** doors and elevators before others.
- Malaysians of the same gender may use **touch** to show friendship (without any sexual overtones).
- Public **demonstration of affection** for members of the opposite

sex is considered bad manners and makes people *malu* (embarrassed).

- **Dating** between foreigners and Malaysians (even when they are both adults) can be rather complicated, as many Malaysian families, especially Muslims, expect dating of their daughters to culminate in marriage. A Muslim man or woman who is suspected of *khalwat*–spending time alone with a person of the opposite sex to whom he or she is not married or otherwise related–loses face in the community and can be taken to court and fined.

Chapter Five

PREPARING FOR THE MOVE

PRE-DEPARTURE ARRANGEMENTS

Advance preparation will help make your move as smooth and trouble free as possible. Below is a checklist of things to do related to documentation, personal finances, health, education for your children, pets and your shipment.

Documentation and Personal Finances

- Consider **opening an account** in an international commercial bank that has a branch in Malaysia.
- Arrange with a bank in your home country to **accept deposit** of your salary cheques.
- Obtain a **letter of introduction from your personal banker** to facilitate opening an account in a Malaysian bank.

- Obtain a **letter from your automobile insurance agent** if you have not made any claims in the past year or longer. A letter stating this fact may make you eligible for a discount on the third-party liability insurance that is required in Malaysia.
- Obtain an **International Driver's Licence** for every member of your family who will be driving abroad.
- Obtain copies of your **marriage licence** and proof of termination of any previous marriages if you plan to give birth to children in Malaysia.

Health and Personal Care
- Obtain copies of your **medical and dental records and X-rays** if you will require treatment for an on-going condition.
- **Refill all medications** for a year, make arrangements to have them sent to you by courier periodically, or contact your embassy to find out if the medication is available in K.L. Obtain the generic names of all medications in case you need to have a doctor in Malaysia write a new prescription. (Pharmacists in Malaysia cannot fill prescriptions written by doctors in other countries.)
- If you take a large supply of medications, to avoid delays at Customs, carry medications in original containers and obtain a **letter from your doctor** stating the generic name and strength of each prescription medicine, and the reason it must be taken.
- If you plan to take **medications containing narcotics**, write to a Malaysian Diplomatic Mission to request permission. (Include a copy of your doctor's letter.) Malaysia has very strict drug laws.
- If you have any **unusual medical concerns**, contact your doctor or other medical authority.
- If you take **insulin** or other timed medication, discuss with your doctor how to adjust your schedule when you cross time zones.

- Women who are particular about **hair styling** may want to ask their hairdresser at home to write down specific instructions for styling, perming or colouring.

Education and Professional Affiliations

Please see the chapter on *Accommodating Children* for information about schools for foreign children.

- Obtain **school records and test results** for any child or adult who will take academic courses in Malaysia.
- Obtain copies of **any educational degrees or certificates** for any child or adult who might join a special interest or professional organisation in Malaysia. (These are sometimes required for application.)
- Try to **pre-register your children** in the school of your choice, as many schools have limited enrolment and fill up quickly.
- If your child has a **special learning need** or a learning disability, be sure to discuss this with school officials, preferably before you arrive in Malaysia.

Pets

- Contact the Malaysian Department of Veterinary Services for current regulations on the **importation of pets**. Please see the section on Regulations for Pets in the chapter on *Complying with Regulations* for addresses.
- Contact the airline you will travel on and enquire about **procedures regarding travel with pets**. Malaysia Airlines will not allow pets to be carried into the passenger cabin, but other airlines may. (Avoid arriving on a weekend, holiday or late evening in any country with quarantine restrictions, as Veterinary Department officials may not be on duty.)
- Hand carry copies of **documents** pertaining to your pet. Originals of the Certificate of Health and Airway Bill should accompany the pet.

- If you prefer to hire an **agent** who will arrange for an Import Licence, pick up your pet at the airport and take it to the quarantine kennel, ask the Malaysian Department of Veterinary Services for a recommendation.

Household
- **MILDEW CAN BE A BIG PROBLEM** in a shipment sent to the tropics. Wood, paper, leather and natural fibres are particularly susceptible. Put moth balls and silica gel packets among books, tapes, papers, clothes, leather goods, canvas paintings, sports equipment, electronic equipment and musical instruments that you will ship. Thoroughly clean and dry (perhaps with a hand-held hair dryer) all kitchen appliances.
- To reduce the chances of damage to or "disappearance" of your belongings during delivery and unpacking of your shipment, seal cartons containing valuable items with duct tape and mark them "Do Not Open". Then unpack these cartons yourself in K.L.

WHAT TO TAKE
Deciding what to take with you to K.L. is no easy task. Below are some suggestions to guide you.

Hand Luggage
In addition to your travel documents, your personal business and employment documents, and the documents mentioned in the checklist earlier in this chapter, you may want to carry the following in your carry-on luggage:
- **Shipping and Storage Papers** (Inventories, insurance certificates, bill of lading, and the name and address of the shipping agent in Malaysia)
- **Title and Registration, Import Licence** and a spare set of **keys** for any vehicle you will ship to Malaysia

- **Birth, Naturalisation and Marriage Certificates** (notarised copies)
- Copies of completed **tax forms** for the previous several years (for reference when you complete tax forms).

Sea or Air Shipment

Some foreigners take almost everything necessary to set up a household, while others take only their clothes and other personal belongings. Most things that you need will probably be available in K.L. in some form or other. When you choose what to ship, keep in mind that the climate is hot and humid. If you plan to have anything custom made, take pictures of styles you like. Below is a list of items that many expatriates think are important to take to Malaysia. The items were selected either because they are impossible or difficult to find in K.L. or are quite expensive there.

Items for Men

Tall or larger-sized men find it difficult to buy good-quality, reasonably priced, properly fitting clothes in K.L. Most tall men have suits tailored or buy them overseas.

- *Clothes:* Take lightweight suits, cotton shirts, a few warm outfits for trips to colder climates, lightweight casual wear, sports clothes, swimwear, cotton underwear, athletic supporters and socks, especially if you wear a large size.
- *Shoes:* Take shoes for work, dress and sports, especially if you wear a large size or have wide feet.
- *Toiletries:* Take deodorant, aftershave, razors and blades, etc. if you prefer specific brands.

Items for Women

Many women find it difficult to buy good-quality, reasonably priced, properly fitting clothes in K.L. The selection is especially limited for women who are tall or anything but quite slim. Most ready-made clothes for women are made from synthetic fabrics. Tailoring is reasonably priced, and silk, wool, cotton and synthetic-blend materials are available. Take pictures, patterns or samples if you have favourite styles.

- *Clothes:* Take lightweight suits, dresses, skirts, blouses and jackets in natural fabrics or blends for work; cool dresses, skirts, blouses and slacks (trousers) for day wear; shorts, halter tops and sleeveless daytime dresses for wear at home; swimwear, cover-ups, towels and bathing caps for the beach; and a few warm outfits for trips to colder climates. Also take natural fibre sleepwear and undergarments, and bras (especially if you prefer unpadded bras or require a large size).

- *Evening Wear:* Take long dresses, hostess dresses and caftans, or plan to have some made of the beautiful batik fabrics that are available in K.L. Women attending palace functions or calling on high-ranking Government officials will need hats, gloves and stockings.

- *Shoes:* You may find it difficult to buy properly fitting shoes if your feet are narrow or larger than European Size 39 or US Size 8, but you can have shoes made in Malaysia. Flat or low-heeled open sandals or lightweight shoes with sturdy (preferably rubber) soles are most comfortable for everyday wear. The uneven pavement and sudden downpours rapidly destroy thin-heeled, thin-soled leather shoes, so you'll want to save your best ones for special occasions. Your feet will swell in the heat, so you may be more comfortable wearing shoes a half-size larger than usual.

- *Personal Care Products:* Japanese, American and European cosmetics are available in K.L. and prices are quite reasonable. If you are particular about brands, however, take a supply of anything you use regularly. Items that many women take include: contraceptives, hair bleach, permanent waves, hair colour (especially for blonde and other light shades) and cosmetics (as your favourite shades may not be available in Asia).
- *Appliances:* A limited variety of small appliances such as hair dryers, curling irons and electric curlers can be purchased in K.L.

Items for Children and Teens

A good variety of children's and teens clothes in small sizes can be found in K.L., but chubby and tall sizes are scarce. Most schools require students to wear uniforms that can be purchased or custom made in K.L.

- *Clothes:* Take play and sports clothes; bathing suits, bathing caps, towels and cover-ups; cotton sleepwear and underwear; athletic supporters for boys; and a few warm outfits for winter travel in colder climates. Students at the International School in K.L. will need solid colour white or navy-blue sweaters.
- *Shoes and Shoelaces:* Take sports shoes, dress shoes, sturdy play shoes; plastic boots, orthopedic shoes. (When choosing shoe sizes, allow room for feet to swell in the heat.)
- *Toys, Books and Sports Equipment:* Take some toys, books, craft supplies, colouring books, educational games, and long-life or rechargeable batteries for toys.
- *School Supplies:* If you have children who will start school soon after your arrival, take backpacks and basic school supplies. (Please note that the standard paper and notebook size used in Malaysia is A4, longer and narrower than the standard used in North America).

Items for Infants

Most items that you will need for infants are available in K.L., but you could take the following: swim diapers; cotton training pants (if you need large sizes); insect repellent for infants; and toiletries and baby formula (if you have preferred brands). If you are travelling with an infant, you will find it convenient to have a month's supply of formula, bottles, nipples, disposable diapers (nappies).

Household Items

- *Furniture:* Some expatriates ship furniture; others buy it or have it made in K.L.
- *Bedroom and Bathroom*: Cervical pillows, shower water purifier/chlorine filters, bed linens and bathroom linens (including commode covers, shower curtains and hooks). (These are sold in K.L., but good quality means high price.)
- *Kitchen:* Large-capacity, dual voltage washers and dryers. (Smaller capacity washers and dryers, most small appliances, as well as adequate cooking and eating utensils can be purchased in K.L.)
- *Miscellaneous:* Kitchen step stool, non-skid throw rugs, and an ironing board, pads and covers (if you are tall and expect to iron), cooler and barbecue.
- *Special Foods:* Spices and flavourings, favourite recipes and cookbooks; packaged foods for special diets.
- *Electronic Equipment:* If your equipment is designed for 120-volts/60-cycles AC, ask your product dealer or manufacturer what accessories you will need to enable you to use it on 230-240-volts/50-cycles AC. Most equipment requires only a transformer and/or an adapter plug, both of which can be purchased in K.L.

- *Converter Plugs:* If any of your electrical/electronic equipment has a US-style three-pronged, grounding plug, take a supply of two-pronged electrical converter plugs so that you can connect your plug to Malaysian plug adapters.
- *Video Cassette Recorder:* Malaysia uses the PAL transmission system, as does Singapore, Australia, the UK and most of Europe. If your country does not use the PAL transmission system, you might want to purchase a multi-system VCR that will play videos that have been made for the PAL transmission system as well as videos made for other transmission systems.

Miscellaneous Items

- *Automobile Parts:* If you ship your automobile to Malaysia, ask your mechanic what extra small parts you should take.
- *Books:* Consider taking novels, cookbooks, first-aid books, children's books, a world atlas, a dictionary, your local phone book, encyclopedias, a book on entertaining, books on child care and development, and copies of your favourite mail order catalogues (include one for gifts in case you want to have gifts sent to people back home). Illustrated cookbooks will be especially useful if a maid does your cooking. Take reference books if you plan to do research, writing, or correspondence courses, or if you might teach a course in a subject that is of special interest to you.
- *Game, Projects and Craft Supplies:* Take plenty of things to keep you busy in your leisure time, especially if you won't be working. If you have a hobby you'd like to share, take some materials and perhaps you can teach a course.
- *Gifts:* Take small items to use as hostess gifts (please see the chapter on *Meeting the People* for suggestions) and presents for Malaysian friends. (For women, take good quality leather

purses and wallets, colourful scarves and cool cotton, silk or cotton/synthetic blend shirts and blouses. For teens, take mugs, posters of popular foreign rock musicians, and tee-shirts and sweatshirts imprinted with the names of well-known foreign universities. For younger children, take toys, educational games or playclothes.)

- *Sewing Supplies:* If you enjoy sewing, take a sewing machine and sewing supplies.
- *Sports Equipment:* Take nose plugs and eye goggles for swimming and a basketball pole and hoop (if you like to practise at home); almost everything else is available in K.L.
- *Stamps:* Take a postage scale as well as a large supply of stamps and a list of postal rates from your home country so that you can prepare letters and packages to send with friends who are going back home.
- *Toiletries and Non-prescription Remedies*: Take a supply of anything you cannot do without.

What Not To Take

Considering the irregular electric supply, the possibility of loss or theft, or the damaging effects of the tropical climate, it is advisable to leave the following items at home: bicycles (there are few safe places to ride); telephones (they may not work well); valuable leather goods (they might mildew); long-haired pets (they feel miserable in the heat); non-PAL televisions and video games (they won't work with the PAL transmission system used in Malaysia); and light bulbs, electric clocks, complicated microwaves and ovens that are made for use with 110-volts, 60-cycles electric current (these will not function properly in Malaysia and ovens should not be run on transformers).

TRAVEL TIPS

Arriving in Malaysia

You probably will enter Malaysia through the primary international gateway, the new KLIA airport. From the airport to town, transportation is provided by taxi and bus. Some hotels will send representatives to the airport to meet arriving guests. For more information, please see the section on Airports and Air Travel in the chapter *Getting Around*.

Hotel Accommodations

You may spend several days, weeks, or possibly even months in a hotel while you are arranging permanent housing. Hotels are available in a variety of categories, and room rates vary, depending on corporate discounts, length of stay, or hotel occupancy rate. All hotels add a 5% tax and a 10% service charge to the bill (known as "plus-plus").

Health and Safety

Newcomers to the tropics may not realise how quickly the heat and humidity can drain energy. If you are not accustomed to the climate, you may find that you will feel more energetic if you modify your diet to include more liquids and several small meals a day; limit your intake of fatty and spicy foods; and resist, however difficult it may be, consumption of an excess of fresh fruits. Should you spend much time outdoors, guard against sunburn and sunstroke by using sunblock or a parasol, and take extra precautions for infants and children. If you are not accustomed to traffic moving on the left, when walking take great care not to step in front of oncoming vehicles. **Teach your children to "Look right, look left, and look right again," and to be extra cautious, even on sidewalks.**

Exploring Your New Surroundings

After you are rested and ready to explore your new surroundings, the first thing you will need is a city map. Your hotel should be able to provide you with one; if not, maps and a wealth of other useful information can be obtained at any office of Tourism Malaysia. A good way to get acquainted with the city is to take a tour.

Embassy Registration

Soon after your arrival you should register with your country's embassy. Registration will speed replacement of lost passports and facilitate contact in case of emergency, illness or disappearance of a family member. Business people can ask their embassy personnel to give them a brief, up-to-the-minute orientation to the business climate.

Adjusting To Life In K.L.

Prior to your departure for Malaysia, your company may offer you the opportunity to take an intercultural training course that will prepare you for living and working in Malaysia. After you arrive, to become better acquainted with the pleasures of living in K.L. and to find answers to your many questions, consider taking the course entitled *Living in KL* that is offered to newcomers of all nationalities by the American Association of Malaysia (Tel: 03-451-9610/9625). Also watch the newspapers and expatriate magazines for announcements of performances of The Expat, a play that highlights in a humorous way, the challenges that expatriates face in adjusting to life in Malaysia and the challenges that Malaysians face in adjusting to expatriates.

~ CHAPTER SIX ~

SETTING UP A HOUSEHOLD

THE HOUSING PICTURE

Kuala Lumpur proper and its suburbs offer accommodations to suit a range of tastes and budgets. However, locating appropriate accommodations can be a time-consuming task. The information in this chapter is designed to assist you in your search. It includes an overview of residential areas; tips on searching for and evaluating a house or apartment; details on negotiating a lease; information on utilities, services, furnishings, maintenance, security and insurance; and suggestions on coping with the climate.

HOUSES, CONDOS AND APARTMENTS

Many foreigners choose to rent spacious, comfortable houses; others prefer modern condos, townhouses, or high-rise apartments. Expatriates on short-term stays often choose to live in **service apartments** which are completely furnished and periodically cleaned by a maintenance staff. The type of accommodation you choose will depend, of course, on personal preference, the benefits your employer offers and the style in which your employer expects you to live. Most employers expect employees to "adjust to what is available"; only a few agree to covering the costs of extensive renovations. When choosing between a house, condo or apartment, consider the advantages and disadvantages mentioned below.

Advantages to living in a house are that you have room for a pet, room to entertain, a place for the kids to play outside, a garden and lawn to cultivate, and probably more privacy and quiet than in an apartment building. **Disadvantages** are that electric bills will be high if you plan to air-condition the whole house; a house is more vulnerable to break-ins than is an apartment or condo with good security; it will be necessary to maintain the garden; and there is usually a problem with insects and occasionally with snakes. Also, most houses that are for rent in K.L are older and may not have been very well maintained.

Advantages of living in a condo or an apartment are that it is easy to meet people, especially if the building has a pool; it may be comforting to know that there are people nearby if you live alone, if you are sick or if your spouse is away; there is no problem with snakes and less of a problem with insects; and the security may be better than in a house. **Disadvantages** are that you might have less room in which to entertain, you probably cannot keep a pet and, unless you have a balcony, you cannot walk outside.

Rental costs change rapidly, depending on the state of the economy as well as on supply and demand. Currently, house rentals for expatriates range from RM1,500 to RM18,000 per month in prime urban residential areas and RM900 to RM8,000 in the suburbs. Apartment rentals range from RM1,300 to RM12,000 per month in the city and RM500 to RM6,000 in the suburbs.

Photo by Lynn Witham

Typical House

RESIDENTIAL AREAS

To help you decide in which area of town to live, you may want to interview your co-workers and acquaintances about where they live and why they have chosen to live there. You may find it helpful

69

to develop a visual picture by locating your work site, schools, shopping areas and recreational facilities on a map, and then circling the residential areas that appear to have the most advantages. As the city grows, traffic is becoming more of a problem, so people generally prefer to live in a location that will require only a short commute to work or school. Suburban areas have good restaurants and shopping facilities so suburban dwellers need not trek back into town after a long day at work.

In the Kuala Lumpur area, the **residential areas** most popular among foreign residents are: 1) Ampang (Ukay Heights, Freeman Road/Taman U Thant, Taman Tun Abdul Razak, Hillview Estate/Taman Hillview); 2) Bangsar, Bukit Bandaraya and Taman Tun Dr. Ismail; 3) Damansara Heights (Bukit Damansara) and Bandar Utama; 4) Kenny Hill (Bukit Tunku); 5) Mont Kiara and Sri Hartamas; 6) Petaling Jaya (also known as "P.J."); and 7) Shah Alam.

SEARCHING FOR A HOUSE

To find houses or apartments that are for rent, most people use a **real estate agent** (estate agent) who has been recommended by acquaintances or whose name they have found listed in the afternoon English-language papers or in the Telephone Directory Yellow Pages under the heading "Real Estate". Some newcomers find homes by asking co-workers, hotel managers and other acquaintances if they know of any vacant or soon-to-be-vacant residences. Still another route is to search the Internet website: **www.propertyzoom.com/pro_aspsearch.asp** which lists properties for rent in K.L. and the suburbs.

If you work with a real estate agent, you will save time by stating clearly **where you want to live, what type of residence you prefer, whether or not you have children and pets, what transportation you have available** and **how much you are prepared to pay**. If at all possible, try to identify an agent before

70

you arrive in Malaysia and correspond with them by e-mail so that they will know your housing requirements and can short-list properties for you to visit when you arrive. One agent providing this service is **JED Realty** (Tel: 60-16-333-22 88 (mobile) or 60-3-651-6619; Fax: 60-3-651-1159; E-mail: tiongp@hotmail.com).

Agents will meet you at your hotel and drive you to potential houses or apartments. Not all agents are dependable, however, so don't be surprised if they miss appointments or neglect to return your calls. The services of agents are paid by the landlord and free to the renter. Some agents may try to collect a fee from the renter as well, however, so don't sign any papers before you read them. As an agent's commission is a percentage of your rent, it is to your advantage to bargain avidly with the agent, as well as with the landlord. Stick to the price you want to pay, as some landlords and agents will ask for as much as they think they can squeeze out. Landlords sometimes sign with two or more agents, so you may be shown the same house twice. If you are taken to a house that you have already seen, tell the agent, and if you rent it, be prepared to get complaints from both agents regarding their fee from the landlord.

EVALUATING A HOUSE

To assist you in evaluating the houses, condos or apartments you visit, take along a notebook in which to record addresses, details, pros, cons and questions. You may find it useful to devise a system to allow you to rate each house on a number of factors such as **cost, space, condition, location, security, terms of the lease** and **personality of the landlord**. The list that follows includes points to consider as you evaluate each house; many of them can also be applied to condos and apartments.

TIPS ON EVALUATING A HOUSE

- How far is the house from your work and how long will it take to commute? What is the commute like when it rains? Are there traffic jams along the route?
- How far is the house from the school(s) your children will attend, and what kind of transportation is available?
- How far is the house from grocery stores? Will the nearest provisioner deliver to your house?
- Is the house located near a river and/or are there many bamboo trees or big old tree trunks? If so, there could be many snakes around.
- Is the house or apartment/condo building located in an area that is prone to flash flooding? Rapid development has made this a problem in some locations in the city.
- What is the crime rate in the area? Some areas, such as those near construction sites or open lots, are more prone to break-ins than others.
- Can the house be made reasonably secure against break-ins? Can all doors be locked? Is outside lighting sufficient? Is the house surrounded by a fence with a gate that can be locked? (Does the apartment building have security guards?)
- What does the neighbourhood look like? Are houses and streets well kept?
- For an apartment or condo, what do the public areas look like? Are the stairwells, hallways, elevators, garbage disposal areas, pool, and other public areas well kept?
- Is there any evidence that the roof leaks? Check all roofs and walls for mildew, brown spots and other signs of leaks.
- Is the water pressure strong and constant? Be sure to check the pressure in the upstairs bathrooms.
- What are the average monthly costs of gas, water and electricity (including air conditioning)?

- Does the house have adequate storage and closet space? Some houses and apartments do not, so you may need to add large wardrobes.
- Are the kitchen counters high enough for your family to use comfortably? Counters in many Malaysian houses are lower than those in Western houses. This will not make much difference if you are in Malaysia on a short assignment or if you will have a maid who will do most of the cooking, but if not, you could avoid back strain by asking the landlord to have the counter raised.
- Will the house accommodate your pets?
- Does the house have suitable quarters for your live-in help? Will the quarters provide your family and your maid with adequate visual and auditory privacy? Consider room use and traffic patterns. Will the quarters provide the maid with a separate bedroom, bathroom and entrance to the house? Some houses, especially older ones, have separate kitchen facilities. Maids' rooms in most condos are very small.
- What repairs and renovations need to be made before you move in, and who will pay for them? Will the landlord allow you to make renovations later at your own expense?
- Will the house be fumigated before you move in? Who is responsible for paying for the pest control programme?
- What is the rent payment schedule? Is a deposit required? What is the refund policy? Can you sublet?
- Is the house furnished? "Furnished" often means only the essentials, many of which should have been thrown out long ago. Finding a house or apartment with a complete set of good-quality furnishings can be difficult, however furnishings can be rented.

NEGOTIATING A LEASE

Lease agreements in Malaysia may be quite different from lease agreements in your country. To review a sample lease, visit the website www.propertyzoom.com. For your own protection, have your personal or company attorney review any lease you intend to sign. Normally the agent will prepare the lease, present it to both parties to sign and arrange for it to receive a stamp (chop) to make it a legal document.

Most landlords require tenants to make a one-month advance rental payment and a two-month deposit, and require tenants to sign a one- or two-year lease with a clause stating that the deposit will be forfeited if tenants break the lease. Try to include in your lease a "diplomatic clause" releasing you from all financial responsibility, except payment of a small penalty, if you are transferred before the lease expires. (Understandably, most landlords will only accept that this clause go into effect after the first year of rental is completed.) After completing a two-year lease, you might be able to negotiate for a lease that will allow you to give only two months' notice prior to moving out. If the house is near a hill or stream, try to incorporate a "snake clause" into the lease that would allow you to move out without penalty in case you are plagued with snakes.

Rents can increase rapidly, so it is to your advantage to negotiate for no rent increase, or for an agreed upon percentage of increase, and to state this in the lease. To protect you from being pushed out by other foreigners who offer to pay more rent, the lease should also include a clause that gives you first option for renewal at a fixed percentage increase.

Any lease should state who is responsible for the following: pest control; roof repairs; ground maintenance; house repainting; phone installation; garbage collection; wind or water damage; utility payments (gas, water, electricity); septic tank servicing and emptying; and plumbing, electrical and hot water heater repairs.

It is advisable to insist that repairs and renovations be made before you move in, otherwise, you may experience long delays in having the work completed. Negotiate who pays: you, your employer, or the landlord. If you or your employer pay, the landlord may let you amortise costs over the length of your contract.

UTILITIES

You can probably make arrangements to initiate service of utilities before you move into your new residence by contacting the utility companies (electricity, water, telephone and gas) and opening an account with each. If you call or visit these offices, for best results, use a quiet, patient, humble approach, and speak slowly and clearly.

Many options exist for payments of electricity, water and telephone bills:

- You can pay all three bills at once at any Bank Simpanan Nasional or at any of the shops (*Kedai*) run by each of the utilities: Kedai Tenaga (electricity), Kedai JBA (water), or Kedai Telekom (telephone). You can pay by mail (with a cheque) or in person (with a cheque or cash). (If you want to pay all three bills at an office of the telephone company, for example, you would make the cheque for the total of all three bills payable to "Telekom Malaysia".)
- You can write a cheque and mail it or take it in person to any local post office.
- You can pay through ATM machines.
- You can pay by credit cards from selected banks (as indicated in the bills).
- You can pay each company separately by mail or in person.

Electricity

The company in charge of electricity is Tenaga Nasional Berhad (TNB). New customers are required to make a deposit equal to one month's estimated bill. Bills, written in Malay and mailed to customers monthly, must be paid within seven days of receipt. It is the responsibility of the customer to enquire about bills not received on time.

If you experience a power failure or other electricity-related problem in your home, contact Tenaga Nasional Berhad. They will send a representative to your home day or night, at no cost to you. In K.L. and Selangor, call 03-282-3711.

Electricity for domestic properties is normally supplied at 230/240 volts AC, 50 cycles, three-phase. Standard plugs are three-pronged British type. Adaptor plugs and step-down transformers are inexpensive and readily available.

Appliances made for 110-volts, 60-cycles can be run on transformers, but some will not operate normally. Dishwashers, washing machines and clothes dryers will operate more slowly, but this probably will not harm the appliances. Small electrical cooking appliances will operate satisfactorily, but to maintain the proper cooking temperature, the heat indicator should be set slightly higher than usual. Appliances such as electric clocks and knives made for 60 cycles, run slower on 50 cycles, even with a transformer. (Transformers convert the voltage but not the cycles.) Electric stoves should not be operated on transformers.

Transformers are safe if used with care. Family members and domestic employees should be warned to take the following precautions: 1) do not overload a transformer; 2) do not use a transformer in a wet place; 3) make sure all transformers have adequate ventilation; 4) unplug a transformer immediately if it is hot; 5) make sure any transformer over 1500 watts is grounded; 6) do not touch a transformer that is plugged into a socket, especially if you have wet hands or feet; and 7) unplug transformers when they are not in use.

Power surges occur frequently, interruptions in power supply occur occasionally, and lightning sometimes strikes modems and fax machines. Consequently, it is wise to protect computer, telephone, fax, modem and other sensitive electronic equipment by using a voltage regulator (surge protector/lightning isolator).

To keep your new home electrically safe, take the following precautions: 1) have an electrician check the wiring before you install large appliances; 2) locate your fuse box and keep extra fuses on hand; 3) make sure that plugs and transformers are in good condition and that outlets are not overloaded; and 4) install smoke detectors, especially if you have a centralised air-conditioning system.

Water

The company in charge of providing water is Jabatan Bekalan Air (JBA). To initiate water service, you must pay a deposit. If you live in a house, bills based on meter readings will be sent to you every two months. It is your responsibility to enquire about bills not received on time. In condos and apartments, the fee for water is automatically included in the monthly rental fee. If your residence has no water or very low water pressure, contact JBA (24 hours) in K.L. at 03-442-0191; in P.J., call 03-7781-2333.

Telephone

The company in charge of telephone service is Jabatan Telekom Malaysia, known as Telekom. To initiate telephone service you must complete an application at any Kedai Telekom. On the application, write your family name before your given name, as your phone number will be listed according to the name you write first. A deposit must be paid at the time of application and an installation/connection fee must be paid later. Each extension phone requires an additional deposit. Many expatriates choose to have two lines: one for telephone/fax and one for the Internet. ISDN lines are available at an extra charge.

While the application process is fairly simple, the process of getting a representative from Telekom to go to your residence to open the telephone line and assure that it is in good working order can be more difficult. Representatives do not necessarily arrive as scheduled and the telephone does not necessarily work properly after the initial visit. To save time, you could try to arrange for your landlord to handle the arrangements with Telekom.

Monthly rental charges are based on radial distance of the phone from the main exchange. There is a minimum monthly rate, with an additional charge for each extension and for long-distance domestic and international calls. Monthly bills must be paid within seven days of receipt. It is the customer's responsibility to enquire about bills not received on time.

Cooking Gas

Gas for cooking comes in cylinders which the gas company will deliver to your home. Purchase two cylinders so that when one runs out you can easily switch to the other and contact the company to bring a replacement. The process of connecting cylinders to the stove and disconnecting them from the stove is simple; the gas company representative can show you how.

You can find a gas company by looking in the Telephone Directory Yellow Pages or by asking your landlord or a neighbour. When your first cylinder is installed, you will be asked to pay a small deposit for the cylinder and a fee for installation of the fittings. Thereafter, you pay each time you receive a new cylinder.

As a safety precaution, if anything on your stove does not seem to be working properly, do not delay in getting it repaired. Gas leaks, for example, can be difficult to detect and can cause serious explosions.

SERVICES

Once you sign the lease, you will need to arrange for services such as pest control and garbage collection.

Pest Control

The warm, humid climate of the tropics provides an ideal breeding ground for a wide variety of insects that will try their best to make their home in your house. Ants, spiders, cockroaches and geckoes are the most prevalent. Their numbers usually can be controlled by having your house and grounds sprayed periodically by an exterminator, and by keeping your house free of dust and crumbs, but it is futile to try to eradicate them completely. If you prefer to use non-chemical deterrents in your home, try using cloves to discourage ants and pandan leaves (ask Malaysians where you can get them) to deter roaches.

For a listing of exterminators in your area, check the Telephone Directory Yellow Pages under the heading "Pest Control". (Some exterminators will use a water-based spray rather than an oil-based spray; the former is reputed to be less problematic for people who are chemically sensitive.) For assistance with eradicating mosquitoes, contact the local Health Department.

You can expect to see mice and even rats in your garden. They may seek refuge in storage areas or other dark warm places in your house where they can nest. Another common household creature is the gecko or cicak, a small grayish-green lizard that makes clicking noises and scurries along ceilings. Geckoes are harmless to people and, as they feed on mosquitoes, are beneficial to have inside your house. To some Malaysians they are symbols of good luck.

Heavily wooded areas are sometimes inhabited by snakes. The most common snakes are pit vipers and cobras. Tall grass attracts snakes, so keep the grass and vines around the doors, windows, gates and walkways of your house well trimmed. Other deterrents are to keep a cat on the premises, cut down dead tree trunks located near the house and spread sulphur around the house and garden. (If you do the latter, be sure that all snakes are outside of the sulphur ring, otherwise you will trap them inside the ring and they may become aggressive.) Most snakes will not attack unless they feel threatened, so it is wise to turn on a light and look around before you enter a room at night, and to use night lights in bathrooms and at the front door of your home.

Garbage Collection

Garbage collection services are provided by each city and financed by yearly assessment taxes paid by landlords. Frequency of collection varies with location. Garbage must be put in a plastic garbage bag, securely closed and placed in a garbage bin. For information concerning collection, call Alam Flora in Kuala Lumpur at 03-984-7255 and in Petaling Jaya at 03-7874-8433.

Recycling is practised by a growing number of people. Garbage collectors will separate the items that are recyclable. It saves them time if you can put bottles, cans and old newspapers in separate bags. There is a centre at Giant Supermarket in USJ 1, Subang Jaya where people can drop off recyclable items. Some organisations, such as Cancerlink in P.J., periodically collect recyclable items as a fund raising project.

Household Emergencies

In the area where you live, if you have problems with snakes, monkeys, stray dogs, mosquitoes, swarms of bees, blocked drainage ditches or roads blocked by fallen trees, a phone call to the proper authorities will usually bring assistance. In K.L., call Dewan Bandaraya at 03-984-3434; in P.J, call Majlis Perbandaran at 03-756-2939/9058/2020 (24 hours). If you need help searching for a missing pet dog or getting rid of a bothersome stray, call 03-4021-1682.

If a problem occurs and you are not sure whom to call, dial 999, the number for police emergencies and ask whom you should contact for help. As the dispatcher may not be accustomed to speaking with foreigners, speak slowly and clearly, and try to stay calm.

Household Renovations and Repairs

If your home requires renovations after you move in, normally your landlord will select the contractor who will do the work. Negotiating to use a contractor of your own choosing will give you more control over the timing of renovations and allow you to more carefully supervise the work. You will need to negotiate with the contractor to stay within the budget you and your landlord have agreed upon and later submit the bills to your landlord or your company.

Repair people who are scheduled to come to your home often do not appear at the scheduled time (or day) and sometimes do not call to let you know that they will be late. Consequently, it can be worthwhile to take the initiative to call the repair people on the day prior to a scheduled visit to check if and when they think they will appear. If you know that you cannot wait at home if the repair person is late, you could ask for the person's handphone number and say that you will call again one hour before the planned visit to check the schedule. Sometimes when repair people fix items, the repair is not permanent or complete. If this occurs more than once with the same item, you could try to get more satisfactory service by asking to speak to the repair person's "senior" (supervisor) or by suggesting that you will find another repair person to do the job.

Expatriate (and Malaysian) women sometimes find that contractors, repair people and other service people seem hesitant to do business with women and will ask to speak with the man of the house. This is especially true if the transaction involves a large sum of money or if the request seems unusual. In such cases, it is necessary for women to explain that they have full authority to make decisions and handle financial transactions and to add that if the business person does not want their business they will find another contractor. This usually brings about a more cooperative attitude.

FURNISHINGS

If you will be staying in K.L. for only a short time, you may choose to rent a furnished apartment. In lower-priced apartments, furnishings may not be of the highest quality and may include only the basic furniture for the living room, dining room, bedrooms and kitchen. If you rent furnished accommodations, make an inventory of all furnishings, have the landlord sign it, and retain a copy. When you terminate your lease, the inventory will be used to verify that you have not removed any items belonging to the landlord.

Most long-term foreign residents rent unfurnished accommodations. "Unfurnished" usually means bare. Renters must supply a stove, washer, dryer and refrigerator, and possibly light fixtures, air conditioners, hot water heaters, wardrobes, drapery tracks, kitchen cabinets, bathroom cabinets, bathroom shelves, shower curtain rods, and ceiling fans.

Furniture

Popular furniture construction materials are cane, teak, glass, wicker, rattan and rosewood. Local furniture makers are skilled at making custom-made furniture from pictures or directions, and many foreigners are so pleased with the results that they ship the pieces back home. Heavy upholstery fabrics, including attractive Indian woven cottons and Thai and Indian silks, are available in K.L. It pays to choose fabrics that are cool and sturdy, in colours that will not fade easily.

Decorative Accessories

When you choose accessories, it is important to consider the effects of heat, humidity and insects. Carpeting, heavy drapes and quilted bedspreads are fine in rooms that are air conditioned, but impractical in rooms that are not, as they are hot and difficult to keep clean, and they attract insects and mildew. In rooms without air-conditioning, easy-to-clean throw rugs and washable lightweight curtains are more functional.

Many Malaysians and foreigners have their accessories custom-made. Seamstresses are prevalent and costs for making drapes or bedspreads and for upholstering furniture are reasonable. Good quality decorating fabric can be purchased in K.L.

COPING WITH THE CLIMATE

High heat and humidity are year-round phenomena in K.L. In rooms that are not air conditioned, the humidity can cause irreparable damage to your belongings. Clothes and linens develop a musty odour. Leather goods turn green from mildew. Books and papers become musty and bug-infested. Records warp, tapes stretch or mildew, and photographic slides mildew and discolour. Pianos and sports, audio/video and photography equipment, and other items with metal parts rust.

A trick to prevent moisture buildup, especially in rooms without air-conditioning, is to install small electric light bulbs or heating elements inside airtight cupboards. In the cupboards, store your clothes, leather goods, tapes, slides, camera equipment, electronic equipment, and valuable books and papers, and leave the light on all the time. Also, place mothballs and silica-gel packets in all closets and bookcases, and in boxes containing shoes, tapes, slides and camera equipment. To minimise musty odour, put sandalwood beads in all these places as well as in luggage and storage boxes, and never put away clothes, linens, shoes or sports

83

equipment until they are completely dry. Keep leather shoes and handbags clean, use a spray to protect them from moisture and wipe them off periodically. If you find mildew to be a major problem in your house, you can wash the walls and ceilings with fungicides (available in hardware stores), or install dehumidifiers in rooms that can be sealed off.

Care of electrical and electronic equipment becomes even more critical than usual in a tropical climate. Take precautions against problems caused by heat, dust, corrosion and power surges.

HOUSEHOLD MAINTENANCE

Your lease should clearly state who is responsible for routine maintenance, and for minor and major household repairs. Tenants usually are responsible for maintenance of the grounds and gardens surrounding the house. You may be tempted to do the work yourself, but if you are not accustomed to the heat, humidity and fast-growing vegetation, you may prefer to hire a gardener or arrange for the landlord to provide a gardener. If you need to select plants for your garden or balcony, nurseries will send a representative to your home to help you.

HOUSEHOLD SECURITY

Household break-ins occur in Malaysia just as they do in many other countries, and most of the precautions you can take to protect your residence are the same as the precautions you may take at home. The most important advice is: do not tempt thieves. Keep in mind that a burglar's enemies—noise, light and time—are your allies, and use them to your advantage. The list that follows gives some commonsense tips for household security.

Tips for Household Security

Before you move into your house or apartment, make sure all doors can be securely locked, all windows are covered with glass or gratings, the house has sufficient outdoor lighting, and (if possible) any repairs or modifications have been completed.

Do not store any of your belongings in the house before you move in.

When your shipment is delivered, be at home to check the inventory and resist the temptation to go off and leave the house filled with packed boxes. Unpack cartons of valuables yourself to avoid possible damage to or loss of those items.

Always lock the doors of your house and car, keep the house gates closed and locked, and don't admit strangers. Keep the shrubs around the house trimmed and put on the outside lights in the evening. If it will make you feel better, keep a dog or install an alarm system.

To avoid tempting your household employees or workmen, keep cash, cameras, valuable jewellery and important documents in a household safe or in a bank safe deposit box. In addition, etch identifying numbers on valuables if they do not already have unremovable serial numbers, and keep a list of the numbers and descriptions of the items in a safe place. Finally, if you have extra supplies of food, cosmetics, clothes or other items, keep them out of sight so that household employees will not be tempted to take them.

To make the house appear occupied, even when it is not, leave on a radio, use a timer to turn on a light, arrange for someone to collect your mail, discontinue delivery of the newspaper, and have the gardener continue to care for the lawn and garden.

Avoid leaving your house unattended while you are out of town. You may be able to join your neighbours in paying for the services of a full-time area guard or to arrange for your domestic help (if you employ any) to take care of the house. Alternatively,

85

you may be able to arrange for someone to house-sit while you are away; newcomers looking for permanent accommodations often prefer house sitting in a "leave house" to staying in a hotel.

INSURANCE

Many people purchase insurance to cover theft, fire damage and storm damage. Fires are uncommon, but storms occasionally cause water damage to personal effects and household break-ins do occur. You will need to itemise valuables such as carpets, watches, antiques, jewellery, cameras, computers and works of art, if you want to have them insured for their full value. Also consider purchasing personal effects insurance to insure you against loss, theft or damage of your valuables outside your home. Your friends and colleagues will be able to offer recommendations about reliable insurance companies and comprehensive policies.

FURTHER INFORMATION

Should you have questions about rental properties in the K.L. area prior to or after your arrival, contact JED Realty (Tel: 60-16-333-2288 (mobile) or 60-3-651-6619; Fax: 60-3-651-1159; E-mail: tiongp@hotmail.com. They will be pleased to answer any questions about the home rental scene in K.L. and to provide referrals to household-related services that are experienced in working with expatriates. Also check the website: www.property.com for property news, real estate terminology, examples of contracts and other useful information.

CHAPTER SEVEN

ARRANGING DOMESTIC HELP

DECIDING ON DOMESTIC HELP

For many foreigners, having domestic help is one of the special pleasures of living in Malaysia. Domestic employees are available and affordable. However, there is more to employing domestic help than meets the eye. Tips to assist you in locating, interviewing, training, supervising, compensating and dismissing domestic employees are discussed below. For more information, take the **Amah Workshop** that is offered by the American Association of Malaysia (Tel: 03-451-9610/9625). (*Amah* is the Chinese term for maid.)

Types of Domestic Help

Among foreign residents of K.L., the services of a part-time or live-in **maid** and a part-time *tukang kebun* (gardener) are in greatest demand. The maid does the cleaning, washing, ironing, mending and may help with cooking, marketing and child care. The gardener stops by two to four times a month to take care of the garden and might serve as a handyman and help with heavy household cleaning.

As protection against break-ins, many families hire a *jaga* (night guard). In residential areas, it is common for a group of neighbours to share the services of an area *jaga*. Although many foreign men and women drive in K.L., a few prefer to have a **driver** to run errands for them, to take them where they need to go and to take the children to school.

Full-time or Part-time Help

The type of help you employ will depend, of course, on your budget, house size, family size, entertainment style and personal preference. Full-time live-in maids work 5 1/2 to 7 days a week and live in the small quarters available in most houses and in some apartments. Expatriates who have never lived with or supervised full-time domestic help may find that they have to make adjustments as their role changes from that of house-keeper to that of house-manager. Many people welcome this role change as it gives them free time to take advantage of a variety of activities, but some people feel a loss of control when the maid takes over. If you feel that you do not need full-time help, or that a live-in maid will interfere with your privacy or control, a part-time maid may better serve your needs. You can arrange to have her come daily, or a few days a week, for as many hours as necessary.

RESPONSIBILITIES OF DOMESTIC EMPLOYEES

Prior to interviewing maids, gardeners and drivers, make a list of the responsibilities you wish each to accept and a list of tasks that members of your family will carry out themselves. During the interview, it is advisable to discuss with potential employees the tasks they will be expected to perform, and to briefly mention details of when and how the tasks should be done. Be sure to ask applicants if there are tasks they cannot or will not do. Muslims prefer not to touch dogs or pork products, and most Hindus and some Buddhists prefer not to cook beef.

In 2000, the Government suggested that Muslim maids be hired only by Muslim employers and implemented regulations that require non-Muslim employers to sign an agreement when they hire Muslim maids. The agreement states that employers will provide Muslim employees with a place to pray, allow them to pray five times a day, allow them to fast during the month of Ramadhan, and will not ask them to do any tasks that involve dogs or pigs.

FINDING DOMESTIC HELP

Most of the experienced Malaysian maids in K.L. are older Chinese women who now prefer to take part-time jobs with two or three clients rather to work for just one client. Many expatriates prefer to hire these maids for part-time positions because they tend to be flexible about the duties they will perform. These maids are most often hired from departing expatriates. To find the names of expatriates who will be departing soon, ask your friends, enquire at the schools for expatriate children, enquire at clubs and organisations, and check for advertisements in the expatriate magazines, *The Finder* and *The Expat*. If none of the above courses of action gets results, try advertising in newsletters or on bulletin boards of companies, places of worship or social organisations, or on bulletin boards in local markets.

In recent years, many young Malaysian women who have not had the opportunity to further their education have chosen factory jobs rather than domestic work, so experienced domestic employees are becoming increasingly hard to find. To fill the demand for maids, the Government has allowed in domestic workers from Indonesia, Thailand, the Philippines, Cambodia and Sri Lanka.

Many expatriates hire full-time maids who are from the Philippines, as many of these young women speak English well and have received training in the duties they will be expected to perform. Also, expatriates sometimes are able to arrange to take their Filipina maids with them to their next postings after they complete their assignments in Malaysia. These maids are usually hired through an agency. Agencies do all the paperwork and are responsible for handling any problems that arise between maids and their employers. Be sure to work through a legal and reputable agency, however, as quality of service varies greatly.

Be aware that some expatriates have attempted to "pinch" maids, especially Filipina maids, from local employers by approaching the maids in churches and shopping malls and offering them salaries higher than those that they were receiving. This has caused trouble for local employers because the maids then complain that they want to be released from their contracts so they can go to work for the expatriates. Such activity is considered an offence and the Immigration Department could respond by deporting the maids and reviewing the work permits of the expatriates involved.

INTERVIEWING

The interview provides the opportunity for you to evaluate each applicant as a prospective employee, and for each applicant to evaluate you as a prospective employer.

Plan for the interview by making a list of questions you want to ask each applicant, a list of hours, duties and regulations you expect each employee to follow, and a list of benefits you are prepared to offer. (If you work through an agency, the benefits will be stated in the contract.)

Request that local applicants take their letters of reference and identification cards to the interview. Plan to interview them in your home so they will be able to see their future work site.

During the interview, describe your family's lifestyle and entertainment habits, and introduce each prospective employee to all family members and pets. Be sure to introduce your children to applicants who will be responsible for child care and to watch their reactions to each other. Then follow your instincts as to whether or not the match will be a good one.

Questions for Applicants

Important considerations are the applicant's trustworthiness, fluency in English or other language that your family speaks, familiarity with household appliances, and experience or training in cooking and taking care of children. If at all possible, discuss these issues with former employers.

Experience and Identification: Find out as much as you can about prospective employees: enquire about whom they have worked for in the past, what their responsibilities were, and why their employment was terminated. Always ask for references and ascertain that applicants are no longer employed and that their termination was favourable. Ask to see each applicant's identification card and check to see that the person you are interviewing is the same as the person pictured on the card. (You may be in for a surprise!) For your records, be sure to keep a copy of the full name, address and identification number of each applicant and employee. When interviewing for a driver, request a copy of the person's driving record. (Malaysians suggest that the most reliable and safe driver will be a recently retired man who has a family and reputation to maintain.)

Family Situation: Ask a prospective local maid what her family situation is, and if appropriate, what she will do when her children are sick or if she becomes pregnant.

Health and Insurance: For the protection of your family, ask applicants if they have any health problems, and inform local maids that they must have a **medical check-up** (at your expense) before you hire them permanently. Foreign maids are given a test for tuberculosis, malaria, leprosy, sexually transmitted diseases and HIV/AIDS when they enter the country. These tests and tests for worms, salmonella and other parasites should be repeated yearly on every employee.

All employees who will be cooking and taking care of children should be in excellent health. Employers usually pay for periodic medical examinations and any treatment employees require during their period of employment. If you hire your maid through a legal agency, the agency's fee will include medical insurance. If you are not happy with the maid's health condition, the agency will replace the maid within one month after she begins employment.

Although not required by law, it is recommended that employers hold **accident liability insurance** for their domestic employees. Domestic employees hired through an agency will be covered by a minimal insurance, the cost of which is included in the fee. However, more comprehensive insurance should include coverage for injuries sustained as a result of accidents occurring while the employee is on the job and compensation of dependants if an on-the-job accident results in death or permanent disability.

Aetna Insurance company, among others, offers a personal accident policy and an in-patient hospital and surgical benefits policy that employers can buy to cover maids. Contact Aetna at Tel: 03-2161-7255; Fax: 03-2162-4939.

Trial Period: It is to your benefit to hire new employees for a trial period of two weeks to three months, and to pay them on a daily or weekly basis during that time. Explain your policy to all applicants. After the trial period, you are legally required to give two weeks' notice of dismissal, or two weeks' pay in lieu of notice.

REGULATIONS

The easiest way to prevent misunderstandings is to discuss with domestic employees the house rules you want them to follow. Maids generally expect to be able to use the family telephone and television. Many employers limit the maid's use of the phone to ten minutes per call and prohibit long distance calls; many provide the maid with a television for her room. Set restrictions based on your maid's need for entertainment and phone contact with family and friends, and your family's need for privacy, quiet and access to the telephone and television.

Instruct employees to refrain from letting strangers in the gate or house, and discuss with your maid whether or not you will allow her to have visitors come into your house when you are home, when you are not home, on her day off, etc. (Most employers will not allow employees to entertain visitors at the house, even when the family is away.) Also, consider how you will handle dating if your maid is single.

If your maid will have responsibility for child care, you can discuss with her the behaviour you expect from your children and the regulations you set for them, but it is unrealistic to expect your maid to discipline your children in the same way you do. Cultural views on child rearing vary greatly, and it is not likely that you and your maid will see eye-to-eye. Most maids feel it is their duty to keep the children happy and will go out of their way to do so.

Ask your local employees to telephone you if they will be late for work or will not come because of illness or family emergency, and request that they give two weeks' notice if they plan to terminate their employment.

SALARIES

If you hire an employee through an agency, compensation is determined by the agency and stated in an employment contract. If you hire a local employee, compensation is an issue for negotiation between you and the employee. Salaries depend on the following: whether employees are part-time or live-in; how many hours they work; the extent of their duties; their previous work experience; their fluency in English; their training in child care; their ability to swim; the size of your house and family; the amount of entertaining you do; the location of your house; and the other benefits you provide.

It is advisable to keep a notebook of all salary and other payments to domestic employees, and if you pay in cash or cheque, to have the employee sign the book to acknowledge receipt of payment.

Average monthly salary ranges that expatriates pay for domestic employees are as follows: full-time, live-in maid who does a variety of tasks (RM700-1200); part-time maid (RM400-700); part-time gardener (RM200-400); full-time driver (RM900-1500); security guard (RM500-700).

BENEFITS

In addition to salary, the employer usually provides all employees with benefits such as time off, holidays, yearly bonuses and payment for medical treatment. Live-in employees are given furnished living quarters and a food allowance or basic staples.

Time Off: Time off for full-time maids depends primarily on their nationality. In K.L., Malaysian maids usually have a day-and-a-half or two days off each week, either from Saturday after lunch to early Monday morning, or from early Sunday morning to Monday afternoon. Filipina maids, most of whom are Christian, take Sunday off as that is the day they go to church and get together with friends. Maids of some other nationalities are discouraged from taking days off because some authorities feel that various social problems are caused by foreign maids mixing freely. Be sure to discuss time off when you interview applicants or talk with employment agencies.

Holidays: All full-time Malaysian employees should receive at least a one-week paid vacation. Malays generally prefer to take their holiday during Hari Raya Puasa (the dates vary yearly). Chinese prefer Chinese New Year (in January or February), or Christmas and Easter if they are Christian. Indians prefer Deepavali (in October or November) if they are Hindu, Hari Raya Puasa if they are Muslim, or Christmas if they are Christian. Some Malaysian applicants may ask to have all public holidays off. If it would be inconvenient to have your maid absent for all those days as well as for a week during a religious holiday, negotiate for a certain number of public holidays. Some employees may prefer to work on public holidays and take a longer religious holiday.

During the interview, ask local applicants which holiday they observe. If they observe the same holiday as you do and you plan to entertain or be away on vacation during the holiday, you may not want to hire them as they will not be able to help you with entertaining or to tend the house in your absence.

Bonuses: It is customary to give bonuses to Malaysian employees before their yearly vacation. The norm is to pay one month's salary if the employee has been with you for a year or more, or to pro-rate the bonus if the employee has been with you for less than a year. Most expatriate families also give small gifts

95

of money, food or clothes to their domestic employees (and garbage collector) during whatever New Year the families celebrate. Policies applied to immigrant maids vary, so discuss this with the employment agency.

Employee Provident Fund: Some Malaysian domestic employees are enrolled in the Employee Provident Fund (EPF), known in Malay as *Kumpulan Wang Simpanan Pekerja* (KWSP). This is a pension plan towards which some employers must contribute a portion of the employee's salary. Regulations vary depending whether the employee is employed by your company or hired through an agent. For details, speak with your employer or agent, or contact the General Manager, E.P.F., Road 5/37, off Jalan Gasing, Petaling Jaya, Selangor, (Tel. 03-755-7550; Fax: 03-756-3386).

Furnished Living Quarters: If you plan to have a live-in maid, it is thoughtful to see that her living quarters are clean and pleasantly decorated. Employers generally furnish a bed, a chest of drawers, a table and chairs, a closet (if none is built in), lamps, a mirror and a ceiling or floor fan (even if there is air conditioning); many also furnish a pillow, sheets, pillow cases, a blanket, a bedspread, curtains, a small desk and a television. Some provide dishes, kitchen utensils and basic condiments if they do not want the maid to use those of the family, or if the maid has a separate eating area and cooking facilities. Many of these items can be purchased at reasonable prices from departing expatriates; watch for announcements of sales in club, church, school and company newsletters and bulletin boards.

Food Allowance: For Malaysian live-in maids, employers customarily provide basic foods (rice, tea, coffee, sugar, etc.), or include a food allowance in the maid's salary so she can select and purchase the foods she prefers. For live-in maids who are from another country, employers are required to provide all food or a food allowance.

Other Benefits: Some employers pay for Malaysian employees' transportation to and from work. For live-in maids who are from another country, employers are required to provide toiletries, clothes and whatever else the maids need to maintain themselves. Be forewarned that when the maids go home to visit, they commonly take with them everything they possess and then return with an empty suitcase.

TRAINING AND SUPERVISION

If you have never trained and supervised domestic employees, you may be surprised to discover that these tasks can require a great deal of time, effort and patience. Keep in mind that because you are working with people who have grown up learning a culture, a language, and probably a religion different from your own, it is only natural that their views of the world and ways of doing things will be different as well. Through interaction with your employees, you will have the opportunity to learn about their culture just as they will learn about yours. Some tips for that interaction follow:

- Be clear about your expectations.
- Be realistic about your expectations.
- Demonstrate tasks.
- Be firm and consistent from the onset.
- Don't meddle.
- Be respectful.
- Be patient.
- Be appreciative.
- Don't make it easy for employees to steal.

DISMISSAL

Dismissal of Unsatisfactory Employees

It is preferable to dismiss an unacceptable employee as soon as possible, as more problems may arise if you try to live with the situation. Avoid firing someone when you are angry. Wait until you are calm and can speak slowly and politely, and wait until your spouse or a friend can be with you. Try to give the employee an explanation that will not cause anyone to lose face. For your own protection, have the employee sign a statement indicating his or her dates of employment and receipt of all outstanding salary.

Malaysian law requires that you give your employees two weeks' notice or two weeks' pay in lieu of notice. The second alternative usually causes less friction. It is inconsiderate to fire employees just before their main religious holiday; if possible, wait until some time after the holiday.

Dismissal of Satisfactory Employees

If you terminate the employment of competent and trustworthy employees, you could do them a favour by trying to find them new employment with other expatriate families. You should at least provide them with letters of recommendation written on company or personal stationery. The letters should include descriptions of duties, wages, performance and dates of employment. It is customary for employers to give Malaysian employees a bonus of half a month's salary for every year they have worked.

CHAPTER EIGHT

COMPLYING WITH REGULATIONS

THE PAPER CHASE

Foreign residents of Malaysia are required to obtain a variety of documents before and after their arrival and are expected to comply with certain regulations established by the Malaysian Government. These documents and regulations are discussed in the following sections.

PASSPORT REQUIREMENTS

All foreign nationals wishing to enter Malaysia must possess **internationally recognised travel documents**, such as passports or certificates of identity, that will remain valid for at least six months after the date of entry into the country.

Each family member, including each infant and child, should have his or her own **passport**. If a child is included in the passport of one of the parents, problems may arise if for some reason the child and the parent cannot travel together. If you leave your child in the care of someone else for a few days, make sure that the caretaker has access to your child's passport, as without it your child cannot leave the country for medical or other emergency reasons.

People who hold dual citizenship should use only one passport for entering and departing Malaysia and applying for work visas, as Malaysia does not recognise dual citizenship.

VISA REQUIREMENTS

Citizens of many countries can enter Malaysia without a visa for a visit of 14 days to three months (depending on nationality). Citizens of some countries cannot enter Malaysia without first obtaining a visa. As regulations change periodically, please check directly with a Malaysian Diplomatic Mission or with the Malaysian Immigration Department (3-6 Wisma Damansara, Jalan Semantan, Damansara Heights; Tel: 03-255-3633). Applications for visas should be made at least six to eight weeks in advance through the nearest Malaysian Diplomatic Mission or British Consular representative and must include the names of sponsors or references in Malaysia.

VISIT PASSES

Visit Passes, issued by the Malaysian Government in addition to or instead of visas, allow foreign citizens to enter and remain in Malaysia for a specific purpose and for a specific period of time. Every foreign national must obtain a Visit Pass before or upon arrival in Malaysia. It is the pass holder's responsibility to be sure that he or she always has a valid and appropriate Visit Pass. Visitors intending to extend their stay should apply at the nearest Immigration Office at least two days prior to the expiration of their Visit Pass. It is an offence (and a hassle) to overstay your Visit Pass, so check your documents carefully. Immigration officials are most likely to grant extensions to visitors who appear clean and neat, and who possess proof of onward passage and sufficient funds.

There are several different types of Visit Passes. **All but the Social Visit Pass and the Business Visit Pass require sponsorship in Malaysia, and should be applied for before arrival.** Sponsors must agree to assume responsibility for financial maintenance and repatriation of the pass holder if the need arises.

Social Visit Pass

Social Visit Passes are issued on arrival to visitors who enter Malaysia for social or tourist visits. They do not authorise holders to engage in any form of business or profession, or to give lectures or political talks.

Business Visit Pass

Business Visit Passes are issued on arrival to visitors who enter Malaysia for the following purposes: investigating business opportunities and investment potential; attending company meetings or seminars: inspecting company accounts; ensuring smooth running of the company; conducting business negotiations; introducing goods that are to be manufactured in Malaysia (not

101

direct sales or distribution); covering a convention or event (journalists); or participating in a sporting event. They do not authorise holders to accept employment, to act as consultants in any capacity, or to supervise the installation of machinery or construction of a factory.

Social Visit Passes may be converted into Business Visit Passes. Applicants must complete the proper forms at the Immigration Department, and submit a letter of recommendation from the Ministry of International Trade and Industry. This ruling does not apply to citizens of Singapore.

Professional Visit Pass

Foreigners invited to visit Malaysia for the purpose of conducting a training course, attending a conference, serving as an expert in any field (including cultural or religious), or performing in any sort of public entertainment must obtain a Professional Visit Pass. Validity of the pass varies, but does not exceed twelve months at one time. The local sponsor must submit the application to the Immigration Headquarters in K.L.

Employment Passes

Foreign nationals who intend to work and reside in Malaysia must obtain a Temporary Employment Pass or a regular Employment Pass from the Director General of Immigration. It is the responsibility of employers to apply for the appropriate pass for all foreign employees. At present, rules are strict, the application process can take many months, and a high percentage of applications are rejected. Foreign organisations with connections to subsidiary or joint venture organisations in Malaysia are strongly encouraged to let the Malaysian organisation apply for the appropriate pass; this tends to be a more effective approach than applying from headquarters through a local, independent representative.

The **Temporary Employment Pass** is issued to foreigners who enter Malaysia as unskilled workers (domestic help or workers in services, plantations, construction or manufacturing) whose contract of employment is for a maximum of two years and whose salary will not exceed RM1,200 a month. This pass is usually issued on a yearly basis.

The **Employment Pass** is issued to foreigners who enter Malaysia with professional expertise not readily available amongst Malaysians and who will be employed in Malaysia for not less than two years at a salary of more than RM1,200 a month. The period of validity of the pass will depend on the length of the employee's work contract. This pass is issued to people who will fill "Executive Posts," act as advisors in technical or engineering projects, oversee the installation of machinery or other equipment, or work in the Government or public sector or in a factory or business establishment.

Applications for Employment Passes must be submitted by the local employer to the Immigration Headquarters in K.L. There can be significant delays with issuance of Employment Passes. Consequently, to address business needs during the waiting period, some expatriates are left with no choice but to enter the country on a Visit Pass, and then to either renew the pass or leave the country for the weekend and obtain a new Visit Pass upon re-entry. Representatives of your sponsoring organisation will probably handle all the details involved in obtaining the appropriate passes for you and your family. If you don't have to handle this personally, it is better not to get involved. If you appear confused or frustrated when meeting Immigration officials you may create a bad image that can lead to complications in obtaining the passes. (The same applies to getting your shipment through Customs). Let the local experts handle these tasks and allow time for them to do their job. Go in person only if you are requested to do so, and then take your behavioural cues from your local company representative.

Dependant Passes and Dependant Employment

Dependants of foreigners who possess Employment Passes are eligible for Dependant Passes. These passes are usually issued for the same time period as the working family member's Employment Pass. Normally this pass is issued only to the wife and children of a male Employment Pass holder, and only after the husband/father has obtained an Employment Pass.

A dependant Pass holder who wishes to accept employment in Malaysia must first obtain permission from Malaysian Immigration authorities. The applicant must follow this procedure: 1) demonstrate possession of a skill that is needed; 2) find a local sponsor who will write an Invitation Letter of Employment; 3) leave the country with the letter; 4) re-enter the country, letter in hand; and 5) check "Business" as Purpose of Visit on the Immigration Control Card.

The applicant must enter on his or her own credentials, without reference to the fact that he or she qualifies as a dependant of someone already working in Malaysia. If the applicant's Employment Pass expires before his or her spouse's Employment Pass and cannot be renewed, the applicant must leave the country and re-enter on a Social Visit Pass. The Social Visit Pass can be converted to a Dependant Pass upon application at the Immigration Department.

Dependants of foreigners who hold a Temporary Employment Pass or a Professional Visit Pass may be issued a Social Visit Pass which is usually valid for the same time period as the Temporary Employment Pass or the Professional Visit Pass.

Employment of Foreign Spouses of Malaysian Citizens

Foreign spouses of Malaysian citizens may apply for Employment Passes, but many restrictions apply. Malaysians married to foreigners joke that their spouses spend more time at the Immigration office than at home. Applicants must have proper credentials and an offer of employment. They are not allowed to participate in local politics or trade unions, nor, in some cases, to start their own businesses. They may, however, apply to work in the firm of their Malaysian spouse or in another organisation. Foreign spouses are cautioned against making any remarks that might be construed as being offensive to the Malaysian people or government, as in such cases the Employment Pass could be revoked.

Student Pass

Foreigners entering Malaysia for the purpose of studying at approved educational institutions will be issued a Student Pass. Children of foreigners working in Malaysia can enter the country on a Dependant Pass. This pass can be converted to a Student Pass after the applicant submits a letter from the school he or she is attending, stating that he or she is a full-time student.

Re-entry Permits

All citizens and permanent residents of Malaysia are required to obtain a Re-entry Permit if they intend to leave the country and then return. A Re-entry Permit may be valid for a single entry or for multiple entries. A Multiple Re-entry Permit is generally valid for the length of one's Visit Pass or up to one year. Most employers obtain Multiple Re-entry Permits for their employees. If yours does not, you must apply in person at the Immigration Department.

Immigration Control

Upon entering Malaysia, foreigners receive an Immigration stamp in their passport, and an Immigration Control Card that must be surrendered to Immigration officials upon departure from the country.

Travel Between Malaysian Territories

Visit Passes for entry into Peninsular Malaysia are not automatically valid for entry into the East Malaysian State of Sarawak. For entry into Sarawak, foreigners must obtain a Visit Pass at the point of entry. A Visit Pass issued in Sarawak (or Sabah) is valid for entry into Peninsular Malaysia, provided the visitor travels directly. Immigration regulations are interpreted strictly in East Malaysia, so to avoid delay when travelling to or from East Malaysia, foreigners should make sure that their international travel document (passport), visa and Employment or other Visit Pass are still valid when they travel to or from East Malaysia.

IDENTIFICATION

Visitors, foreign residents and local residents are expected to carry identification at all times. If you intend to reside in Malaysia for one year or more, you are requested to obtain a National Registration Identity Card from the Registration Office nearest your residence, and to carry it with you.

LOSS OF PASSPORT

If you lose your passport in Malaysia, you should lodge a police report at the nearest police station and contact your embassy to request a new passport. Finally, to obtain a new endorsement, take your new passport and evidence of your date of arrival in the country to the Immigration Office.

DEPARTURE TAX

All travellers are required to pay an airport departure tax when flying to any domestic or international destination from any airport in Malaysia. The amount of tax varies according to the destination and is usually automatically added to the price of the plane ticket.

HEALTH REGULATIONS

Prior to your departure for Malaysia, it is advisable
Malaysian Diplomatic Mission and enquire about curr
regulations and requirements for immunisations. If you
passing through other countries on your way to Malaysia, be
to check health regulations for them all. At the time of writing
Certificates of Vaccination for Yellow Fever are required from
visitors above one year of age who have been in an affected area
(such as Africa or South America) within six days prior to their
arrival in Malaysia. In addition, if you intend to import
medications containing narcotics, request a letter of permission
from the Malaysian Diplomatic Mission in your country.

REGULATIONS FOR PETS

Import Licence

All pets entering Malaysia will require an **Import Licence** and a
Certificate of Health. Some pets imported from certain countries
will require a **Certificate of Inoculation against Rabies** and a

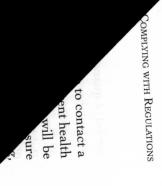

ns vary depending on the type of
details, contact the Department
at Perkhidmatan Haiwan), Blok
Perdana, off Jalan Semantan,
umpur, Malaysia (Tel: 60-3-254-
60-3-254-0092; Website:
dogcat.html).

Export Licence

If you will export your pet at the end of your stay, you must obtain
an Export Licence and a Certificate of Health within fourteen
days of your departure.

Dog Licences

All dogs must be licensed yearly. K.L. residents can purchase
licences at **Dewan Bandaraya** located on Jalan Raja Laut (Tel:
03-291-6011). Residents of P.J. and other towns can purchase
licences at City Council (*Padung Kota*) offices. In K.L., dogs must
be kept on one's own property, either in a cage, on a leash or
restricted by a fence.

CUSTOMS REGULATIONS

All residents and non-residents entering Malaysia are required
by law to declare to Customs officials all dutiable or prohibited
goods in their possession, whether carried on their person or in
their baggage. Failure to do so could result in heavy fines, forfeiture
of goods, or prosecution in court. Honesty is the best approach.

The regulations outlined below are subject to change. If
you have any questions, write to the Public Relations Unit, Royal
Customs and Excise Department, 4th Floor, Block 11,
Government Offices Complex, Jalan Duta, 50596 Kuala Lumpur,
Malaysia; Tel: 60-3-651-2563/6088; Fax: 60-3-651-2548.

Shipment of Household Effects

Expatriates who ship their household effects and personal belongings to Malaysia, are not generally charged Customs duty or sales tax. You or your shipping agent, however, may be called upon to satisfy Customs officials that you are the owner of all the goods, that the goods have been in your possession and use for at least three months, and that they will remain in your possession for at least three months beyond the date of importation.

Duty-free Allowance

As a rule, residents and non-residents entering Malaysia may import used personal effects and equipment intended for private use without paying duty, but Customs officials may require registration of valuables. In addition, the following items are admitted duty free: tobacco not exceeding 225 grams (the equivalent of 200 cigarettes or 50 cigars); wine, spirits or malt liquor not exceeding a total of one litre; dutiable foods not exceeding a total value of RM75; cosmetics and soap not exceeding a total value of RM200; unused footwear not exceeding one pair; unused wearing apparel not exceeding three pieces; portable electric and battery-operated appliances for personal care and hygiene not exceeding one unit each; and gifts and souvenirs to the value of not more than RM200. Items totalling not more than RM500 (excluding liquor and cigarettes) purchased at the Free Ports of Labuan and Langkawi may be imported duty free by people who have spent at least 72 hours on one of the islands.

The following goods, even if new, may also be imported duty free: pocket calculators; cigarette lighters; computers; perfume and skin care products; fishing equipment; fountain pens; gold coins; golf clubs; photographic equipment; pocket watches; wrist watches and clocks; printed books, newspapers and journals; racquets for sports; video tapes; camera equipment and most film.

Duty and Tax Liability

Duty payable on wine, liquor, spirits, tobacco, cigarettes and motor vehicles is variable. Duty payable on all other non-commercial goods is 30% of the value. Sales tax also may be charged. Foreign residents of Malaysia may or may not be charged duty on items they import upon any entry after their first entry and upon any packages they receive by mail or courier.

If you are charged duty that seems unreasonable, or if you have any questions about Customs duty, ask to see a Senior Customs Officer. If you know you will be importing items that might be subject to high duty, allow plenty of extra time for your border crossing so that time won't force you to give in and rush off if a problem arises. If time and patience are on your side you may be able to work something out, but don't expect to accomplish anything in a hurry or by force. Do settle the claim while you are at Customs, as according to Customs laws, once an item has been released from Customs control, the owner can make no claim against the duty imposed upon it. Be sure to obtain an official receipt for any duty you pay.

Temporary Visitor's Deposits

Short-term visitors who wish to import dutiable items and to keep them in Malaysia for a maximum of three months, may be able to avoid payment of Customs duty by depositing the sum equivalent to the duty (30% of value) with the Customs Office at any main point of entry, and by requesting a refund when the items are exported. Presentation of the receipt of purchase for dutiable items will speed the process of determining the duty. Be sure to keep the official deposit receipt as you will have to present it, along with the actual items, to obtain a refund upon your departure.

ATA Carnet

The ATA Carnet allows duty-free temporary import of exhibition goods, advertising materials and trade samples of commercial value. The items covered by the Carnet must not be sold and must be exported within the time period specified on the Carnet. Trade samples with no commercial value may be admitted duty free and do not require an ATA Carnet, but their importation must be justified to the Customs officer upon entry.

Import and Export of Motor Vehicles

Motor vehicles that are manufactured and assembled abroad and not more than seven years old may be imported. An Import Permit is required, and Customs duty (140% to 300% depending on the value of the vehicle) and sales tax (10%) will be assessed upon delivery. Diplomatic personnel may be exempt from duty and tax. Foreign nationals may take motor vehicles into Malaysia free of duty for three months by registering them with Customs at the point of entry and by obtaining an International Circulation Permit. If an imported vehicle is not exported after three months, the owner must pay Customs duty and sales tax.

Import and Export of Antiques

Antiques imported into Malaysia should be declared at Customs Arrival Checkpoints so that they can be exported later without difficulty. The export of Malaysian antiques is strictly regulated and requires a permit obtainable from the Director General of Museums.

Censored Imports

All films, laser discs, video tapes and CD-ROMs, including those intended for personal viewing, must be handed over to Customs on arrival. The items may be approved for import on the spot or may be taken temporarily for review. After obtaining approval for import, you may be required to complete a Customs declaration form.

Mail

Documents with no commercial value are seldom subject to delays at Customs. Parcels generally have commercial value and are subject to Customs inspection; the contents might be taxable or dutiable. Please note that to expedite Customs clearance, if you are having prescription medicines sent to you, request that a copy of the prescription be enclosed in the package. Also, expect delays of up to three weeks for Customs clearance of packages containing videotapes.

ADDITIONAL REGULATIONS

Appearance

Authorities throughout Southeast Asia frown on people who look unclean and untidy as this sort of appearance is associated with "hippies" and illegal drugs. Immigration authorities may deny entrance to people whose appearance raises questions about their involvement with drugs or about their financial solvency. Therefore, it is to your benefit to look neat, clean and conservatively dressed when you pass through Customs or visit embassies or government offices.

To show proper respect, visitors to mosques are expected to cover their shoulders and legs (no tank tops or shorts). In addition, nudity on beaches is illegal.

Arrests

Foreign citizens residing in Malaysia are subject to Malaysian laws. In the event that you are arrested and imprisoned, your embassy does not have the power to demand your release, provide you with legal advice, obtain favoured status for you, or otherwise interfere with due process of Malaysian law. Malaysian laws are strict, and punishments are more severe than in many Western countries. In serious cases that require expert legal counsel, you may want to contact representatives of the International Legal Defence Counsel (Tel: 1-215-977-9982, Fax: 1-215-564-2859).

Gambling

The only gambling games officially allowed in Malaysia are those sanctioned by the Government. They are: weekly sports Toto, the casino in Genting, the Social Welfare Lottery, weekend turf-club race course betting, three-digit lotteries organised by turf clubs and their authorised agents, and four-digit lotteries run by Empat Nombor Ekor Berhad (ENE). It is illegal to play cards or games of chance for money, even in the privacy of one's home or hotel room.

Illegal Drugs

Malaysia has launched a serious campaign against drug abuse. **TRAFFICKING OF ILLEGAL DRUGS (DADAH) CARRIES A DEATH PENALTY THAT IS STRICTLY ENFORCED. THE ABUSE OF DRUGS IS ALSO CONSIDERED A SERIOUS OFFENCE.**

Under Malaysian law, anyone convicted as a drug trafficker is subject to the death penalty, regardless of the amount of drugs in his or her possession. Any person found in possession of 15 or more grams of heroin, or slightly larger amounts of other drugs (including marijuana), is automatically considered to be a drug trafficker. Foreigners detained by authorities for possession or sales of drugs face the same penalties as Malaysians.

If drugs are found in your possession, the burden of proof of innocence rests on you. Warn every member of your family to avoid using drugs or associating with people whom they know or suspect to be using or selling drugs. Also warn them not to agree to carry anything through Customs for anyone whom they do not know well; and warn them not to leave their bags unattended in airports, bus stations or train stations, or on planes, buses or trains, especially prior to crossing borders.

Liquor

For most Malaysians, drinking is not a typical pastime, but beer, wine and hard liquor are served in pubs, hotels and some restaurants; beer is also available in some coffee shops. The minimum legal drinking age is eighteen.

Smoking

Smoking is prohibited in some public places such as mosques, cinemas, theatres, elevators and public buses. Watch for signs that say *Jangan Merokok!* (Don't Smoke!) or *Dilarang Merokok!* (Smoking Prohibited!). Most large restaurants in K.L. have smoking and non-smoking sections.

Tipping

Most leading hotels and restaurants add a 10% service charge (and a 5% Government tax) to the bill, so tipping is not necessary. The 10% service charge, however, is used to pay employees' salaries, so if you receive excellent service, you could leave an additional tip. In small establishments that do not include a tip in the bill, tip 10% of your bill for good service. Tipping in some hotels and restaurants is not encouraged and these establishments may advertise a "No Tipping Policy". For car jockeys and special errands run by a porter, bellman or messenger, a tip of RM4 is appropriate. Taxi drivers may be tipped a small amount, but tipping is not necessary. Office clerks, airport employees, Government employees and employees of private clubs should not be tipped.

EMBASSY SERVICES

Nearly 100 countries have diplomatic missions in K.L. Most missions are closed on Saturdays, Sundays, Malaysian public holidays and holidays celebrated in their respective countries. Many embassies offer the following services: business briefings, lists of Malaysian lawyers and doctors, regulations and procedures for getting married in Malaysia, medical evacuation, notarial services, power of attorney, renewal or replacement of passports, registration for military service, registration of the birth of children (to establish citizenship for travel and other purposes), tax information and forms, and absentee ballot forms for voting in your country's national elections.

In the unlikely event that a member of your family dies in Malaysia, you should notify your embassy and your employer immediately. Both should assist you in making necessary arrangements. Another source of help, if you are a member, is a travellers' assistance service which will arrange and cover costs for transportation of the remains of a deceased insured individual to the place of burial.

Please note that if your spouse is not a citizen or permanent resident of your country, he or she may have to apply to your embassy for an **Immigrant Visa** before returning permanently to your country. Immigrant Visas can take several months to process.

CHAPTER NINE

MANAGING YOUR FINANCES

THE FINANCIAL SCENE

In Malaysia, a wide range of financial services is offered through a network of domestic and foreign-incorporated commercial banks, and many foreigners are able to do their business in a Malaysian branch of a bank based in their home country. However, managing your finances in Malaysia may be somewhat different than managing your finances at home. The following sections briefly cover many aspects of personal finances that may be of concern to you.

For more detailed information on banking and finance in Malaysia, refer to the book *Banking and Finance in Malaysia* by Johnson Pang and visit the **Bank Negara** Website: www.bnm.gov.my/.

MALAYSIAN CURRENCY

Legal tender of Malaysia is the Ringgit Malaysia or Malaysian Dollar, denoted by the symbol RM. Paper currency is issued by the Central Bank (Bank Negara Malaysia) in denominations of RM1, RM2, RM5, RM10, RM20, RM50, RM100; RM500 and RM1,000 notes were phased out of circulation in 1999. Banks do not accept any bank notes that are significantly defaced. The Ringgit is divided into 100 sen. Coins in circulation include the 1-sen made of copper, the 5-sen, 10-sen, 20-sen and 50-sen denominations made of nickel, and the gold-coloured MR1 denomination.

CURRENCY RESTRICTIONS

There are some restrictions on the amount of money people may take in or out of Malaysia. For complete information on foreign exchange controls, visit the **Bank Negara** Website: www.bnm.gov.my/. Residents and non-residents may carry into and out of Malaysia up to RM1,000 in Ringgit notes. There is no limit on the amount of foreign currency notes and travellers' cheques they may carry into Malaysia. Non-residents may carry out of Malaysia foreign currency notes, including travellers' cheques, not exceeding the amount brought in. Residents may carry out foreign currency notes, including travellers' cheques, not exceeding the equivalent of RM10,000. All arriving and departing travellers (including children) must complete a Travellers' Declaration Card regardless of the amount of currency carried.

You may carry money to Malaysia in the form of cash, travellers' cheques or Demand Drafts. The latter are issued by your bank to a branch bank or correspondent bank in Malaysia. You present the Demand Draft (and positive identification) at the appropriate bank and receive your money. In some banks payment is immediate; in others there is a delay of up to 21 days,

117

especially if you do not yet have an account in the bank. Plan for this possible delay by taking sufficient cash or travellers' cheques, or by making arrangements with your bank and a credit card company so that you will be able to withdraw cash from an ATM.

CURRENCY EXCHANGE

The ringgit is backed by gold and foreign assets, and until the economic downturn in the late 1990s, it remained quite strong and stable. Since that time it has been pegged to the dollar at the rate of RM3.80 to US$1.00. The best **exchange rates** for foreign cash and travellers' cheques are given by licensed money changers; slightly lower rates are given by large banks. Generally, hotels and banks in airport arrival halls give the lowest rates.

Licensed money changers operate legally in Malaysia. They can be found in small sundry, jewellery or stationery shops along main streets and in office buildings and shopping centres. Interestingly, most money changers are Indian Muslims who have taken over the business from their fathers and grandfathers. Money changers accept cash in most major currencies. Transactions seldom take more than a few minutes and generally no service charge is levied. Not all money changers offer the same rate of exchange, however, so it pays to compare and to request a better rate if you are changing a large amount of money. Most money changers operate from 8:30 a.m. to 6:00 p.m. daily, except Sundays and holidays. Some commercial banks are also licensed to exchange foreign currency, but they levy a service charge and a single transaction can take up to an hour if the bank is busy.

Please note that outside of Malaysia, it may be impossible to convert Malaysian Ringgit to other currencies except at branches of Malayan Banking Berhad.

TRAVELLERS' CHEQUES

Travellers' cheques can be cashed at most licensed money changers and at many commercial banks in K.L., all state capitals and some smaller towns. Some large tourist shops, many leading restaurants and all international-class hotels accept them, but at a low rate of exchange. Smaller shops in shopping complexes usually do not accept travellers' cheques. To facilitate cheque cashing, carry cheques issued by well-known internationally recognised companies such as American Express, Bank of America, Barclay's, Citicorp, and Thomas Cooke. Travellers' cheques may be purchased in Malaysia in a variety of foreign currencies. In most cases, banks charge a commission and a stamp duty.

CREDIT CARDS

Major hotels, leading stores and restaurants, and some small shops accept credit cards such as Visa, MasterCard, Diners Club, JCB and American Express. When you use a credit card to make purchases in small shops, merchants may charge an extra 3%-5% to cover the percentage they must pay the credit card company.

Many foreigners maintain accounts in Malaysia as well as at home. In Malaysia, credit and charge cards are issued by numerous commercial banks and a few finance companies. Foreign residents can apply for a card issued in Malaysia by presenting a valid Employment Pass which has at least six months' validity remaining. Most companies require proof of an annual income of RM18,000 for a classic card and RM40,000 for a gold card. Cards for foreigners are usually issued with an expiration date that corresponds to the date of expiration of the Employment Pass. For security reasons in case cards are lost or stolen, some expatriates opt for a low credit limit for cards they will use in Malaysia and the region. They use the cards to pay local bills, and then pay off the balance monthly. Also, in order to protect

119

their accounts, many people use a paper shredder (available in Malaysia) to destroy credit card receipts and other personal documents.

BANKS

The Malaysian banking system is dominated by a few large banks with numerous branches. The largest are Bank Negara Malaysia, the country's central bank, and Malayan Banking and Bumiputra-Commerce Bank, in which the Government has financial interests.

Most foreigners do their banking in a full-service branch of a foreign commercial bank. It may be worthwhile to make contact with a bank official in a bank in your country that has a branch in Malaysia and to ask for the name of an official in the Malaysian branch. Bank officials may be able to assist you in an emergency if you have previously made contact with them. As a safeguard, give your attorney and spouse or other family member the names, addresses, phone numbers and fax numbers of bank officials.

A list of foreign commercial banks with full-service branches appears below. For a list of all banks, consult the Telephone Directory under the heading "Banks".

Branches of Foreign Banks in Malaysia
- **Australia** (Westpac Banking Corporation)
- **Canada** (Bank of Nova Scotia)
- **England** (Standard Chartered Bank)
- **France** (Bank Paribas)
- **Germany** (Deutsche Bank)
- **Hong Kong** (HongKong Bank Malaysia, Hongkong & Shanghai Banking Corporation)
- **Japan** (Bank of Tokyo)
- **Middle East** (Arab Malaysian Bank)
- **Singapore** (Chung Khiaw Bank, Overseas Chinese Banking

Corporation, Overseas Union Bank, United Overseas Bank)
* **Thailand** (Bangkok Bank)
* **United States** (Bank of America, Chase Manhattan Bank, Citibank)

Automated Teller Machines

Many banks have Automated Teller Machines (ATMs) that allow customers to make transactions in Savings and Current (Checking) Accounts during and after regular bank hours. Customers can withdraw cash, deposit cheques or cash, make payments, or transfer funds between accounts within the branch or between other branches.

Many credit card companies allow holders to obtain cash advances through ATMs. Fees, interest rates and restrictions vary. Some credit card companies charge a high rate of interest from the day the advance is made until the balance has been cleared. American Express does not charge interest for advances. Amex card holders can withdraw cash at ATMs of Bank Simpanan Nasional in locations throughout the country. They can also cash personal cheques at the main office of Amex in K.L. (18th Floor, Menara Weld, Jalan Raja Chulan; Tel: 03-213-0000; Fax: 03-206-2410). Green Card holders can purchase the equivalent of US$200 in local currency and the equivalent of US$800 in travellers' cheques every 21 days, subject to local regulations and cash availability; Gold Card and Platinum Card holders can draw up to US$2000.

Electronic Banking

Some expatriates maintain their home country bank accounts while they are in Malaysia and access those accounts through the Internet. Electronic banking for accounts established in Malaysia is currently being developed.

Safe Deposit Boxes

Safe deposit boxes can be rented at most banks for a small fee. To be on the safe side, store your important papers and small valuables such as jewellery in safe deposit boxes rather than at home.

FINANCIAL SERVICES

Most full-service commercial banks offer a wide range of financial services including the following: transfer of funds, current (checking) accounts, savings accounts, term deposit accounts, and status enquiries (credit reports), direct salary deposits, loans, investments, credit cards, and safe deposit box rentals.

Domestic Transfer of Funds

All transfers of funds within Malaysia must be made in Malaysian currency and can be made as follows:

- **Cashier's Orders**, also known as Banker's Cheques and Manager's Cheques, can be purchased at banks for unlimited amounts. They are generally used only for payments within the same locality as the issuing bank.
- **Demand Drafts**, also known as Banker's Drafts, can be purchased at banks for unlimited amounts and may be used to make payments anywhere in the country. A Demand Draft is a written request from an issuing bank to a receiving bank, requiring that the receiving bank pay on demand the sum stated on the draft. To apply for a draft you must specify the name of the beneficiary (an individual or an account), the passport number and local address of the beneficiary, the currency and amount, and the name and address·of the bank at which the draft will be paid.
- **Telegraphic Transfer** allows rapid transfer of funds. The issuing bank will send instructions to the receiving bank by cable, telex or telephone. Applicants are required to provide the same information as for a Demand Draft and to pay a fee.

122

International Transfer of Funds

Non-residents who are working in Malaysia can make international transfers in foreign currency. No approval is required for transfers from one non-resident to another non-resident regardless of amount. For transfers in excess of the equivalent of RM10,000 between a resident and a non-resident, a Form P (for payments) or Form R (for receipts) must be completed. It is not an approval per se, but a declaration of the purpose of the movement of funds between the resident and non-resident. Transfers may be made in any foreign currency, but banks may automatically change incoming foreign currency into Malaysian currency (at the current buying rate) unless instructions on the transfer state otherwise.

If you plan to transfer funds in or out of Malaysia, you can expedite the process before you leave home by opening an account in a bank in your country that has a full-service branch in Malaysia, or by asking your local bank if they correspond with a large commercial bank that has a branch there. Through one of these avenues, you should be able to arrange for direct transfer of funds between your home country bank account and an account you open in the commercial bank branch in Malaysia.

There are two primary methods for international transfer of private funds: Demand Draft and Telegraphic Transfer. The latter is the fastest, but the first is more economical.

An **International Demand Draft** is usually drawn in a foreign currency on an overseas branch of a bank in Malaysia or on a foreign correspondent or agent bank. The draft is issued to the applicant for a small fee. Recipients must pay Malaysian stamp duty on all Inward Drafts. The application is the same as for the Domestic Demand Draft.

Telegraphic Transfer allows rapid international transfer of funds. The issuing bank will cable, telex or telephone instructions to the receiving bank . Applicants are required to provide the same information as for a Demand Draft and to pay a fee.

123

Most banks will not accept transfer of funds unless the recipient has an account with the bank. Please note that the initial transfer with which you open a new account can take up to three weeks to clear. It can be difficult to arrange telegraphic transfers to Malaysia through small rural banks abroad that have no direct connections with banks in Malaysia, and in most cases the service charges are high.

Standing Instructions (Standing Orders) allow a customer to instruct his bank to periodically transfer money from his account to a specified recipient. The recipient can be an individual, an organisation or a bank account. Foreigners sometimes use this service to make deposits into their home country accounts, to pay insurance premiums, or to pay loan instalments. Regulations are similar to those for other transfer instruments.

Current Accounts (Checking Accounts)

Most foreigners maintain their old current account back home, and open a Malaysian Ringgit account in Malaysia. The home-country account is useful for paying taxes, paying off loans, making investments, depositing salary cheques, ordering something from home, paying college tuition for children, or having access to cash while you are on home leave. A Malaysian Ringgit current account is useful for paying local rent, grocery, utility and other bills.

Before opening an account, compare the services and account requirements of several large full-service banks, as both vary somewhat. Many banks allow deposits and withdrawals at any branch, and some have Express Deposit facilities that allow you to pay into your account without waiting in line. In some banks, overdraft protection can be arranged. Few banks pay interest on individual current accounts, but some have a system to transfer balances into interest-bearing savings accounts. Most banks do not have a system for returning cancelled cheques with bank statements.

To open an account, you will need your passport for identification. Also, you might be asked to present a letter from your present employer, from the bank with which you have done business most recently, or from a current customer of the bank in which you wish to open an account.

Writing Cheques

Malaysian banks follow the British system for issuing and cashing cheques. Issued cheques are of two types, **"bearer"** and **"to order"**. Cheques made out to "bearer" may be cashed by anyone, while cheques made out to "to order" require endorsement by the recipient. A "bearer" cheque may be converted to a "to order" cheque by deleting the word "bearer".

Either type of cheque may be **"crossed"** so that it can be deposited into an account but cannot be cashed by an individual. To cross a cheque, draw two parallel diagonal lines on the upper left corner. Cheques sent in the mail should be protected by writing the words **"Account Payee Only"** inside the crossing so that the cheque can be paid only into the recipient's account. Businesses cross cheques by stamping them with "For Deposit Into Payee A/C Only".

A "crossed bearer" cheque can be paid into any account, while a "crossed to order" cheque can be deposited only into the recipient's account. The recipient of a "crossed to order" cheque may convert it into a "crossed bearer" cheque by endorsing it on the reverse side.

To avoid confusion, follow these suggestions when writing cheques:

- date your cheques according to the British system of day-month-year;
- sign your full name, not just your initials, if you alter a cheque (or, better yet, rewrite the cheque as banks may not accept corrected cheques);

- write your invoice number or credit card number on the back of your cheques, rather than on the front; and
- **IF YOU WANT A CHEQUE TO BE CONVERTIBLE TO CASH, DO NOT CROSS IT.**

Savings Accounts

Savings accounts are available only in Malaysian Ringgit. Individuals wishing to open an account usually need only present identification and a minimum deposit (the amount of which varies). Children over age twelve can open accounts in their own names. Interest rates for savings accounts are set by individual banks. Some banks calculate interest daily (based on the balance at the end of each day); others do so monthly (based on the balance from the 15th day to the end of the month); some compound interest. Some banks credit interest to savings accounts monthly; others do it every six months. All interest earned on savings accounts is subject to withholding tax.

Most banks allow deposits or withdrawals at any branch in the country with the presentation of a savings passbook; many allow purchase of Demand Drafts and Cashiers' Cheques as well as transfer payments on savings accounts at any branch.

It is suggested that foreign couples residing in Malaysia open both separate and joint savings accounts so that both husband and wife will have the authority to deposit, withdraw and transfer money without the signature of the other. This is essential as spouses may travel separately for business, pleasure or emergencies, and because, in the unfortunate event of one spouse dying, joint bank accounts, assets and safe deposit boxes would be frozen and the surviving spouse would not be allowed access to them.

Term Deposit Accounts

A Term Deposit Account (or Fixed Deposit Account) allows a depositor to earn a pre-set rate of interest on a deposit placed in a bank for a fixed period of time. The minimum deposit required varies. It is possible for non-residents who are working in Malaysia (with valid Employment Passes) to open term deposit accounts in Malaysian Ringgit and in several foreign currencies. Interest rates for Term Deposit Accounts are quoted at the discretion of individual banks. Penalties apply if a deposit is withdrawn prior to maturity. No tax is levied on interest earned on Term Deposit accounts of up to RM100,000 for a period of up to twelve months or for interest earned on Term Deposits of any amount for periods of twelve months or more.

Credit Reports (Status Enquiries)

Before closing a business deal, an individual may want to request from his banker a report on the financial standing of another individual. Some local banks and branches of foreign banks will provide such reports for their customers. The person making the inquiry must supply the name and address of the bank at which the firm in question has an account. Banks disclaim any liability on the credit reports they provide.

WILLS

To avoid legal problems in case of death, it is suggested that all expatriate adults living in Malaysia (including each spouse) have a will that states who should receive their assets and in what proportion. Under Malaysian law, if a woman dies intestate (without a will), her whole estate goes to her husband; if a man dies intestate, one-third of the estate goes to his wife and two-thirds to his issue (children). If you have children, be sure to appoint a legal guardian in your will.

When preparing your will, it is helpful to have the assistance of an attorney who is familiar with Malaysian laws regarding assets, property rights, government taxes and inheritance taxes, as these might influence the execution of your will, especially if you claim Malaysia as your place of residence. Place a copy of your will in your safe deposit box, give a copy to your attorney and keep a copy at home. Be sure to revise your will after you leave Malaysia.

ATTORNEYS

Foreign residents of Malaysia may wish to consult a local attorney concerning matters such as taxes, divorce, house leases or traffic accident settlements. Before engaging an attorney, enquire about fees. For driving-related situations, the Malaysian Automobile Association offers some legal assistance to members. Foreigners with complicated legal problems can contact the **International Legal Defence Counsel** (24th Floor, Packard Bldg., 111 South 15th St., Philadelphia, Pennsylvania, 19102 USA; Tel: 1-215-977-9982, Fax: 1-215-564-2859). ILDC specialises in international law cases and maintains contacts with law firms throughout the world.

ACCOUNTANTS

Most internationally known firms offer accounting, auditing and tax services in Malaysia. Among them are Arthur Andersen, Deloitte & Touche, Ernst & Young, KPMG (formerly Peat Marwick) and Price WaterhouseCoopers.

PERSONAL INCOME TAX

Malaysian personal income taxes have been reduced over the past few years due to the country's economic success. Tax laws change frequently and are quite complicated. Many employers pay full or partial Malaysian taxes for their expatriate employees. Before you sign your employment contract, make sure you have a clear understanding of what your tax liability will be. Your employer should be able to provide you with clear up-to-date information.

Residents are taxed at progressive rates from 2% to 29% on all income accrued in or derived from Malaysia, and are also taxed on income from sources outside Malaysia that is remitted to Malaysia. Deductions are allowed for self, spouse (if the couple lived together during the year), dependent children, dependent relatives, disabled family members, certain business and education expenses, life insurance premiums, and contributions to pension plans, provident funds and approved charities. Interest received is taxable at a flat rate of 5%, except for tax-exempt interest. In addition, expatriate residents are required to contribute 11% of their income to the EPF (Employee Provident Fund). All monies are returned upon departure.

Non-residents are exempt from taxation on income remitted to Malaysia, but at present are taxed at a flat rate of 29% on chargeable income derived from Malaysia and are not allowed personal deductions. Generally a person who resides in Malaysia for 182 days during a twelve-month period will be regarded as a tax resident. Short-term visiting employees who work in Malaysia less than sixty days in one year are not subject to tax on income from employment in Malaysia.

Taxable income includes salary, allowances, rent-free accommodations, and benefits such as furniture, utilities, leave tickets, motor vehicles, medical treatment, medical insurance, domestic employees, income tax paid by employer, etc. Payments made outside Malaysia for work done in Malaysia are also taxable, as is investment income accrued in or derived from Malaysia or remitted to Malaysia.

Foreign residents are allowed to claim **foreign tax credits** against their Malaysian tax. If a tax treaty with the foreign country exists, the credit covers the entire foreign tax paid or the Malaysian tax levied on the income, whichever is less. If no treaty exists, the credit is limited to one-half the foreign tax paid. Your embassy can tell you if a tax treaty is in effect for your country.

Tax returns are issued to tax payers in late February and must be completed and returned to the Inland Revenue Department within thirty days (unless an extension is granted). Monthly deductions from pay are made for individuals whose annual taxable income exceeds a specified amount. Tax audits are conducted if tax evasion is suspected. The statute of limitations, during which taxpayers may claim relief for an error in a previously filed tax return, is six years. If you have **tax questions** during your stay in Malaysia, your country's embassy in K.L. may be able to refer you to a tax expert who can answer specific questions about how Malaysian taxes affect you. When leaving Malaysia at the end of your contract, you may be required to show written proof that all your personal income taxes have been paid by you and your employers. Be sure to resolve any outstanding matters prior to your departure.

MAINTAINING CREDIT

In order to avoid the hassle of having to re-establish credit back home after completing an assignment in Malaysia, most people maintain a current account (checking account) and at least one credit card in their home country. This also provides access to cash after departure from Malaysia, an important consideration as you will probably close your checking accounts when you leave and credit cards issued in Malaysia may expire along with your Employment Pass.

INSURANCE

Most insurance policies in Malaysia are filled with loopholes. It is to your advantage to read them carefully and to negotiate, although it is doubtful that you will be able to arrange policies exactly like the ones you have at home.

WORK DAYS AND HOURS

Sunday is the day of rest in the Federal Territory (K.L. and environs) and in the States of Johor, Pahang, Penang, Perak, Perlis, Melaka, Selangor and Negeri Sembilan, all of which were united under British rule. It is also the day of rest in Sabah and Sarawak. In addition, government offices are closed on the first and third Saturdays of each month and on Fridays there is an extended lunch break so that Muslims can go to a mosque for afternoon prayers. Friday, the Moslem holy day, is the day of rest in the States of Kedah, Kelantan and Terengganu, which retained semi-autonomy under the British. Saturday is also a day off as is Thursday afternoon for some people.

Banks
10:00 a.m. to 3:30 p.m. or 4:00 p.m., Monday–Friday
9:30 a.m. to 11:00 a.m. or 11:30 a.m., Saturday
Banks are closed on the first Saturday of each month.

Money Changers
8:30 a.m. to 6:00 p.m. (variable)

Supermarkets and Departmental Stores
10:00 a.m. to 9:30 p.m. or 10:00 p.m., Monday–Saturday
Some complexes open later and close earlier.
Most complexes are open on holidays.

Shops
9:30 a.m. to 6:30 p.m. or 7:00 p.m., Monday–Saturday
Many shops are open on Sundays.

Government Offices
8:15 a.m. to 12:45 p.m.,   Monday–Friday
2:00 p.m. to 4:45 p.m.,   Monday–Thursday
2:45 p.m. to 4:45 p.m.,   Friday
8:15 a.m. to 1:15 p.m.,   Saturday
Government offices are closed on the first and third Saturday of
each month

Commercial Offices
8:30 a.m. or 9:00 a.m. to 1:00 p.m., Monday–Friday
2:00 p.m. to 4:30 p.m. or 5:00 p.m., Monday–Friday
8:30 a.m. or 9:00 a.m. to 12:30 p.m. or 1:00 p.m., Saturday

Airline Offices
Airline offices follow the commercial office schedule.
MAS Reservations Department is open 24 hours.
(Tel: 03-746-3000)

DATES, NUMBERS AND NAMES
Dates are written in the order of day/month/year: 18 August 2008
or 18.8.08 for example. Follow this format to avoid confusion.
Numbers are written with commas denoting thousands, and
periods denoting fractions: RM32,650.85 for example. On
cheques, a dash is often used in place of a period so that no
alteration is possible: RM32,650-85.

    Names are often written with the surname (family name)
first and the given name last: Richardson, Robert for example.
When you fill in forms or make reservations, give your surname
first. If you have made a reservation for transportation or
accommodations, but find that your name is not listed when you

check in, ask the agent to check listings under both your surname, given name and middle name. If you expect to be paged or met at an airport, listen and look for either your surname or your first name.

TIME

Time in Malaysia is often stated according to the 24-hour time system rather than the 12-hour system. Bus, train and airline schedules are written this way. Foreigners not familiar with the 24-hour system will not find it difficult to learn. From 1:00 a.m. to 12:00 noon the numbers are the same, but they are written as 0100 to 1200. No punctuation or indication of "a.m." is necessary. Thus, 10:30 a.m. is written as 1030. After 1200, the numbers change. The 12-hour system repeats itself, while the 24-hour system continues on. Thus, 1:00 p.m. is 1300, 6:30 p.m. is 1830, and 12:00 midnight is 2400. To find 12-hour time from 24-hour time, simply subtract twelve hours if the time is 1300 hours or later. Time in the 24-hour system is read as:

- 0800: eight hours;
- 1030: ten hours thirty;
- 1200: twelve hours;
- 1609: sixteen hours nine; and
- 2400: twenty-four hours.

Chapter Ten

STAYING HEALTHY

GENERAL CONDITIONS

Malaysia is basically a healthy place in which to live. Standards of sanitation are quite high, and medical care and facilities in hospitals and clinics are, for the most part, adequate and continually being updated. Serious tropical diseases are uncommon, except in areas in which sanitation is sub-standard, and the minor health problems that are common are easily prevented or treated. This chapter covers a variety of health-related topics that may be of interest to newcomers. Please note that the information in this chapter is offered only as a guide and is not meant to replace the advice of your doctor.

CHALLENGES TO YOUR HEALTH

The tropical climate brings with it a variety of ailments with which you may not be familiar. Try to inform yourself about these ailments by talking with your doctor and by reading any information you can find in books and on the Internet. Then try to take precautions daily as well as when you travel.

The minor ailments common in Malaysia and other tropical climates include the following: tropical fatigue, sunburn and heat disorders, dry skin and skin rash, stomach upset and diarrhoea, colds and bronchial disturbances, fungus and other infections, eye and ear infections, worms and head lice.

Some serious diseases are found in Malaysia. They include the following: malaria, dengue fever, cholera, typhoid, hepatitis, tuberculosis, sexually transmitted diseases, AIDS, Nipah virus and coxsakie virus.

RECOMMENDED IMMUNISATIONS

At present, the only immunisation required for entry is **yellow fever** and it is only required of people over age one who have passed through a yellow fever endemic zone (Africa and South America) within six days prior to their arrival in Malaysia. The following immunisations are widely recommended for foreign adults living in Malaysia: diphtheria and tetanus, poliomyelitis, typhoid, hepatitis A, hepatitis B, cholera, malaria and measles, mumps and rubella. The following immunisations are recommended for foreign children living in Malaysia: typhoid, cholera, hepatitis A, hepatitis B, and malaria. Some medical personnel believe that the risks of contracting these diseases are not great enough to warrant the risks inherent in the immunisations, however, so be sure to discuss these recommendations with your doctors.

NATURAL HAZARDS

During your stay in the tropics, you may want to guard against the following natural hazards: polluted drinking water, haze, poisonous snakes and certain insects, plants, and marine life.

Water in Kuala Lumpur and other major Malaysian cities is fluoridated, chemically treated and considered safe to drink, except during droughts, after severe rainstorms or during outbreaks of cholera. However, most people prefer to purify or boil their water or drink mineral water, especially if they are sensitive to chlorine.

In recent years, K.L. has been experiencing periodic problems with lingering haze, probably due to agricultural burning and heavy traffic; the Government is addressing this issue.

The most common poisonous snakes are pit vipers and cobras. Consider any snake potentially harmful and keep your distance. In the case of snake bite, take emergency action immediately.

Beware of scorpions, black and dark-brown spiders, and spiders with bright splashes of colour on their backs. Shake out your shoes before putting them on and treat poisonous bites and stings rapidly.

Several plants common in Malaysia are toxic if ingested, or cause severe skin irritation if touched. They include bamboo, cashew nut tree, dieffenbachia, frangipani, mango tree, oleander, palm, papaya tree, philodendron and poinsettia.

When you visit Malaysia's beaches, watch out for poisonous jelly fish, sea snakes, sea urchins and catfish, as well as for dangerous undercurrents and polluted water. While not widespread or constant, these hazards do occasionally appear at some beaches.

MEDICAL CARE AND FACILITIES

Good medical care and facilities are available in K.L. The sections below give details about pharmacies, specialists, hospitals, ambulances and support groups.

Pharmacies (Chemists)

There are large modern pharmacies in most shopping complexes and smaller ones in some hotels and supermarkets. Among the largest chain pharmacies are **Apex, City Chemist, Georgetown, Guardian** and **Watson's**. Most pharmacies are open during regular business hours; those in shopping complexes are open seven days a week. To obtain medications after hours, it is necessary to go to a clinic or hospital.

Pharmacies carry Malaysian, Chinese, Western and some Japanese medications. When you purchase medications, carefully check the package for signs of tampering and note the date of expiration.

Medical Specialists

Below are some notes about various kinds of medical specialists available in K.L. The best way to find a specialist is to ask friends and acquaintances for recommendations.

- *Acupuncturists:* Acupuncture is practised widely in K.L. As in other countries, the training, experience and skill of practitioners vary greatly. Please note that some medical doctors who practise acupuncture may not be highly trained or experienced in doing so. Look for a practitioner who is experienced in using both herbs and acupuncture, and ask to do an informational interview before receiving any treatment. One experienced and highly respected fourth-generation practitioner in K.L. is Leong Hong Tole of **The Tole Acupuncture and Herbal Medical Centre** (Suite 4.08, 4th Floor, Menara Promet, Jalan Sultan Ismail, 50250 K.L.; Tel: 03-241-8370, 254-1671). The Tole Centre treats a variety of health problems including autism, Alzheimer's disease, and the after-effects of chemotherapy and stroke, and offers training courses for people wanting to learn acupuncture.

- *Audiologists:* Reliable hearing tests for children and adults are available. Good-quality hearing aids can be purchased for reasonable prices, but care should be taken to buy them from a well-qualified practitioner or after consulting an ENT (Ear, Nose and Throat) specialist.

- *Chiropractors:* Chiropractic, a procedure for re-aligning the joints of the body by specific manual manipulation, is gaining in popularity and several practitioners are available.

- *Dentists and Orthodontists:* Good dental and orthodontic care are widely available in Malaysia. Many dentists have international training and are familiar with the latest techniques. Costs are less than in many countries. Some doctors use a local anaesthetic and a lead X-ray shield only at the patient's request.

139

- *General Practitioners and Specialists:* Many general practitioners in private practice belong to a medical group. They can make arrangements for you to enter a hospital, but cannot care for you while you are hospitalised. Some specialists will only see patients who are referred by general practitioners. Most doctors speak English fluently, but the doctor/patient relationship may be rather distant, formal and dogmatic. If you are doubtful about the diagnosis, or if surgery or treatment with medications known to have potentially harmful side effects is recommended, a second opinion is always advisable.

- *Opticians:* Numerous foreign-trained opticians have offices in K.L. They offer well-known, international-brand contact lenses and spectacle (eyeglass) frames, and high-quality prescription lenses for reasonable prices. Some "opticians" who give eye tests and fit contacts are not properly qualified to do so. To assure best results when being fitted for contacts, seek the advice of a qualified optician, optometrist or ophthalmologist. When you buy eyeglasses or contact lenses, specify every detail (size, color, tint, finish, etc.) in writing. If alternatives are not acceptable to you, say so clearly. Shop around to compare price, quality and answers to your questions, and bargain when you finally find what you want. (Some expatriates have lasik vision correction surgery, which is available in K.L.)

- *Gynaecologists:* Well-trained male and female gynaecologists work in hospitals and private clinics.

- *Herbalists:* Chinese, Malays, Indians and Indonesians have a long tradition of using herbs to tone the body and cure a variety of ills. Check the Yellow Pages of your Telephone Directory for a list of shops and practitioners, or better yet, ask friends for recommendations.

- *Homeopaths:* There are some homeopathic practitioners in K.L. Although not all are medical doctors, some have extensive training and numerous years of experience. To find them, ask around or check the Yellow Pages under the heading "Homeopathy". If you are in Singapore, a well-respected and reasonably priced homeopathic clinic is the **Hahnemann Homeopathy Centre** (320 Serangoon Road, #04-19, Serangoon Plaza; Tel: 02-291-9440).

- *Massage Therapists and Foot Reflexologists:* Many hotels and health centres have massage therapists on staff. A traditional form of therapeutic Malaysian massage, known as *Urut Tradisional*, is helpful for relieving sore muscles and stimulating blood circulation. Foot reflexology is gaining in popularity. Check the Yellow Pages of your Telephone Directory for addresses and watch for advertisements in shopping malls and health food shops.
- *Psychologists:* Most embassies maintain a list of qualified psychologists and psychiatrists. Also check *The Expat* and *The Finder* magazines for advertisements.

Other Medical Services

- *Blood Transfusions:* Rh-negative blood is rare in Malaysia and other parts of Southeast Asia. If you or anyone in your family in Malaysia has Rh-negative blood, discuss with your doctor what steps should be taken if a transfusion is needed. The **Ibu Family Resources Group** (Tel: 262-8589) maintains a blood donor register of members who would be willing to donate blood to another member in an emergency.
- *Medical Alert:* The system of medical alert in Malaysia is called *Medik Awas*. Members wear bracelets or carry cards to warn medical personnel of medical problems or allergies to medications. This information, which is kept on file at the University Hospital in K.L., can help save lives in emergencies. You can become a member by asking your Malaysian doctor to complete and submit the necessary forms.

- *Medical Check-ups:* Most expatriates have a complete physical when they go on home leave. Complete physicals are available at many hospitals and private clinics in K.L., however, and at the American Hospital, Mount Elizabeth Hospital and Executive Health Screeners (EHS) in Singapore. It is advisable to arrange for your domestic employees to have a health examination prior to their employment and periodically after they have been hired.

Maternity Care and Support

Good obstetric care is available in K.L. Many Malaysian doctors advocate natural childbirth. Classes for expectant mothers and fathers are held at hospitals and community organisations. Some of the pre- and post-natal tests which are routinely performed in your country may not be routinely performed in Malaysia. It is advisable to talk this over with a physician at home if you are planning to give birth while you are abroad.

Photo courtesy of Pucuk Rebung

Beadwork depicting the Mantree, a stylised tree-of-life from a baby carrier, native art. Circa 1950s, Kenyah, Sarawak.

Most hospitals will allow advance visits to the maternity ward and delivery rooms; some will allow pre-registration and advance choice of room category. Prior to their due date, women should contact the hospital and ask what they will need to take with them for the hospital stay. Some private hospitals will allow husbands to accompany their wives in the delivery room during birth.

Both **La Leche League** and the **Breast Feeding Association** are active in Malaysia. Many expatriate mothers and mothers-to-be join the **Ibu Family Resources Group** (Tel: 03-262-8589), started by a group of expatriate mothers in 1987 to offer friendly support to mothers and fathers of all nationalities. The organisation can help with questions about hospitals, playgroups, child care and child development. *Ibu* (which means "Mother" in Malay) is a volunteer-run, non-profit, non-political organisation. It holds monthly meetings and frequent coffee mornings, and offers a pregnancy support group for mothers-to-be, a breast feeding support group for new mothers, and weekly Well Baby Clinics to provide mothers and fathers with needed advice and support. It also has a Helpline, a reference library, and a loan service for maternity clothes, baby equipment and winter clothes for children and mums.

Medical Care for Children

Good paediatric care is available in K.L. and medical personnel generally show children much care and attention. Parents usually are allowed to stay in hospital while their children are being treated.

In case of illness or emergency, school officials or the school nurse should always have telephone numbers where you and your spouse, or other people responsible for your children, can be reached. If you leave your child in the care of your maid or friends when you go out of town, be sure to leave the following with the caretakers:

- some form of identification for the child (preferably a passport

143

so that the child can be evacuated in case of extreme medical emergency);
- a letter stating who is responsible for the child while you are away; and
- a letter from your employer guaranteeing payment of medical bills.

Hospitals and Clinics

Kuala Lumpur has a variety of private clinics and hospitals, as well as Government hospitals. The most well known are listed below:

- **Ampang Puteri Specialist Hospital:** 1 Jalan Mamanda 9, Taman Dato Ahmad Razali, 68000 Ampang (Tel: 03-470-2500; Fax: 03-470-2443; Emergency Tel: 03-470-7060). A 250-bed hospital with 24-hour emergency care.
- **Assunta Hospital:** Jalan Templer, 46990 Petaling Jaya (Tel: 03-778-3433 [8 lines]–hospital and ambulance; Fax: 03-7781-4933; Emergency: 03-7780-6118, 7780-6108). Older 420-bed private hospital with 24-hour ambulance service and emergency care.
- **Kuala Lumpur General Hospital ("Hospital Besar"):** Jalan Pahang (near Jalan Tun Razak Circle), 50586, K.L. Tel: 03-292-1044/1086/1139). Government-run, 2000-bed facility with an emergency room staffed by a doctor 24 hours a day. Emergency treatment for snake bites and an ICU for severe burns.
- **Gleneagles Intan Medical Centre:** 286 Jalan Ampang, 50450 K.L. (Tel: 03-457-1300; Fax: 03-457-9233). A 330-bed hospital, opened in 1996, with specialists services and 24-hour emergency facilities.
- **Mont Kiara Medical City:** Suria KLCC (Tel: 03-382-2000). Private polyclinic housing medical, diagnostic, dental and outpatient surgery services.

- **Pantai Medical Centre:** 8 Jalan Bukit Pantai, 59100 K.L. (Tel: 03-282-5077; Ambulance: 03-756-8879). Small private hospital run by specialists. No accident/emergency unit; emergency cases admitted only if they have been accepted by one of the specialists.
- **Subang Jaya Medical Centre:** 1 Jalan SS 12/1A. Subang Jaya (Tel: 03-734-1212). Located 20 minutes from K.L. and 10 minutes from Shah Alam and P.J. Modern, 224-bed, full-service hospital with a 24-hour emergency room. Managed by a Malaysian-American joint venture.
- **Tawakal Specialist Hospital:** 202-A Jalan Pahang, 53000 K.L. (Tel: 03-4023-3599; Fax: 03-4022-8063; Emergencies: 03-4023-0733). Modern, 150-bed hospital with an accident unit, 24-hour operating room and emergency unit staffed by a doctor after hours.
- **University Hospital:** Jalan University, 46200 Petaling Jaya (Tel: 03-756-4422; Ambulance: 03-750-2500). Well-staffed and well-equipped teaching hospital with a wide variety of services.

Hospital Admittance and Payment

For hospital admittance, some form of **identification**, such as a passport or identity card, is required, even for children. Most hospitals accept major credit cards. Prior to medical treatment, especially surgery, request a **written estimate of costs**. Also, request **itemised bills** for all medical treatment and review them carefully. If any charges seem unreasonable or far beyond what your insurance will cover, approach your doctor and explain the details of your insurance coverage. Doctors might assume your insurance will pay any amount that is charged. Do not be shy about negotiating prices for medical services, even if you would not think of doing so in your own country. Keep copies of receipts for all paid medical bills.

Emergency Treatment

Prepare for medical emergencies by talking with your family physician in Malaysia about what procedures to follow. Also, contact ambulance services to enquire about their protocol, and visit the emergency room of the hospital nearest you so that in case of emergency you will know how to get to the hospital, what gate to enter and what admitting procedures to follow. Do this especially if you have children. Also ask your insurance carrier or your employer about the procedures for Medivac (medical evacuation).

Ambulances

Several ambulance services operate in K.L. The most reliable are the **Red Crescent** (Tel: 03-201-0280) and **St. Johns** (Tel: 03-985-2008). In case of emergency, dialling one of these services directly is faster than dialling 999. When you call, explain the urgency of the situation to the operator and describe exactly where you are located. If the location is obscure and extra help is available, arrange to have someone meet the ambulance at a better-known location. Ambulance personnel are paramedics trained to stabilise the patient and take the patient to the nearest hospital that provides the relevant services.

Support Groups

K.L. hosts branches of several international and local support groups, many of which offer counselling and accept volunteer assistants.

- **Alcoholics Anonymous (Al-Anon):** (Tel: 03-986-2102).
- **Alcoholism Foundation Malaysia:** (Tel: 03-2274-3167).
- **Alzheimer's Disease Foundation:** (Tel: 03-758-1522).
- **The Befrienders:** (Tel: 03-756-8144/45). Counselling for the suicidal, lonely and depressed.
- **Cancerlink Foundation:** (Tel: 03-757-9310).

- **Malaysian Red Crescent Society:** (Tel: 03-457-8122). Counselling for teenagers and adults regarding personal and family problems, including HIV, drug abuse and teen pregnancies.
- **Natural Therapy Centre AIDS Hotline:** (Tel: 03-781-7474).
- **Wesley Methodist Church Kuala Lumpur:** (Tel: 03-238-1214). Counselling.

INSURANCE

Specialists' fees and the costs of medical care in private hospitals can add up if you require treatment and do not have insurance coverage. If your employer does not provide you with medical insurance coverage, you can purchase your own policy in Malaysia.

You might want to purchase travel accident insurance that will provide indemnity against injury sustained anywhere in the world while you ride in a bus, train, taxi, subway, airplane, steamship or automobile, or if you are involved in a pedestrian accident. Some credit card companies offer travel accident plans for cardholders, their spouses and their dependent children.

EMERGENCY ASSISTANCE

A full range of travellers' assistance services is offered for a small fee to subscribers of emergency assistance programmes. The spirit of the programmes is "call and we will do whatever we can to get you out of trouble". The largest company that provides these services is International SOS Assistance. SOS has several branches, including the following:

- *Malaysia*–Level 10, Menara Chan, 139 Jalan Ampang, 50450 K.L. (Tel: 03-926-3000; Fax: 03-925-1311).
- *Switzerland*–12 Chemin Riantbosson, 1217 Meyrin-1, Switzerland (Tel: 41-22-785-0000; Fax: 41-22-785-6426).

147

- *USA*–P.O. Box 11568, Philadelphia, PA 19116, USA (Tel: 1-800-523-8930 or 1-215-244-1500; Fax: 1-215-244-2227).

HEALTH CARE FOR PETS

Pets living in a tropical climate are subject to many of the same ailments as humans. In order for pets to stay healthy, they should have plenty of water, a cool place to rest, adequate exercise and a well-balanced diet.

Pets should be vaccinated against distemper, hepatitis, parvovirus and leptospirosis. Check them for worms and parasites every three months and follow a heartworm preventive treatment for your dog. Pets can get skin infections easily, so immediate treatment of open wounds is essential. To keep your pets free of ticks, use a wash prescribed by your veterinarian, and have an exterminator treat your house and grounds before you move in and as necessary thereafter.

For pet food and supplies, visit large supermarkets. Most carry a variety of local and imported brands. Even *halal* cat food (which contains no pork by-products) is available.

Veterinary Services

Many well-qualified veterinarians practise in K.L. To find them, ask friends or check the Telephone Directory Yellow Pages under the headings "Veterinarians" and "Veterinary Hospitals".

Kennels

The **SPCA** (Jalan Kerri Air Lama, off Jalan Ulu Klang, Ampang Jaya; Tel: 03-456-5312) arranges adoption of animals, and runs a birth control clinic (by appointment only) and a boarding kennel for cats.

CHAPTER ELEVEN

STAYING IN TOUCH

COMMUNICATION SERVICES

Malaysia's modern communication system makes it easy to keep in touch with family, friends and business associates in Malaysia and abroad through mail, telephone and the Internet. This chapter gives an overview of postal and telecommunications services and connections to cyberspace.

POSTAL SERVICES

Malaysia's computerised postal system (POS) is operated by Pos Malaysia Berhad. The system is becoming more efficient and reliable. However, as letters, magazines and parcels occasionally go missing, many people choose to send important documents (including cheques) and valuable items by courier service or with someone who is travelling to the destination.

Post Offices

Post offices in K.L. and the Klang Valley offer a full range of postal services, issue money orders, accept payment of road taxes and phone, water and electricity bills, and deliver mail to residences and businesses daily. Most are open every day except Sundays, public holidays and the first Saturday of every month.

Post Office Hours

The post offices listed below are open every day except Sundays, public holidays and the first Saturday of every month, unless otherwise indicated.

- **Main Post Office:** Dayabumi Complex, Jalan Sultan Hishamuddin. Open 8:30 a.m. to 6:00 p.m. Handles only stamps, parcels and registrations after 5:00 p.m. (Tel: 03-2275-6725).
- **KLIA Sepang Airport:** Open for all services 8:30 a.m. to 6:00 p.m. Located on Level 5.
- **Suria KLCC:** Open 10:30 a.m. to 6:00 p.m., seven days a week, except holidays. (Tel: 03-2161-8069).
- **Kuala Lumpur Plaza:** Open 8 a.m. to 5 p.m.
- **Petaling Jaya:** Open 8 a.m. to 5 p.m.
- **Bangsar Baru:** Open 8:30 a.m. to 10 p.m.
- **Mid Valley Megamall** and **Ampang Point Mall:** Open 10:30 a.m. to 6:00 p.m.

Addressing Mail

All mail to addresses in Malaysia should include a Poskod (Postal Code/Zip Code). A booklet of codes can be purchased at any post office for a small fee. When you address mail to addresses in Malaysia, write the Poskod before the city name and write the state name last. For example: 30300 Ipoh, Perak. There is no need to add "Malaysia" on mail sent to addresses within the country. Write the return address on the reverse side of the envelope.

Letters

Letters mailed within Peninsular Malaysia take up to five days to arrive at their destination. Letters between Peninsular Malaysia and Sabah and Sarawak can take up to two weeks, and as service is somewhat unreliable, sending letters (and packages) by registered mail may improve the chances of delivery. Airmail letters normally take seven days to reach Japan, Europe, the U.K., Australia and the Middle East, and ten days to reach North and South America. International airmail letters must have an airmail sticker (available at the post office) or the words "By Airmail" on the envelope.

Parcels and Small Packets

Post offices do not offer wrapping services, but small shops known as POS 2020, located next to selected post offices, sell stationery and offer wrapping, strapping and binding services.

- *Surface Parcel Post:* Seamail is economical but slow. Parcels to Japan, Europe, the U.K. and Australia take one to two months; those to the Middle East and North America take two to three months. Send Christmas parcels prior to 15 October to ensure arrival before 25 December.

  For international and domestic surface parcel post, the maximum weight per parcel is ten kilograms (22 pounds). The maximum length for a parcel is one metre or a combination of length and girth not exceeding two metres. Parcels should be securely boxed, wrapped in waxed brown paper and secured with twine. Drops of sealing wax must be placed on the joints and flaps of the parcels that are to be insured. Parcels may be insured to a maximum of RM1,000.

- *Airmail Parcel Post:* The maximum weight for airmail parcel post is ten kilograms (22 pounds). Regulations are the same as for surface parcel post. Be sure to save your postal receipts so packages can be traced if they do not arrive at their destinations.

- **_Small Packets:_** A small packet, with a maximum weight of one kilogram (2.2 pounds), travels faster than parcel post. Packets should be marked "Small Packet" in the upper left-hand corner and may be registered, but not insured. They may be used for domestic or international mail. A Customs Declaration form must be attached to each small packet sent outside Malaysia.
- **_Incoming Parcels:_** Incoming parcels will sometimes be delivered to your door and sometimes detained for Customs inspection. If a package in your name is detained you will be notified. You must then go to the Customs Office with proper identification (Passport or Driver's Licence), or send someone with your identification and written authorisation to pick up the package. Customs officials may open the package and charge you applicable duty.

Registered Mail

Registered mail may be sent to addresses within Malaysia and abroad. You will be given a receipt when the article is mailed and an acknowledgment of receipt will be obtained from the recipient when the item is delivered. For a small extra charge you can purchase an **Advice of Delivery Reply Card** that will be returned to you as proof of delivery.

Registered letters and small parcels are delivered directly to the addressee's home. Heavy parcels are held at the General Post Office, and the addressee is notified and requested to collect them. If you need proof of having posted an unregistered article, you can obtain a **Certificate of Posting** for a small fee.

Insured Mail

Any registered letter or parcel containing items of value, addressed to any country with which there is an agreement for remittance, can be insured. It is not possible to insure letters or parcels mailed to addresses in Peninsular Malaysia or Singapore. The maximum insurance for a letter or parcel is RM1,000. Envelopes of insured letters must be sealed with three drops of sealing wax. For a small fee, the post office, by means of an **Advice of Delivery Reply Card**, will advise the sender when a registered or insured letter or parcel has been delivered.

Express Mail

Domestic and international express mail service, called **Poslaju** (Speedpost) or Expedited Mail Service (EMS), is available to points within Malaysia and many other countries. The maximum weight is 20 kilograms within Malaysia and up to 30 kilograms to some countries. Size restrictions also apply. Poslaju items travel separately from ordinary mail and are delivered by special courier in many overseas destinations. A receipt is given for all items posted and a signature is required at transfer and delivery points. Refund is given for failure to deliver, prices are competitive and there are no hidden charges. However, service is not always speedy.

Other Postal Services

- *Cash on Delivery:* This service allows the sender to specify the cost of goods mailed and the recipient to pay this amount upon receipt of the goods. The Postal Department then remits the amount to the sender by special money order. A letter or parcel mailed COD can be insured.
- *Postal Money Orders:* Money up to certain amounts can be remitted by Postal Money Order. However, Postal Money Orders do sometimes "go missing" and if they are claimed by someone other than the addressee, the Post Office bears no responsibility and may not have a record of the claimant.
- *Private Letter Boxes:* Private boxes can be reserved for a small charge at most larger post offices.
- *Vacation Mail:* It is not possible to arrange for the post office to hold your mail while you are away on vacation.

- *Mail Forwarding/Redirection:* When you leave Malaysia, and if your address changes while you are a resident, you can arrange to have your mail forwarded to your new address by submitting a Redirection Form at your local post office. Mail is redirected free of charge for six months; however, if an item is forwarded to a country in which the postal charges are higher than the original charge, a surcharge may apply.

COURIER SERVICES

Private courier services offer rapid pick-up and delivery for documents and parcels. The Telephone Directory Yellow Pages lists them under the heading "Courier Service". Couriers serving Malaysia include DHL Worldwide Express, Federal Express, Nationwide Express, SkyNet Worldwide Courier Systems, Overseas Courier Service (OCS), TNT Express Worldwide, and United Parcel Service (UPS). Rates vary widely, so it pays to comparison shop.

TELEPHONE

Satellites, submarine cables and radio relay systems operated by Telekom Malaysia Berhad (Wisma Telekom, Jalan Pantai Baharu, 59200 K.L.; Tel: 03-208-9494; Website: **www.telekom.com.my**) provide telephone connections between East and West Malaysia and most countries of the world. The country's rapid economic development has placed heavy demand on the system, and expansion has not yet caught up with utilisation. Overloading results in frequent delays, bad connections, disconnections and failures to connect, in both local and long distance calls. Use of the telephone still requires patience, but service continues to improve and should be fully modernised by the year 2005.

For assistance when you use the phone, dial 0 for the **Operator** (Telephonist), 108 for the **International Operator**, and

103 for **Telephone Number Enquiries** (Directory Assistance). If you need the police or an ambulance, you can dial 999 from almost anywhere in Malaysia. To report a fire, dial 994. Please note that it can be dangerous to use the phone during **thunderstorms** as power surges through telephones have been known to cause personal injury as well as household damage.

Telephone Talk

To use the phone you will need to recognise the following signals: **Dial Tone**, a continuous "beep," indicates that the line is clear for you to make a call. **Ringing Tone** "beep, beep ... beep, beep," indicates that the number called is ringing. **Engaged Tone**, "beep" ... "beep" ... "beep," indicates the number called or the circuits are busy. **Number Unobtainable Tone**, "beeeep"... "beeeep," indicates the number you have called is not in use or is out of order.

Numbers that are in pairs or triplets are often read as a unit, so a telephone number such as "888-2008 would usually be read as "triple eight, two, double zero, eight". Also, some things that you frequently hear on voicemail and Telekom messages might be unfamiliar to you. "Press hash" means "Press the # (pound) button on the phone". *"Nombor yang anda dial, tiada dalam perkhidmatan"* means "The number you have dialled is not in service". As many numbers in the Klang Valley are being changed from 7 to 8 digits, you will sometimes hear, *"Sila dial xxx* (a 3-digit number) *diikuti dengan lima nombor terakhir"* which means "Please dial xxx followed by the last five digits of the number".

Calls from Hotels

Most hotels in Malaysia add a hefty surcharge to domestic trunk calls and international calls made from guest rooms. These surcharges are rarely published and may amount to 50%. Most hotels will allow guests to make Home Country Dial Direct or Collect Calls, but many assess a service charge for each connection. Rates for sending faxes may also be high as some hotels charge for a minimum of two pages in addition to the telephone surcharge. To avoid surprises when you see your bill, ask specific questions about charges when you make a reservation or register.

Local Calls

Local calls are billed to subscriber phones at a set number of *sen* per unit, irrespective of the duration of the call. Telephone subscribers are entitled to a rebate of 100 charge units per month.

Public telephones can be found in most supermarkets, post offices and shopping complexes, and are of three types. **Coin phones** accept 20- and 50-*sen* coins; some accept RM1 coins. The cost is 10-*sen* for a three-minute local call. Watch the monitor to see how much time you have left to talk, as when the money runs out the phone disconnects without an audible warning. **Prepay Cardphones** take Phonecards rather than coins. Phonecards can be purchased in denominations of RM5, RM10, RM20, RM50 and RM100, from news agents, post offices, money changers, convenience stores, petrol stations and shopping complexes. **Credit Cardphones** accept Phonecards as well as major credit cards.

Long Distance Domestic Calls

Direct dialling between all Malaysian cities and Singapore is possible from phones equipped with Subscriber Trunk Dialling (STD) facilities. Use of an appropriate area code is required; a complete list appears in the Telephone Directory.

Long distance (trunk) domestic calls are billed to STD subscribers according to charge units which vary depending on the distance between call centres and the time of day the call is made. Reduced rates apply to calls made between 6:00 p.m. and 7:00 a.m. Charges for STD calls appear on the phone bill as "Metered Calls" and will be itemised only if the subscriber pays a small monthly fee.

International Calls

Direct dialling from home to nearly all countries is possible if subscribers have International Direct Dialling (IDD). (Malaysians who do not need to make international calls do not subscribe to IDD service.) Dial 181, plus 00, plus the country code and the telephone number to make calls or send faxes.

For example, to call London from Malaysia, dial:
International Access Code: 181–00
Country Code: 44 +
Area/City Code: 171
Phone Number: 9155055

Charges for IDD calls are itemised on monthly phone bills and are charged in six-second blocks. The charge per block depends on the country to which the call is made, and the day and time at which the call is made. Reduced rates apply to calls made daily during off-peak hours (which vary according to the country called) and between 6:00 p.m. on Saturday and 6:00 a.m. on Monday, Malaysian time. Both reduced rates and regular rates for most countries are listed in the Telephone Directory.

An alternative approach to making international calls is to use the **Home Country Direct** toll-free access number to connect with your home country telephone service and then to dial the telephone number you wish to reach. To obtain the Home Country Direct number, check the introductory pages of your Telephone Directory or dial 102 for Enquiries and be patient while the telephonist searches for the number. Calls can be charged as collect calls or to home-country telephone calling cards. For Malaysian telephone subscribers travelling out of the country, the same service, known as **Malaysia Direct**, is available. A list of toll-free access numbers appears in the introductory pages of the Telephone Directory.

Calls to countries that cannot be dialled directly can be made with Operator (Telephonist) assistance. To ensure a connection at a specific time, book your call in advance by dialling 108 for the International Telephone Exchange Operator. Bookings can be made up to four days in advance. Operator-assisted calls can be made Station-to-Station, Person-to-Person or Collect. The minimum charge is for three minutes; subsequent charges are by the minute. Rates are higher than for IDD calls; reduced rates apply during off-peak hours (which vary according to the country called) and on weekends.

Rates for calls from Malaysia to certain other countries may be higher than calls made from those countries to Malaysia. Many foreign residents of Malaysia arrange for friends and relatives to call them.

To call K.L. from abroad, dial:
International Access Code: (Check with your local operator.) +
Country Code for Malaysia: 60 +
City Code: 3+
Phone Number: (7 to 8 digits)

Telephone Billing

Telephone bills are sent to subscribers monthly and must be paid within seven days by post or in person at a telephone office or post office. International calls are itemised; domestic trunk calls and local calls are itemised only if you pay a small monthly fee for the service. If you have questions about your bill or think that an error has been made in billing, go to the Telekom office to ask for clarification. You may have to be persistent to get mistakes rectified. Be sure to save your receipts as proof of payment.

If problems in reception arise during a call, inform the telephonist at once by dialling 108. It is not the policy of Telekom to give credit for poor connections or for calls that are inadvertently disconnected.

Telephone Calling Cards

Telekom offers a calling card known as **Telecard**. With it, sub-scribers can use any tone-phone in Malaysia to make calls and charge them to their Telecard account. The card also can be used in other countries by dialling the access code and can be used to dial Malaysia from abroad through Malaysia Direct. Personal and Executive Telecards are available to anyone above 21 years of age with a minimum monthly income of RM1,200 and RM2,000 respectively. Supplementary cards can be obtained for family members above age twelve. For information, call 1-800-88-8887, toll free, or visit the website at **www.telekom.com.my/telecard**.

An alternative to arranging for a calling card in Malaysia is to set up a calling card account in your home country. If you do not have a home country billing address during your assignment in Malaysia, you may be able to arrange for the monthly calling card charges to be automatically billed to a home country credit card.

Telephone Directories

Telephone Directories may be obtained by submitting the Direc-tory Entitlement Form at a designated telephone distribution centre. Distribution dates and centres are announced yearly in the press. The Directory contains a Yellow Pages Consumers' Guide, useful information about telephone and telegraph services, and a listing of Government departments in Malay and English.

Directories for areas to which you are not a subscriber may be purchased for a small fee. Directories of other countries may be ordered by writing to: Manager, Directory Management and Information, Customer Assistance Services, Pusat Telekom, Jalan Tun Sambanthan, 50470 K.L. (Fax: 03-273-9093).

It is not always possible to find **residential telephone num-bers** in the Telephone Directory or by contacting Telephone Information, as records are not always up-to-date and many telephones are listed under the name of the landlord rather than under the name of the tenant. The same problem exists with **businesses** as they are often listed under the name of the holding company rather than the name of the business. The *Kuala Lumpur A to Z* directory published by the American Association and the *Welcome to Kuala Lumpur* directory published by the British Women's Association in Malaysia are useful guides as they list the telephone numbers of many businesses used by expatriates. For a list of emergency numbers, telephone service numbers and Malaysian city telephone code numbers, please see the Appendices.

Mobile Telephones

Many working expatriates and family members use mobile telephones (handphones/cellular phones) for convenience and in case of emergency. Mobile telephone service is available through several wireless service providers (WSP). Among them are Telekom Malaysia (Tel: 03-932-4379 or just 1050) and Maxis (Tel: 03-784-3211; E-mail: onetoone@maxis.net.my). Global mobile telephone service is also available. Fees for mobile telephone services vary, so it pays to comparison shop.

TELEGRAMS

Telegrams can be sent to points in Malaysia and most countries from private phones, hotels, post offices and telegraph offices. There is a minimum charge for ten words, with the address counted as regular wording. If you are a telephone subscriber, you can send telegrams from your home by dialling 104 and dictating your telegram to the operator. Charges for telegrams will appear on your monthly bill. Telegrams also can be dictated from public phone booths and charged to your account. Both services operate 24 hours a day. If you are not a telephone subscriber, you can send telegrams from any *Kedai Telekom* (Telekom Office) during business hours.

INTERNET ACCESS AND E-MAIL

The Internet is rapidly gaining popularity in Malaysia and is being used for the purposes of message transmission, data transmission, education, research and pleasure. To keep up with the changing scene, read *PC Magazine Malaysia*, *Jaring Internet Magazine* and *The Web*. Home access requires a computer, a modem, a phone line and appropriate software, as well as an Internet service account. People who do not have Internet access at home can visit any of the growing number of Cybercafés springing up throughout K.L.

Internet service providers available in Malaysia are MIMOS Berhad **(Jaring)** (www.jaring.my) and Telekom Malaysia Berhad **(Tmnet)** (www.tm.net.my). Connection is some-times slow and unstable as lines are overcrowded. If you have difficulty maintaining a connection, do the following:

- disable any "Call Waiting" feature on your telephone;
- check that your telephone line is in good condition;
- check the configuration of your modem; and
- close other applications while you surf.

When you surf for information about Malaysia, you can use an international search engine such as Yahoo, AltaVista or Ask Jeeves, or a local search engine. Two of the most **popular local search engines** are: www.cari.com.my and www.mol.com.molynks (Malaysia Online MOLynks). Some other useful local web addresses are listed in the Appendices of this book.

Chapter Twelve

GETTING AROUND

Malaysia's transportation system is modern and efficient. International air service, provided by the country's own flag carrier, Malaysia Airlines, and over forty foreign airlines, links Malaysia with most countries of the world. Domestic air service connects all state capitals and numerous smaller towns. A dependable train system runs the length of the West Coast offering service from Thailand to Singapore. Taxis, a light-rail train (LRT) and buses provide inexpensive local and inter-city transportation, and people who prefer to drive themselves can rent or purchase cars. Information on each of these means of transportation is provided in this chapter.

AIRPORTS AND AIR SERVICE

Kuala Lumpur has two airports, the new KLIA airport at Sepang and the old airport at Subang. When you book a flight, make sure you know from which airport you will depart and into which airport you will arrive.

KLIA Airport at Sepang

Known as KLIA, the new world-class Kuala Lumpur International Airport has a sleek, space-age design and offers the conveniences to which international travellers are accustomed. There is a 450-room hotel and two floors of shops, restaurants and services. (For information, call: 03-8777-8888.) When completed, recreational facilities surrounding the airport will include shopping centres, golf courses and theme parks. Already up and running nearby is one of Malaysia's prides, the Formula One racing circuit.

The airport is located in Sepang in the Multimedia Super Corridor (MSC), close to the new administrative city of Putrajaya. Malaysians are still adjusting to their new airport. For them it seems too far from K.L. and not very intimate. As one taxi driver put it, "No one likes to go see people off anymore because you can't wave to them when they get on the airplane". This is characteristic of a challenge facing the country: how to address the "people needs" and retain the heart and soul of Malaysia while taking it to full development.

Taxi service is available from KLIA to anywhere in Klang Valley and to outstation (out-of-town) locations. In good weather the ride to the centre of K.L. will take less than an hour; in bad weather, traffic jams and flooding can cause long delays to and from the airport. You must pay for the ride in advance at the Taxi Counter located near the exit from the Arrival Hall; you will receive a coupon that you should give to the driver when you reach your destination. Fares depend on the distance you will travel and whether you choose a Budget (small) or Premier (large) taxi. Independent taxi drivers may try to entice you to ride with them; it is best to decline such offers, as fares tend to be higher than the coupon fares. To go to KLIA, take any red and white city taxi (the metered fare should apply) or call in advance to book a **KLIA Airport Limousine** (Tel: 03-8787-1010, 8787-3030).

Public buses depart for the city and surrounding towns from the bus stands on the floor below the Arrival Hall. Fares are low and vary according to the distance travelled. The ride to central K.L. takes about an hour.

KLIA will soon be linked to K.L. Sentral (the new K.L. Railway Station on Jalan Travers in the Brickfields section of K.L.) and Putrajaya by an **Express Rail Link (ERL)**. The trip to K.L. will take 35 minutes. K.L. Sentral will have a City Air Terminal with check-in facilities for air travellers. Passengers will be able to connect with inter-city rail services (KTM) and the intra-city light rail system (LRT).

Subang Airport (SAAS)

Until 1998, Malaysia's largest airport was located in Subang, 22 kilometres from the centre of K.L. Currently, a few domestic flights still depart from Subang, as the airport is commonly called, and it remains a centre for small planes and executive jets. Facilities include a nearby hotel, shops, restaurants, and services such as currency exchange, baggage deposits, hotel reservations, tourist information and rental cars. For information, call: 03-746-1833.

Taxi service is available to anywhere in Klang Valley and to outstation locations. In good weather the ride to the centre of K.L. takes forty minutes to an hour; during a rainstorm it can take much longer. You must pay for the ride in advance at the Taxi Counter in the Public Arrival area. Bus service operates from the Departure Concourse to and from Kuala Lumpur, Petaling Jaya and Klang.

International Flights

Malaysia's national flag carrier is **Malaysia Airlines**, formerly known as the Malaysian Airline System, and still known by the acronym MAS. The acronym is auspicious as the word *mas* means "gold" in Malay. MAS, which has won several international awards for inflight service, flies to over 110 destinations in six continents. For information, call the **MAS 24-hour reservation number** in K.L.: 03-746-3000, 774-7000 or visit the website at malaysia-airlines.com.my/gst.

More than **forty international airlines** link K.L to major cities of the world. For a list of airline offices in Malaysia, consult the Telephone Directory Yellow Pages under the heading "Air Line Companies".

Between K.L. and **Singapore**, MAS and SIA (Singapore Airlines) operate frequent regular-fare flights and reduced-fare shuttle flights. For the latter, reservations cannot be made, tickets are sold at counters at both airports, and seats are allotted on a first-come, first-serve basis. Singapore is about 35 minutes by air from K.L.

Domestic Flights

MAS, Pelangi Air, Air Asia, Berjaya Air, Island Air and **Transmile Air** provide daily or near daily service between K.L. and more than thirty domestic destinations. Private light aircraft and helicopters can be hired to fly to areas not on scheduled airline routes. Contact **Wira Keris** (Subang) or the **Royal Selangor Flying Club.**

MAS Services

Frequent flyers (age 12 and above) will benefit from becoming members of the MAS **Enrich Programme**, which features two-way point exchange with Swissair, KLM, Virgin Atlantic, Northwest Airlines, Korean Air and other affiliated airlines. Points in Enrich can also be obtained by making purchases at affiliated hotels, credit and charge cards and car rental companies. There is a small enrolment fee. For information, in K.L. call 263-3689 or visit the website at malaysia-airlines.com/enrich.my.

Three check-in services speed the process of checking in for flights. The **Return Check-in** service, which provides passengers with a boarding pass for both departure and return flights, is available when both flights are on the same day, the return flight has been confirmed and there is no baggage to check in. **Telephone Check-In Service** is available for First and Golden Club Class (Business Class) passengers and Enrich Gold members. Simply call MAS to confirm your flight details and MAS will prepare your boarding pass so that you will need to arrive at the airport only 30 minutes in advance (40 minutes if you have luggage to check in) for domestic flights. Allow at least 65 minutes when you fly internationally. At KLIA, MAS has a **No Baggage Check-in Counter**.

MAS has a good reputation for taking care of passengers who require **special assistance**. Airline personnel can provide the following services: assist adults travelling with children; assist young passengers (between age 5 and 15) who are travelling alone; provide escort service for children aged three months to five years (for a fee); provide wheelchair transport from plane seat to airport transportation; accompany travellers who must catch connecting flights; and accompany travellers through Customs and Immigration formalities. These services can bring peace of mind to expatriates in Malaysia who are visited by their children and their parents. Arrange for the services at least 24 hours in advance by contacting MAS.

In addition to regular flights, MAS offers numerous **domestic and international tour packages,** called Golden Holidays, some with themes such as golf, scuba, shopping and nature.

MAS Regulations

- Passengers must arrive at the airport **check-in** desk within a specified period of time before the flight (30 to 120 minutes depending on the destination and the size of the aircraft). Ask about check-in time when you book your ticket.

- Specific regulations apply to flights within Malaysia and to Singapore and Brunei. Passengers must pay a 25% **cancellation fee** for the following: 1) cancellation of a confirmed booking within 24 hours of departure; and 2) failure to present the ticket for rebooking, re-issue or refund at least 24 hours before the original flight departure time, even if the reservations were cancelled before the 24-hour time limit; 3) failure to travel on a flight on which they have a confirmed booking; 4) failure to check in by the official check-in time; 5) inability to travel due to improper travel documents.

MAS Fares

- MAS offers special fares for the following: **Night Tourist Flights** and **Advance Purchase Excursions** between certain locations, **ASEAN Circle Trips** (which also allow two to five stopovers), a **Family Fare** (head of family accompanied by spouse and/or children aged 12-19), **Groups** (three or more people, including children), **Senior Citizens** (people aged 55 and over), **Journalists** (based in Malaysia and on assignment to cover events of national interest), and **Blind or Severely Disabled Passengers** and their companions.
- An adult, accompanied by one **infant** under two years old who does not occupy an individual seat, will be charged the regular adult fare plus 10%. Half the regular fare is charged for additional accompanying infants, or for children ages two through eleven.
- **Students** age twelve or above who are enrolled in a Government-recognised school or institution of higher learning in Malaysia for a full-time or at least a six-month course are eligible to apply for a **MAS Grads Card** which allows students to fly standby for a reduced fare.

167

Cruises

International cruise liners and passenger cargo ships make regular calls at Malaysian ports and a number of cruise lines offer regional cruises. **Star Cruises**, for example, offers cruises popular among individuals, couples, families, extended families and business groups striving to rest, recreate and celebrate. The ships also can be chartered for short trips to a variety of destinations, including fishing in the South China Sea. For information, contact Star Cruises in Port Klang (Tel: 03-301-1313; Fax: 03-301-1322; Website: www.starcruises.com).

For most cruise lines, reservations can be made through travel agents or directly with cruise line offices. When you travel out of Malaysian waters you will need to take your passport (be sure that it has at least six months' validity) and obtain any necessary visas.

TRAINS

Long Distance Trains

Travel by train offers a leisurely way to see the lush green Malaysian countryside. The main line of the Malaysian Railway, **Keretapi Tanah Melayu** (KTM or KTM Berhad), operates from Singapore to the southern border of Thailand, passing through Johor Bahru, K.L., Ipoh, Butterworth and Alor Setar to Haadyai in Thailand. This line will eventually become part of the Trans-Asia Rail Link that will connect Singapore, Malaysia, Vietnam, Cambodia, Laos and Myanmar by rail to Kunming in China, with connections to Beijing. A long branch line extends from Gemas northeast to Tumpat near the East Coast border with Thailand.

Regular day and night **express trains** connect Singapore, K.L., Butterworth and Bangkok. The journey between K.L. and Singapore takes nearly seven hours; between K.L. and Butterworth over six hours; and between K.L. and Bangkok about twenty-nine hours. The fastest trains are the Ekspres Rakyat (ER), the Ekspres Sinaran (XSP), and the Senandung Malam night train. **Express trains** are quite comfortable; all have sleeping berths, dining cars and air conditioning, and offer a variety of seating options.

The **Express Langkawi** leaves nightly from K.L. and arrives in Arau the following morning, with connecting service to Haadyai in Southern Thailand. The train returns through Arau in the evening and arrives in K.L. the next morning.

The **International Express (IE) to Bangkok, Thailand**, with connections from K.L. and Singapore, operates daily from Butterworth. Passengers departing K.L. in the evening and arriving in Butterworth the next morning can arrange a six-hour stopover in Butterworth before the mid-day departure for Bangkok. The journey from Butterworth to Bangkok takes about 22 hours (longer if there is a delay at the border). First- and second-class coach seats and sleeping berths are available. All railway passengers crossing the borders of Malaysia, Thailand and Singapore are subject to normal Customs and Immigration procedures.

The hub of rail travel in the country is the **K.L. Railway Station** on Jalan Hishamuddin, easily recognisable by its classic Moorish style architecture. Over the next few years the hub will shift to the new K.L. railway station known as **K.L. Sentral** in Brickfields.

Train Travel Fares and Regulations

- **Tickets** for all trains may be purchased sixty days in advance, inclusive of the day of travel. Payment for tickets may be in cash, Visa or MasterCard at all major stations and at ticketing outlets.
- **Purchase tickets** for all trains at the K.L. Railway Station, the KTM ticket booth in **Sungei Wang Plaza** (at the entrance to Parkson Grand Department Store; Tel: 03-245-6902), or at

169

Heritage Travel and Tours (near Gate 4 in the train station; Tel: 03-2273-3973; Fax: 03-2273-5007; E-mail: heritage@pd.jaring.my).

- A **Ticket Delivery Service** is also available; call: 03-2274-3377, 2274-4366.
- **Reservations** are necessary for first-class seats and sleeping compartments and may be made up to sixty days in advance. Confirmation of reservations is recommended, especially during public and school holidays.
- Hefty charges apply to passengers in possession of valid tickets who want to **change** the date or time of their scheduled departure. Enquire prior to purchasing tickets.
- **Reduced fares** for regular tickets may apply to family groups (minimum four persons), persons over 65, handicapped persons and groups of ten or more adults travelling together.
- **Children** between the ages of four and twelve are charged half the adult fare; children under age four travel free of charge.
- Money-saving **Tourist Railpasses**, good for unlimited travel within Peninsular Malaysia and Singapore for ten days or thirty days, may be purchased by foreign tourists (except Singaporeans). There are different rates for adults and for children under age twelve. The passes are sold at several railway stations including K.L., Singapore, Johor Bahru, and Butterworth. They allow travel on any class of train, but do not include the cost of berths.
- Students/youths under age 30 holding an International Student Identity Card (ISIC) or a Youth Hostel Card can obtain a special fare **Explorer Pass–Malaysia**, valid for seven, 14 or 21 days of unlimited second or economy class travel on all KTM services in Peninsular Malaysia, Thailand and Singapore.
- KTM offers groups, families, couples and individuals **packaged holiday tours** to popular destinations. For information on holiday packages, watch the newspapers or contact KTM, your

travel agent, or **Heritage Travel and Tours** (Tel: 03-2273-3973; Fax: 03-2273-5007; E-mail: heritage@pd.jaring.my).

Luxury Tourist Trains

For a special journey, take the **Eastern & Oriental Express**, which runs between Singapore and Bangkok about once a week. The 1,943-kilometre (1,200-mile) trip takes 42 hours and is carefully timed to pass through the most scenic areas during daylight hours. The fully air-conditioned train offers compartments in three levels of luxury and maintains high standards of cuisine and service. For more information, contact **Heritage Travel and Tours**, the E&O representative agent in K.L. (Tel: 03-2273-3973; Fax: 03-2273-5007; E-mail: heritage@pd.jaring.my).

Commuter Services

Many people in K.L. and the Klang Valley avoid driving in the heavy traffic by taking the LRT, the Monorail or the KTM Komuter rail service to and from work or when running errands. The combined service is known as Putra; the **Putra Hotline** is 03-469-6999. Single-journey, return-journey and stored value tickets as well as monthly Travelcards are available. Request information and a map at a customer service kiosk in any station.

Light Rail Transit (LRT)

The rapid and inexpensive LRT is an elevated train system that runs from Petaling Jaya through K.L. (Ampang and Brickfields) to Gombak. The **Star Line** (Tel: 03-298-4977) runs a north-south route from Sentul Timur through Masjid Jamek and Pudu, where it divides into a line running south to Sukan Negara and east to Ampang. The **Putra Line** runs a southeast route from Gombak (near the International Islamic University Malaysia) and intersects with the Star Line at Masjid Jamek. It continues in a southwest direction via K.L. Sentral, Bangsar and the University of Malaya to Kelana Jaya. Trains operate at three- to seven-minute intervals from 6:00 a.m. to 12:00 midnight. Feeder buses provide transport between outlying areas and LRT stations, however the bus service is not always reliable.

Monorail (PRT)

PRT, the People Mover Rapid Transit, is an elevated monorail running southwest from Jalan Tun Razak (near the Pekeliling Bus Station) via the Golden Triangle and K.L. Sentral to Kampung Pasir. It intersects with the Star LRT Line at Hang Tuah and Titiwangsa stations with the Putra LRT Line at Bukit Nanas and K.L. Sentral stations. An extension line from the Tun Sambanthan PRT station runs to K.L. Sentral train station in Brickfields. The Monorail line will soon cross Shah Alam with main stations at the Section 14 Commercial Centre and Universiti Institute of Technology Mara (UITM).

KTM Komuter

The KTM Komuter, an electric train, provides quick, comfortable and inexpensive transportation between K.L. and the Klang Valley (with routes between Rawang and Seremban, and between Sentul and Port Klang), and stops at several points along the way. Note that once you arrive at your destination, taxis might not be waiting at the station, so plan your time and energy accordingly. An Express Rail Link expected to open in 2001 will connect the K.L. International Airport at Sepang to the K.L. Sentral Railway Station in Brickfields. (KTM Komuter: Tel: 03- 2274-7435).

INTRA-CITY BUSES

Intrakota (Tel: 03-7727-2727) and **Cityliner** (Tel: 03-7826-6904) provide air-conditioned bus transportation throughout the Klang Valley. Intrakota serves K.L., P.J. and Ampang. The fare (90 *sen*) is the same irrespective of the distance travelled and should be

172

deposited in the coin box when you board the bus; no change is returned if you deposit a MR1 coin. Cityliner covers other routes. The fare depends on the number of stages travelled. Carry plenty of change, especially during rush hour. Enter buses at the front and exit at the back.

OUTSTATION BUSES

Economical bus transportation is available between K.L. and all cities and major towns in Peninsular Malaysia. Regular bus services also connect K.L. and Singapore. On outstation (long-distance) routes, most buses depart during the morning, seats can be reserved and tickets must be paid for in cash. At holiday times, tickets are often sold out weeks in advance. Most buses are air-conditioned; as air-conditioned can mean cold, take a sweater and socks. Schedule information for long-distance buses can be obtained at bus terminals.

BUS TERMINALS

Main bus terminals in K.L., from which outstation buses depart, are the following:

- **Pudu Raya** (Jalan Cheng Lock: Tel: 03-230 0145). North, northwest- and south-bound service (including Singapore).
- **Bangunan MARA** (Medan MARA, Jalan Raja Laut; Tel: 03-291-8113). North- and south-bound service; Executive Coach to Johor Bahru, Singapore, Penang and Ipoh.
- **Putra (Dewan Bandaraya)** (Opposite Putra World Trade Centre; Tel: 03-442-9530). East Coast express bus service.
- **Pekeliling** (Jalan Tun Razak, near Jalan Ipoh Junction; Tel: 03-442-1256). East Coast and Genting Highlands service.
- **Kelang (Toshiba)** (In the multi-storey car park on Jalan Sultan Mohammad). West-bound service.
- **Hentian Duta** (Persiaran Duta, off Jalan Duta; Tel: 1-800-880-495 or 03-653-3064/67). Buses to KLIA and Genting.

Photo by Lynn Witham

Getting Around in K.L.

LOCAL TAXIS

A fast and fairly economical way to get around in K.L. is by taxi. Taxis are usually easy to find, except during rush hours and rain storms, when many taxi drivers seem to prefer to wait it out on the roadside. Taxis can be hired at all major hotels and shopping centres, hailed on the streets, or called by phone. All licensed taxis are metered and easily identified by their red and white colour, by the letter "H" on their number plates, and by the sign "Teksi Kuala Lumpur" on both front doors.

Metered Taxis

When you use a metered taxi, check to see that the meter is on and that it reads RM2.00 when your ride begins. (In van taxis the meter reading begins at RM4.00.) Some drivers may decline to go to a certain location, especially if they are changing shifts. During heavy traffic and rainstorms, around major bus stations and shopping centres, and for trips to remote destinations, some drivers will refuse to use the meter and will quote a flat rate. The practice is against regulations. Try to bargain, or if you have time, wait for another taxi. To lodge a complaint with the Road Transport Department (Kompleks Pejabat Damansara, Blok A, Jalan Dungun, Damansara Heights, K.L.), note the taxi registration number, the driver's name and the date, time and place. If you leave any personal possessions in a taxi, contact the local branch of the Road Transport Department.

Taxi Fares In K.L. (subject to inflation)

- RM2.00 for the first kilometre or part thereof
- 10 *sen* for every additional 200 metres
- 20 *sen* for every additional passenger
- RM1.00 for each piece of luggage in the boot (trunk)
- Waiting charge is RM2.50 for the first 15 minutes and RM2.50 for every subsequent 15 minutes
- Highway tolls are paid by passengers
- A 50-percent surcharge is assessed for taxi service between midnight and 6:00 a.m.

Telephone Taxis

Telephone taxis can be obtained through the radio-paging system for a surcharge of RM1.00 and rented by the hour at a charge of RM20. A list of telephone taxi companies can be found in the Telephone Directory Yellow Pages under the heading "Taxicabs".

Two reliable companies are: Comfort Radio Taxi Service (Tel: 03-733-0507, 724-2727) and Federal Territory and Selangor Radio Taxi (Tel: 03-293-6211, 291-8361).

Hourly Taxis

A convenient way to run a series of errands or to see the sites is to hire a taxi by the hour. The usual rate is RM25 per hour, with a minimum of three hours; there is no limit to the distance or number of stops. Many expatriates and Malaysians ask for the telephone numbers of drivers they like and call those drivers rather than telephone taxis when they need transportation.

OUTSTATION TAXIS

Fast, economical (and sometimes hair-raising) outstation (long distance) taxi service operates between all cities in Malaysia, as well as to Singapore and Haadyai, Thailand. Taxis depart when they have four passengers, so departure and arrival times are unpredictable, but there is seldom a long wait for rides on major routes. Long-distance taxis may be chartered for groups or hired by individuals who are willing to pay four times the individual fare. Passengers often arrange for outstation taxis to pick them up and drop them off at specific locations. Fares are about double the bus fare for most routes. In K.L., walk-in long-distance taxi offices are located along Jalan Pudu Raya and upstairs in the Pudu Raya Bus Terminal. To book an outstation taxi to points in Malaysia or Singapore, contact the **Outstation Taxi Service Station**, Jalan Stadium, K.L. (Tel: 03-238-3525).

MAPS AND DIRECTIONS

Maps of Malaysia and its major cities are available free at offices of Tourism Malaysia and sold at bookshops, some gasoline (petrol) stations and the Automobile Association of Malaysia. Check that maps are up-to-date, as the road system is changing rapidly.

When giving directions, Malaysians sometimes say "At the T-junction, go straight on about one-half 'k'". A "T-junction" is a three-way intersection and "k" means kilometre. Please note that a street address such as 12 Jalan SS16/2 refers to house or building number 12, section 16, street number 2. A street address such as 9 Jalan 1/2 means building number 9 on street number 1, stroke 2, and is read as "nine Jalan One stroke two".

As the architectural landscape and the road system in the K.L. area are changing rapidly, check that you have complete, preferably written, directions before you go in search of an unfamiliar place, and enquire if there is a landmark (school, hospital, well-known restaurant or store) near the location. You may wonder why so many streets are named Jalan Sehala. Well, it isn't actually the name of the street; it means "One Way".

RENTAL CARS

Both self-drive and chauffeur-driven rental (hire) cars are available through international companies such as **Budget** and **Hertz**, and regional companies such as **Orix, Sintat, Pacific, Mayflower, SIA** and **SMAS.** Car rental companies maintain offices in airports, hotels, and shopping and office complexes. A complete listing can be found in the Telephone Directory Yellow Pages under the heading "Motorcar Renting and Leasing".

Regulations for renters and drivers of self-drive cars vary, but most companies stipulate the following: a minimum age of 23 (age 30 for luxury cars), and a maximum age of 60; a minimum of two years' driving experience; and possession of a valid local or international licence. In addition, the renter must present either a credit card or cash equivalent to the estimated rental charge when the car is received. For long-term cash payments, two letters of guarantee from local bank officials may be required. In addition to the rental fee, most companies require a refundable cash deposit. Extra hourly charges are assessed for late return of rental cars.

Rental rates, which range from RM160 to RM450 a day, depending on the vehicle make and model, are calculated on a daily (24-hour) or weekly basis. Rates do not include the cost of petrol (gasoline), collision damage waiver, personal accident injury insurance or long-distance delivery and collection fees. Rates may include mileage, car insurance and reimbursement for any repairs or maintenance required while you have the car. Some companies offer special promotional, weekend and long-term rental rates; some also offer leasing. Chauffeur-driven cars rent from RM40 an hour, subject to a minimum of three hours' rental.

Enquire about the amount for which you are liable in the event of an accident. Some companies will charge you the full amount if the accident is your fault, even if you buy the **collision damage waiver** (CDW). Also enquire about the need for extra CDW or insurance if there is a **second driver**. It is compulsory for renters to lodge a police report at the nearest police station for any accident, theft or vandalism involving the rented vehicle. Failure to lodge a report may void all liability protection.

Most rental companies do not charge for **collection and delivery**, within five kilometres in the city limits, on weekdays between 8:00 a.m. and 5:00 p.m. After hours, and on weekends and holidays, some companies charge for this service. A rent-it-here/leave-it-there option is available between major cities (including Singapore), usually for an extra charge.

For your protection, whenever you rent a car you are advised to **check for body damage**. If you find a serious dent or scratch, ask the agent to record the damage (along with his or her signature) on the rental agreement so that you cannot be held responsible for the damage when you return the car.

Be sure to write down the **emergency service number** of the rental firm, and ask how you should pay for repairs and where you should get help if the emergency service does not function 24 hours a day. If you will be driving a long distance, rent from a company that has 24-hour, nation-wide emergency service.

THE AUTOMOBILE ASSOCIATION OF MALAYSIA (AAM)

The AAM, a national motoring organisation with offices throughout the country, is a valuable source of information for the motorist. Among the **services** offered to members are: claims recovery; 24-hour breakdown service; 24-hour battery delivery service; legal aid and free legal advice; motoring insurance and other insurance; technical advice for any motoring problems; car inspection and valuation; vehicle maintenance courses; issuance of international driving permits; rental of child restraint seats and baby bassinets; arrangement of Carnets for international car shipment; transfer and cancellation of car ownership; and reminders and arrangements for renewals of driving licences and road tax payments. The AAM also publishes the *Malaysia Motoring Guide* and a monthly magazine, provides travel information, offers discounts on rental cars and hotel accommodations, and makes arrangements for tours and fly/drive programmes.

Foreigners who belong to motoring organisations affiliated with AAM may be given free **reciprocal membership** until the expiration of their home-country membership or up to a maximum of twelve months. Affiliated organisations include over 90 automobile associations and clubs in nearly 90 countries. Those who are not members of an affiliated organisation may join the AAM at reasonable rates.

For further **information**, contact the Chief Executive, Automobile Association of Malaysia (191 Jalan Tun Razak, 50450 K.L.; Tel: 03-262-5777; Fax: 03-262-5358). The AAM also has a branch at Unit No AM-18, Mezzanine Floor, PJ Industrial Park, Jalan Kemajuan, 46200 Petaling Jaya; Tel: 03-756-3043, 758-1163.

PRIVATE CARS

Many foreigners living in Malaysia have their own cars. Some import and others buy locally, depending on their shipping privileges or, for diplomatic personnel, duty-free privileges. If you decide to import or purchase a car in Malaysia, choose a car that handles well in rain, is solid enough to give some protection in accidents, and has rust proofing, air conditioning and a tropical radiator that will not overheat in traffic. Some people prefer to have a vehicle with a standard transmission.

IMPORTATION OF MOTOR VEHICLES

An **Import Permit** issued by the Ministry of International Trade and Industry is required for all imported vehicles. Usually the company responsible for shipping your car will obtain the permit. Some national automobile associations, such as the Automobile Association of Malaysia, offer a vehicle reception and shipping service for members. People wishing to import a new car can make the arrangements while they are still in their home country or after they arrive in Malaysia. Delivery to K.L. usually takes two to three months. **Only motor vehicles not more than seven years old may be imported.**

Duty charges on new and used imported cars range from 140% to 300%, depending on the value of the car. There is also a 10% **tax** on every imported vehicle. **Road taxes** for large cars are high. **Resale values** for certain makes and models and left-hand drive cars are low; foreign compact cars and locally assembled used cars in good condition usually retain their resale values.

Parts for unpopular foreign-made cars in Malaysia are not readily available and must be ordered from the country of manufacture and assembly. If you import a car, you can save time and energy by taking a supply of small spare parts. The Automobile Association of Malaysia can suggest where to find parts locally.

Local Purchase of Motor Vehicles

In 1985, Malaysia began production of the first made-in-Malaysia car, the **Proton Saga**, for the domestic and export markets. The Saga and other Proton models offer efficient performance for a reasonable price and are the market leaders.

A variety of foreign cars such as **Ford, Mazda, Toyota, Nissan, Honda, Daihatsu, Isuzu, Volvo, Peugeot, Fiat, Renault, Mercedes, BMW, Volvo, Saab** and **Audi** also can be purchased in Malaysia. You may not be able to find exactly what you want, however, as the models, colours and options available are limited.

Prices for imported cars are much higher than in the countries of origin because of the extra charges for tax and duty added to factory costs. Prices for foreign-manufactured but locally assembled cars are more reasonable.

Used cars in good condition often can be purchased from departing expatriates. If you have colleagues in Malaysia who are about to complete their assignments, you may be able to make arrangements to buy a car from them even before you arrive. Used cars can also be bought on the local market, but to get a good deal, take the time to shop around and bargain, and have a mechanic check the car before you buy. Also, make sure that the previous owner has paid up any traffic violations. **Locally assembled cars** are the best buy, as parts are prevalent. The *Automobile Association of Malaysia (AAM) Motoring Guide* offers valuable tips about choosing a used car. Open-market used car sales are held on Sundays at several locations; contact the AAM.

Financing for the purchase of motor vehicles is available to foreigners through Malaysian branches of many foreign-based banks. Loans are generally short term (12months -18 months) and command a high rate of interest.

181

Automobile Registration and Road Tax

Registration of new cars is arranged by sales agents. To register a used car, the new owner must:

- sign form MV4;
- obtain the blue registration card and a signed form MV3 from the seller; and
- present all three along with proof of insurance to the Road Transport Department.

Registration procedures for an imported car must be initiated within **30 days** after the car arrives in Malaysia. Presentation of title and proof of insurance is a prerequisite to being granted a registration. All necessary forms are available from local offices of the Road Transport Department. As traffic moves on the left in Malaysia, most vehicles are right-hand drive. A **left-hand drive** vehicle may be registered, but it must display a sign indicating that it is left-hand drive.

When you buy a car, the dealer will supply you with **licence plates**. If you import a car, you must obtain plates from an office of the Road Transport Department.

Road tax is payable annually to the Road Transport Department in K.L. Contact them at: 03-254-9044. The amount depends on the make, model and age of the vehicle.

Insurance

Third-party liability insurance coverage is the mandatory minimum requirement. It is best to purchase a comprehensive policy that will provide insurance coverage for third party liability, fire, theft and damage to the vehicle caused by a malicious act or an accidental collision or overturning. Premiums are reasonable, and you may be eligible for a **No Claim Discount** if you have made no claims on your current insurance for the past year or more. You must have a letter from your previous insurance company as proof in order to qualify for the discount. You are required to carry in your car at all times **proof of registration and liability insurance**.

MOTORING

Motoring is quite convenient. Malaysian roads are adequate in most areas and traffic is lighter and more regulated than in many countries. Topics of interest to motorists are discussed below.

Driving Licences

Driving licences from other ASEAN nations are valid in Malaysia (and vice versa). Driving licences from other countries (except India, Pakistan, Bangladesh and certain other countries) are valid after being endorsed by the Road Transport Department, and remain valid for 90 days. Valid **international driving licences** are acceptable until their date of expiration.

Malaysian licences may be obtained at the Road Transport Department office nearest to the area in which you reside. The main office is at Blok A, Kompleks Pejabat Damana, Jalan Dungun, Damansara Heights, 50620, K.L.; Tel: 03-254-9044). Applicants must present two passport pictures and their foreign or international licence, and pay a small fee. No driving test is given, but applicants may be required to exhibit knowledge of international road signs and traffic signals. These are explained in a booklet prepared by the Road Transport Department. If for some reason authorities do not issue a licence, the driver must take a series of lessons and then pass a written test and a road test. The minimum age to apply for a licence is eighteen; it is not possible to obtain a Learner's Permit at a younger age.

Traffic Signs and Signals

Malaysia uses a combination of local and international traffic signs. Local signs include the following: *Utara* (North), *Selatan* (South),

Timur (East), *Barat* (West), *Ikut Kiri* (Keep Left), *Jalan Sehala* (One Way), *Kosongkan* (Do Not Block), *Awas* (Caution), *Perlahan-lahan* (Slow) and *Kurangkan Had Laju* (Reduce Speed).

Malaysian drivers have devised three signals to communicate with each other. **Flashing headlights** mean, "Watch out, I'm claiming the right of way". A **flashing left blinker** (directional indicator) means, "I'm going to turn left" or "Go ahead and pass me, but do so with caution". A **flashing right blinker** means, "Do not pass (overtake) me now". Drivers use this signal to warn the driver behind them that another vehicle is approaching, that there is a dangerous curve ahead, or that they are about to pass the car ahead of them.

Regulations

If you are stopped by police and required to pay a fine, be polite and cooperative. You will be given a **summons** that must be paid in person or by mail within one week at the police station through which the summons was issued. Under no circumstances should you try to bribe a policeman; the result may be a greater fine and your name in the local newspapers. A few motoring regulations that may be new to you are mentioned below.

Seat belts must be worn by the driver and all front seat passengers. People who fail to comply with this regulation can be fined a maximum of RM200 or be imprisoned for up to six weeks.

It is illegal to hold a **mobile telephone** while driving and violators will be fined RM300. Buy a hands-free device for your phone.

Horns (hooters) should not be used near a hospital, or between 12-midnight and 7:00 a.m., except in an emergency.

The car on the right legally has the **right of way** at roundabouts (traffic circles) and intersections, but use caution as not all drivers follow this rule.

Do not enter a **yellow box** unless your exit is clear.

When **turning left or right**, drivers must give way to through traffic and to pedestrians.

Drivers should give way to **pedestrians** at zebra crossings (black and white striped crosswalks) and to vision-impaired pedestrians who carry white walking sticks.

Drivers must stop at the request of the owner of a **horse**.

In Malaysia it is *not* illegal to pass (overtake) a stopped school bus. Warn your children who ride buses that vehicles may pass stopped buses. **Teach children to be extra careful in crossing the road when they get out of a school bus.**

When an **emergency vehicle** (such as the police, an ambulance or a fire engine) signals its approach, drivers must pull over and stop to let the vehicle pass.

In K.L., some traffic lanes (marked with yellow lines) are designated as **bus and taxi lanes** during certain hours.

A regulation pending approval is that toddlers must be placed in **child restraint seats**.

Do not take the risk of **drinking and driving.** Penalties are high, the hassles are great, and the impressions that expatriates make on Malaysians, especially in the case of injury accidents, is extremely negative.

Driving Hazards

Driving in K.L. demands close attention. The main streets are crowded and traffic in and out of the city can be heavy at rush hour and slow moving during torrential downpours. When driving out of town, motorists must be alert to **unexpected hazards** such as speeding taxis and transport trucks, slow-moving trucks and buses (often with non-functioning tail and brake lights), wandering people or animals, unmarked fender-bending pot holes and washouts, and cars that cut in without warning.

Motorcyclists pose a host of dangers to motorists as they weave around lanes of traffic, drive on the wrong side of the road to get around traffic jams, and do not necessarily flow with the speed of other traffic. Many motorcyclists have never driven cars and do not understand the differences in manoeuvreability. Honking your horn at them is dangerous as they may panic and lose control, causing an accident. Motorcycle drivers who are inexperienced, risk-taking, and often unlicensed have become so prevalent that their characteristic style of driving has gained the uncomplimentary name, "Mat Motor Syndrome".

Be forewarned that some drivers have the habit of **driving on the edge** rather than in the centre of traffic lanes and that rather than formally passing other cars, they informally "slide" in front of them. Also, the use of **directional signals (blinkers)** is overlooked by many local drivers. Drivers will, with no warning, cut in front of others. A common scenario for accidents is when a motorcyclist slides up alongside a car, intending to pass, and the driver of the car, not seeing the motorcycle, makes a turn. In accidents, motorcyclists will often claim that the driver was not using a directional signal. Consequently, do use your directional signal whenever you intend to change your path, and in the unfortunate case of an accident, leave the signal on as proof.

Another hazard is **"road bullies,"** drivers who do whatever they can to slide in ahead of you and then display unfriendly signs of "road rage" if you respond. This overt, aggressive behaviour has increased along with the increase in traffic congestion and is a puzzle to Malaysians themselves as it is in stark contrast to the non-aggressive behaviour that is traditionally valued in Malaysian society.

Driving on the left may be a new experience for you. Try to get a feeling for it by sitting behind the driver of a taxi or private car, and then begin practising on uncrowded streets. When you make turns, keep in mind that drivers are always seated closest to the middle of the road. Learning how to flow with the local driving style takes practice.

Be extremely careful when backing up or when **parking** along the deep storm drains. Double check for children, animals, adults and other vehicles behind you as they have the habit of appearing from out of nowhere. During **rainstorms**, it is safest to drive slowly with the headlights on, and to avoid stopping on the highway unless it is possible to pull far off the road, as visibility is poor and the danger of being hit from the rear is great.

In summary, motorists are urged to avoid taking chances; to pass, change lanes and make turns with great caution; to be especially cautious of motorcyclists; and to expect that people will not drive defensively.

Accidents and Emergencies

According to strict interpretation of the law, accidents should be reported to the police even if there is only minor injury or property damage. By law the drivers involved may leave the scene of an accident, and have 24 hours in which to report it. **Minor accidents**, especially those involving motorcycles, are common. Most minor accidents are settled on the spot between the parties involved, usually by the driver at fault giving the other driver enough cash to cover the damage. Such accidents might also be reported to the police, but are usually not reported to insurance agents.

If you are involved in, or at fault for, a **serious accident** resulting in the injury or death of a local person or a valuable animal such as a cow, goat or sheep, some people suggest that you should not stop or get out of your car. You may risk injury if you stop, especially in rural areas, as a crowd might gather and become angry, especially if they assume you have been drinking. Instead, do as many Malaysians do–lock your car doors and proceed directly to the nearest police station to report the accident.

Other authorities, however, suggest that you should stop to help the injured and to obtain the name, address and vehicle registration number of any other drivers involved. Give the same

187

information about yourself to other drivers, to the injured or to witnesses if they ask for it. Also ask for the names and addresses of any injured persons, passengers or witnesses, and make a diagram of the accident. You are under no obligation to sign any type of document at the scene. If you intend to file an insurance claim, do not discuss at the scene whose fault the accident was as this may create difficulties for your insurers in their handling of your claim. Also, to prevent theft of accessories, do not leave your car unattended or unlocked at the site.

Similarly, if you see an accident, your instinct may be to stop and try to help. Consider, however, that it may be dangerous for you to stop to assist or to give first aid if there is a chance a crowd will congregate and assume that you are responsible for the accident. Again, this is especially true in rural areas. In case of a **highway emergency**, flag down a passing motorist or call the Automobile Association of Malaysia (AAM), or the nearest garage, hospital or police station for assistance.

Parking and Tolls

In K.L., public parking areas are equipped with meters or staffed by attendants. Metered parking is free in some areas of K.L. after 6:00 p.m. and on Sundays and public holidays. (Look for instructions on the meter.) In areas with attendants, the attendant gives you a coupon when you arrive and you pay the designated amount when you depart. In Selangor, parking coupons are available from vending machines at a cost of 60 *sen* per hour. Place the coupons on the dashboard of the parked car for inspection.

Several highways in the Klang Valley are toll roads. Frequent users can purchase a stored-value **Smartcard** usable on any toll road, a **Metrakad** monthly pass valid for travel on a specific toll road, or a booklet of 30 **Toll Vouchers** that are valid for three months and offer a 10% savings.

Gasoline and Service Stations

Companies such as **Petronas, Caltex, Shell, Esso, Mobil and BP (British Petroleum)** operate gasoline (petrol) stations throughout the country. Urban centres and small towns have service stations that stock spare parts and employ experienced mechanics who can repair most locally assembled makes of cars. **Towing** charges can be high, so contact AAM or bargain hard and specify exactly where you want the vehicle taken.

Driving Out of K.L.

A well-developed and fairly well-maintained road system connects K.L. to other urban areas. Before you embark on a long drive, arm yourself with an up-to-date map and speak with the AAM to request information about the route you will be travelling. The main **North-South Expressway**, a toll road, runs from Singapore through K.L to the Thai border. The 400km drive from K.L. to Singapore takes about four hours (depending on traffic at the Causeway), and the 370km drive from K.L. to Butterworth takes just under four hours. **Highway 8** runs northeast from K.L. to Kota Bahru near the Thai border (474km) and **Highway 2** links K.L. with the East Coast at Kuantan (259km). Both link with the main **East Coast Highway** which runs from Johor Bahru in the south to Kota Bharu in the north (689km). Crossing the Peninsula in the north, the **East-West Highway** links Gerik in the State of Perak to Jeli in the State of Kelantan, and extends to Butterworth in the west and Kota Bharu in the east. The total distance is about 363 kilometres (225 miles).

Driving Across International Borders

Motorists driving a Malaysian-registered vehicle to Thailand, Singapore or Brunei must obtain an Entry Permit at the border by showing the following documents: proof of registration; proof of insurance coverage; and a valid driver's licence issued by the

Malaysian Road Transport Department or a valid international driving licence. To re-import the vehicle into Malaysia motorists must show the same documents. There is often a delay at Customs at the border.

If you drive to **Singapore**, you should know the following:

- All vehicles entering and leaving Singapore must pay a cash toll or buy a stored-value Autopass from which the toll fee will be deducted.
- Near the border you can rent an "In Vehicle Unit" (IVU) which will be installed in your car. You must insert your Autopass if you travel on an Electronic Road Pricing (ERP) highway or enter the Central Business District (CBD) during certain times of day. When you leave Singapore you must stop near the border and have the IVU removed.
- The country has a coupon parking system. Buy the coupons at parking lot kiosks or in post offices, indicate on a coupon the date and length of time you wish to park, and place the coupon on the inside of your car windshield.

WALKING

Walking, like driving, demands your full attention. If you are not accustomed to traffic moving on the left, **be sure to look both ways before crossing streets or driveways**, and to take great care not to step in front of oncoming vehicles. Teach your children to be extra cautious and to **"Look right, look left, and look right again"**. In all Southeast Asian cities, watch out for **buses** travelling in bus lanes and don't count on buses coming to a complete stop to let passengers on or off. Watch also for speeding motorbikes, the terror of K.L. streets. Motorbikes weave through stopped traffic (look around each lane of traffic when you cross the street) and drive on sidewalks (walk in a straight line or look behind you before you vary from your straight path).

Sidewalks in some areas are uneven or non-existent, and man-hole covers are sometimes missing or unsturdy. To guard against foot injuries, watch for uneven surfaces and unexpected holes in the road or sidewalk, and wear comfortable low-heeled shoes. Pedestrians in Malaysia are expected to cross roads at **designated crossings**, but the law is seldom strictly enforced. Sometimes jaywalking is the only way to avoid a long walk to the nearest crosswalk or pedestrian bridge.

Hitchhiking is not common among Malaysians and is not recommended for foreigners.

Chapter Thirteen

ENJOYING THE FOOD

SAVOURING THE FLAVOURS

Adventurous diners will delight in the variety of cuisines available
in Malaysia. Malaysia's three major culture groups produce
distinctly different cuisines. Common to all are rice, tomatoes,
chilli peppers, green and root vegetables, and a variety of aromatic
spices including cloves, ginger, cumin, turmeric, cinnamon,
tamarind, galingale, cardamom and lemon grass. When it comes
to the main course, however, people of different groups have
diverse preferences. Malays and other Muslims are forbidden to
eat pork, and prefer beef, lamb, chicken and fish. Chinese opt for
seafood, poultry and pork; some do not eat beef (especially if they
are devotees of Kuan Yin, the Goddess of Mercy). Indian Hindus
do not eat beef and some do not eat pork; some Hindus and
Buddhists are vegetarians.

Much of Malaysian food is spicy. To ensure the absorption of spices and to make the food easier to eat with the fingers, meat and vegetables are cut into small pieces before cooking. Foreigners not familiar with the powerful kick chilli peppers can give the palate may be interested to know that the seeds are the most potent, and that yogurt, white rice and raw cucumber are more effective coolants than water or carbonated beverages.

Malay Cuisine

Foods preferred by Malays are rice, fish, fruit, beef, lamb, chicken, curries and green vegetables. A typical meal consists of rice served with a variety of spicy curries, fried foods and vegetable dishes and garnished with *sambal blacan*, a relish of chillies and shrimp paste or *sambal ikan bilis*, a relish of ground chillies and anchovy-like fish. Cheese, bland foods and sweet Western-style desserts are not popular. Islam forbids Muslims to drink alcohol or to eat pork, any product that comes from a pig, or any food containing or fried in pork fat. Also forbidden is the flesh of predatory birds and animals, and the flesh of rodents, reptiles and amphibians such as frogs. According to Islamic law, Muslims should eat only meat that is *halal* (ritually slaughtered by a Muslim).

Chinese Cuisine

Chinese cuisine features a wide variety of foods prepared according to regional traditions. Staple foods include noodles, rice, fish, seafood, chicken, duck, pork, beef, vegetables and beancurd. A typical meal might consist of a noodle dish, a fish dish, a poultry dish and a vegetable dish. Chinese Buddhists often prefer not to eat products that come from a cow, and staunch Buddhists observe vegetarian diets, especially on the first and fifteenth day of every Chinese lunar month. For some Chinese, as well as many other Asians, eating milk products can result in stomach upset. Iced drinks are also unpopular, as many Chinese believe that drinking cold liquids is unhealthy; even after martial arts exercises warm tea is served.

Chinese believe that foods prepared with herbs promote good health and harmony in the body, and that proper food combinations are basic to good health. Various foods are assumed to have specific effects on the body's internal harmony or balance of *yin* and *yang*. *Yin* foods are believed to be cooling and soothing to the spirit, while *yang* foods are body-heating and energy-producing. (Sample *yin* foods are beer, cucumbers, cooked vegetables, certain fruits and many herbal teas; sample *yang* foods are chicken, red meat, the durian fruit, and many varieties of nuts.) Too much of either type of food will cause disharmony in the body, resulting in sickness or problems of temperament.

Photo by Lynn Witham

Time for Tea

Nyonya Cuisine

Nyonya cuisine is a tasty blend of Malay and Chinese cooking that originated in Melaka among the Straits-born Chinese. Traditionally, family recipes were carefully guarded by the Nyonya and few specialties were prepared in restaurants. Today, however, several modest restaurants in Melaka, Penang and K.L. serve authentic Nyonya food.

Indian Cuisine

Religious beliefs influence the food preferences among Malaysia's people of Indian origin. Devout Hindus do not eat beef and many are vegetarians. Indian Muslims do not eat pork and many do not drink alcohol. Most Indians prefer spicy curries served with rice, yogurt, chilli sauce, wholewheat breads and rich sweet desserts, and are not fond of shellfish, raw vegetables, strong-flavoured cheeses, or foods that are bland, boiled or steamed. A traditional Indian meal consists of meat, fish, poultry, or vegetable curry served with a rice dish, several vegetable dishes, at least one kind of freshly baked Indian bread, and perhaps *lassi*, a cool yogurt drink. The curries are often served on banana leaves and accompanied by yogurt.

MALAYSIAN DINING ETIQUETTE

While Malays, Chinese and Indians each have their own rules of etiquette, some customs are shared by all groups. Malaysians customarily accept food or drink which is offered to them so that they will not offend the host or hostess, but they do not drink until the host or hostess has invited them to do so. Any food or drink that a guest cannot eat for medical or religious reasons is simply not consumed; otherwise, it is at least tasted. Malaysians seldom divide the cost of restaurant meals or other entertainment among the guests. The person who suggests the outing is usually the one who pays.

Malay Dining Etiquette

Malays and other Muslims prefer to hand and receive objects, especially food, with the right hand or both hands. Strictly speaking, it is considered bad manners to use the left hand alone, as that hand is reserved for personal hygiene. Malays often eat rice and its accompanying dishes with a spoon or with the right hand. They will be glad to show you the proper way of scooping rice with your hand. Malays consider it impolite to blow their noses or to laugh or cough loudly at the table.

During the holy month of **Ramadhan** (the dates of which vary yearly), Muslims abstain from eating and drinking from sunrise to sunset. Most Malaysians break their daily fast with dates or other fruits and a glass of cool water, or with sweet cakes *(kueh)* and a hot drink.

When invited to a Malay home for a meal, guests sometimes take a gift to show appreciation. Appropriate gifts are fruit, biscuits or chocolates, but not flowers or alcohol. Other possibilities are small decorative items for the home, handicrafts, toys or clothing for the children, and brightly coloured, good-quality Malaysian or Indonesian batik and sarongs. Toys, clothing or household items made outside Southeast Asia are especially appreciated. The proper time to present gifts to a Malay host and hostess is upon departure. Malays feel it is impolite to open gifts in the presence of the giver, so they usually put gifts aside until the guests leave.

Chinese Dining Etiquette

Most formal Chinese dinners are multi-course affairs. The more important the guests, the more courses in the dinner. The host usually sits facing the door and honoured guests sit to the left of the host. (An important assistant to a Chinese is his "left-hand man," not his "right-hand man".) The host usually begins the affair by raising his glass and offering a toast to his guests. Diners begin eating when the host raises his chopsticks. Chopsticks should not be waved in the air, used to point, or stuck upright in a bowl of rice. (The latter action is especially inappropriate, as it resembles the burning of incense sticks in a ceremony to honour the spirits of the dead.) During the meal, chopsticks are rested on the small chopstick holder; at the end of the meal, they are placed on the table beside one's bowl or plate. Chinese do not turn over a fish on a plate, as the action is a bad omen, especially for sailors or fishermen for whom it may signify the capsizing of a boat. Burping after the meal is a sign of contentment and is not impolite in traditional Chinese etiquette. Guests leave immediately after the meal is completed.

When people are invited to a home for a meal, they may take gifts of fruits or biscuits. The Chinese custom is to give gifts in pairs or even numbers (symbols of good luck), but never singly or in odd numbers (symbols of bad luck). Appropriate gifts are imported cakes, two boxes of sweets, a basket of food delicacies, or an even number of pieces of fruit. (Sometimes the host may return a few pieces of fruit to the guest as a token of good luck.) Some Chinese may appreciate a gift of imported liquor.

Photo courtesy of Mines Beach Resort and Wonderland

Dim Sum

Indian Dining Etiquette

Indians traditionally eat with the right hand or with a spoon. The left hand is used to lift one's glass or to pass dishes if the right hand is soiled from eating. When Indians finish eating food that is served on a banana leaf, they quickly fold the leaf (by taking hold of the stem side and folding it up over the other side) if they do not want a second helping. Otherwise the leaf will be refilled and the diner will be obliged to eat.

In an Indian home, men are usually the first to be served and the first to eat. At a buffet, women usually serve themselves first and men follow. Guests at Indian dinners usually stay a while after the meal to chat. When visiting an Indian home, thoughtful guests take a bowl of fruit, tins of cakes or candies, toys for the children, or good quality material for a sari. It is not customary for Indians to open gifts in the presence of guests.

FRUITS

Malaysia's succulent tropical fruits make a tasty finale to any meal. The most unusual of fruits is the durian. It looks like a spiked green football and to many foreigners smells something like a mixture of licorice and kerosene. Its smooth, creamy pulp is a favourite among many Asians and is used to make a variety of dishes. It is said that a Malaysian will pawn his best sarong to get a good durian. The fruit is reputed to be a powerful aphrodisiac and according to a local joke, when the durians begin to fall, so do the sarongs. Consumption along with alcohol, tea or coffee is not recommended, as stomach upset or heartburn is often the result. Fruits and other foods take on special significance in Malaysia. They are categorised as "heaty" (stimulating) or "cooling" (calming), depending on how they affect the body. Durians, for example, are "heaty" as are rambutans and pineapples.

Photo by Lynn Witham

The Mysterious Durian Fruit

Mangosteens are "cooling," as are bananas, oranges and watermelons. To balance the heating effect of durians, people often follow them up with mangosteens.

DRINKS

Common drinks in Malaysia include the traditional *teh tarik* (tea mixed with condensed milk and poured into a glass from a pitcher high above) and *kopi O* (black coffee). Other local drinks include fresh fruit juices, coconut juice, sugarcane juice and soya bean milk. For delicious 100% fruit and vegetable "smoothies", try the shop **Juice Fusion** (branches in Suria KLCC and Mid Valley Megamall). Internationally known brands of soft drinks are widely available. Beer, wine and hard liquor are heavily taxed and generally quite expensive. Prices for alcoholic beverages are fairly reasonable at Carrefour stores, but some people prefer to save money by buying the maximum allowance at the duty free liquor shop at the airport each time they fly into the country and by asking visiting family and friends to do the same. Water in K.L and major cities is potable, but many people prefer to drink bottled water. Several companies offer home delivery of bottled water; one praised for excellent customer service is **Sterling Pure Water** (Tel: 03-634-7088).

Photo by Lynn Witham

Pausing for Refreshing Sugarcane Juice

Photo by Lynn Witham

Time for Cooling "Cats' Eyes Drink"

EATING OUT

Even the most demanding gourmet will enjoy eating out in K.L. While numerous restaurants offer local Malay, Nyonya, Chinese and Indian fare, others feature specialties from France, Japan, Britain, Thailand, Korea, Italy, Indonesia and the Middle East, as well as "fusion" cuisine. The choice of eating places ranges from elegant, expensive restaurants, to foreign fast-food chains, to inexpensive open-air stalls. Sanitation standards are high in most restaurants and hawkers stalls; if one eating establishment does not meet your standards, there is sure to be another nearby that will.

For a list of recommended restaurants, consult *Malaysia's Best Restaurants* guide published by Malaysia Tatler, "The Expat Going Out Guide" in the monthly magazine called *The Expat,* and announcements in the local newspapers. Note that some restaurants (including Bombay Palace) offer home and office delivery.

A Few Favourites

The following are just a few small restaurants offering international culinary delights. For authentic Nyonya food served in a traditional setting, visit the **Old China Café** (No. 11, Jalan Balai Polis, K.L.; 03-232-5915). To savour traditional Malay food while surrounded by Malaysian art and artifacts, try the **Kafe Kayu Manis** (Lot G9, Level 2, Block G, Pusat Bandar Damansara, K.L., behind 7-11 Shop). Another good place for *kampung*-style Malay food is **Restoran Puteri** (Jalan Tun Sambanthan). For North and South Indian Vegetarian delicacies, go to **Madras New Woodlands** (42A, Jalan Telawi Lima, Bangsar Baru). To sample authentic Persian food, visit the **Persian House** (04 Lorong Kolam Air Lama Satu, Ampang Jaya), a tiny outdoor restaurant near ISKL. For a Vietnamese-Thai culinary experience, visit **Tamarind Hill** (1 Jalan Kerja Air Lama, Ampang). Finally, to enjoy some Asian dishes during your hunting and gathering sprees at the Central Market, stop at the **Ginger Restaurant** (Central Market, 2nd Floor).

Local Fast Food

Malaysia has its own version of fast food. When Malaysians are in a rush, don't want to cook, or just want some good food, they go to food courts in shopping malls or to the hawkers' centres or street stalls located throughout the city. Ask Malaysians to recommend their favourites to you. They will be pleased that you asked and might even invite you to join them. If so, you will be in for a treat, especially if you are an adventurous diner. Dining in food courts is informal and when empty tables are few, it is not uncommon for people to ask strangers if they can share a table; you can do the same.

Photo by Lynn Witham

A Quick Snack

International Fast Food and Coffee

Connoisseurs of Western and Japanese fast food will be relieved to know that in many locations in K.L. they can find familiar foods: burgers at **A&W, Wendy's, McDonald's** and **Burger King**; pizzas and submarines at **Shakey's, Pizza Hut** and **California Pizza**; chicken at **Kentucky Fried Chicken**; roast beef sandwiches at **Arby's**; sushi at **Sushi King** and **Genki Sushi**; fresh croissants at **Delifrance**; donuts at **Dunkin Donuts**; freshly baked cookies at **Famous Amos** and **Aunt Annie's**; ice cream at **Swenson's** and **Haagen-Dazs**; and specialty coffees at **Starbucks, The Coffee**

Bean, **Gloria Jeans** and numerous other cafés. One of the trendiest places to enjoy refreshments and pastries is **Bintang Walk** near the Marriott Hotel in K.L.

SHOPPING FOR FOOD

As Malaysia depends on imports for much of its food supply, certain items that are a regular part of your diet at home may be available only sporadically, if at all. Consequently, menu planning may be a challenge. You may want to stock up on your favourite non-perishable foods whenever you find the items for sale. Some of the specialty grocers will try to order items for you if you show them the label and the manufacturer's address.

When you purchase foods, check expiration dates; when you open packages, check for weevils. Payment for groceries is by cash or credit card. Some small shops will allow you to pay monthly, a time saver if you frequently run into the corner store to pick up one or two items.

Supermarkets

K.L. and the suburbs have numerous large and modern supermarkets, many of which are located in or near shopping complexes and stay open until 9:30 p.m. or later. Most supermarkets carry a wide variety of local and imported fresh and processed foods, as well as toys, books, liquors, magazines, cosmetics, toiletries and household articles. The supermarkets most popular among expatriates include the following:

- **Ampang Grocers/ Ampang Minimarket:** 387 Jalan Ampang, K.L. (This small store is a favourite among expatriates as it is packed with imported foods and has a delivery service.)
- **Bi-Lo:** Desa Pandan, K.L.
- **Carrefour:** 5 Jalan SS16/1, near Subang Parade Shopping Centre in Subang Jaya; Mid Valley Megamall in P.J.; Jaya; Endah Parade in Seri Petaling

- **Cold Storage:** Jaya Shopping Centre, Section 14, Jalan 14/17, P.J.; Bangsar Shopping Centre on Jalan Maarof in Bangsar; Komplex PKNS in Shah Alam
- **Euro-Orient Boutique Butcher and Delicatessen:** Bangsar Shopping Centre
- **Giant:** 244 Jalan Bandar 13, Taman Melawati, K.L.; 2 Jalan SS 6/3, Pusat Bandar Kelana Jaya in P.J.; 1 Jalan Pinang 18/D, Seksyen 18, Kawasan Perniagaan, Shah Alam; 672 USJ 1, Subang Jaya
- **Hock Choon:** 241-1 Jalan Ampang
- **Hock Lee Minimarket:** 6-1 Jalan Batai in Damansara Heights
- **Isetan:** Lot 10 Shopping Centre on Jalan Sultan Ismail; Suria KLCC, 3rd Fl.
- **Jaya Jusco:** Alpha Angle; Bandar Baru in Wangsa Maju; One Utama in P.J.; Mid Valley Megamall in P.J.
- **Lifestyle:** (formerly Yaohan) The Mall on Jalan Chow Kit Baru; Sunway Pyramid Shopping Mall in Bandar Sunway; Plaza OUG on Jalan Klang Lama
- **Sogo:** 190 Jalan Tuanku Abdul Rahman, K.L.
- **Tops:** (in Parkson Grand) Sungei Wang Plaza on Jalan Sultan Ismail; Subang Parade in Subang Jaya; The Atria in Damansara Jaya
- **TMC:** Taman Lucky in Bangsar
- **Thrifty:** 19 Jalan Barat, Petaling Jaya
- **Xtra:** Ampang Point; The Mines Shopping Fair

Provisioners

One of the luxuries of living in Malaysia is the provisioner, or "van man" or "van lady," as they are often called, who will deliver food and household supplies to your home and possibly cash cheques for you. Some provisioners are delivery services from small grocery stores; others circulate with well-stocked vans. A provisioner may come to your home soon after you move in; if not, you can find one by asking your neighbours.

205

You can arrange for the provisioner to stop at your house as often as you want. Provisioners can even deliver milk, bread and water on a regular basis, but the cost can be high. Most provisioners accept monthly payments. Keeping careful records and checking your bill before you pay it will help avoid misunderstandings.

Wet Markets

Daily outdoor wet markets offer the greatest variety of fresh meats, eggs, poultry, seafood, fruits, vegetables and flowers. Arrive early for the best selection. Note that the prices for some food items tend to rise on weekends and holidays, and sometimes for foreigners. Get to know the sellers and compare prices with market prices. Two large markets are the **Chow Kit Market** and the **Jalan Pasar Pudu Market**. There are also several popular night markets, known as *pasar malam*, that sell food and other items.

Photo by Lynn Witham

Thoughtful Shopping

Health Foods

Health foods are slowly gaining in popularity. Larger supermarkets often carry some health foods imported from Europe, Australia and North America. New health food shops open periodically; check the Yellow Pages of your Telephone Directory for addresses. Current shops in K.L. include the **General Nutrition Centre** (GNC) (in many locations) and **Body Basics** (Bangsar Shopping Centre, Sunway Pyramid, Subang Parade, The Ampwalk). When you are in Singapore, visit Brown Rice Paradise (03-15 Tanglin Mall; Tel: 02-738-1121) and Planet Organic (Wheelock Place, 3rd Floor). These shops carry quite a wide variety of products from around the world and will try to special order items they do not stock.

The Web

If you are yearning for a special food or ingredient and you cannot find it in Malaysia, try searching the following website: **www.theglobalgrocer.com**. The Global Grocer, based in Singapore, offers home delivery of hard-to-find foods and will ship to Malaysia.

ENTERTAINING

Most entertaining takes place in clubs, restaurants and private homes, and preparations for formal occasions are quite elaborate. If you invite Malaysians to your home or to a restaurant banquet, prepare the **menu** with dietary restrictions in mind. If you are not sure about the eating habits of your guests, ask them in advance. When entertaining Muslim guests, it is considerate to refrain from serving any dishes containing pork, alcohol or other ingredients that are *haram* (forbidden), and to cook only meats that are *halal*. It is also considerate to provide a variety of non-alcoholic beverages. If you are having both Muslim and Hindu guests, omit both pork and beef from the menu. If you invite

Chinese guests, omit beef, cheese and dairy dishes, unless you know they are fond of these.

The safest approach is to serve a buffet from which guests can serve themselves whenever they arrive, and to provide many different dishes, including at least one rice dish along with several meat and vegetable dishes, some of them with spicy gravies.

If you are interested in learning how to prepare Malaysian cuisine, the popular recipe book *Traditional Malaysian Cuisine*, gives some useful cooking tips and clear explanations of how to prepare a wide variety of favourite foods.

ATTENDING SOCIAL FUNCTIONS

One of the great pleasures of living in Malaysia is attending festivals, religious celebrations and social functions. If work colleagues offer invitations, accept freely, but be sure that you do not show favouritism to colleagues of one particular race. Also, try to arrive on time as Malaysians expect this of foreigners.

Dinner invitations from Malays or Indians may be to a restaurant or private home and will usually include spouses and sometimes children. Invitations from Chinese will probably be to a restaurant and may not include spouses. Many official functions and dinner engagements begin at 8:30 p.m. or later, after Muslim evening prayers.

Alcohol is served at some business-related social functions (although not at government functions). It is best to avoid drinking excessively and showing signs of inebriation in public, however, especially in the presence of Malaysian colleagues who are not imbibing. The foreigner who begins to speak loudly, gesture wildly and use profane language at a social or business occasion will make a negative impression that is not likely to be forgotten. If you choose not to drink alcoholic beverages, you can politely refuse. At a Chinese banquet you can participate in the *yam seng* toasts by simply raising your glass along with the other guests.

The drinking of alcohol is a sensitive subject among Muslims in Malaysia. While some Muslims may drink in private settings, they do not expect to have their indiscretion referred to after the fact. To maintain relationships, foreigners too must be discreet about the activities of their Malaysian colleagues and themselves.

CHAPTER FOURTEEN

MAKING PURCHASES

THE SHOPPING EXPERIENCE

Fast developing as a regional shopping hub, K.L. and its suburbs offer more than 60 large shopping complexes and over 300 smaller ones, as well as narrow streets lined with small shops and bustling night markets that rotate about the city and suburbs. Malaysian-made products are interspersed with a wide range of products imported from East and West. Almost everything you might need will be available in some form or another, if you are willing to search and pay the price. This chapter contains information that will guide you through the process of hunting and gathering.

Photo by Lynn Witham

Shopping is an Adventure

When you shop, you might find it necessary to adjust your shopping patterns and expectations to local conditions. You'll probably have to go to several small stores rather than to one large one to find what you need. Also, you will find that items that were available at one time are suddenly "out of stock" and that while products of a certain brand are available, the specific item you are looking for is not. By the time you leave Malaysia, you may well have become an expert at bargaining, stocking up and making do with substitutes.

211

Prices in department stores and in many small shops in up-scale shopping complexes are fixed and items are marked with price tags. Prices can vary greatly, though, so you may save money by comparing prices before you buy and by asking about a discount if you buy in quantity. Prices in small retail shops along streets, in small shopping centres, in hotel shopping arcades and in roadside stalls are often negotiable, sometimes up to 60%, even if the prices are marked.

Payment in large departmental stores, supermarkets, pharmacies, major bookshops, jewellery stores and many boutiques can be by cash, travellers' cheque or credit card. Many small shops accept only Visa and MasterCard and sometimes add 3% to 5% onto the purchase price to cover their administrative costs. If you plan to pay in cash, you can sometimes use this as a bargaining point. Many small shops do not accept travellers' cheques.

Whenever you make a major purchase, ask for and **save the receipt** if you plan to export the item. Customs officials may ask to see purchase receipts if you export expensive items out of Malaysia or import them into your own country. (Note that to export antiquities, you must obtain an **export licence** from the Director-General of the Museums Department.)

Return or exchange of purchased goods is an option only at a few large departmental stores. In most cases the item, accompanied by the receipt, must be returned within one week. The customer is then issued a credit voucher that remains valid for a short period of time.

Shopping hours are quite convenient, even for people who work long days. Shopping complexes and departmental stores open between 10:00 a.m. and 11:00 a.m., and close between 8:30 p.m. and 10:00 p.m.; most are open seven days a week. Private shops open between 9:00 a.m. and 10:00 a.m., and close at 6:00 p.m. or 7:00 p.m.; many are closed on Sundays. Night bazaars

(*Pasar Malam*) stay open until 10:00 p.m. or later.

Special conveniences of shopping in Malaysia are that service people such as the dressmaker, shoemaker, furniture maker and plant nursery representative will come to your residence, and almost anything (including photos, plants, clothes, furniture, plane tickets and groceries) can be delivered to your home for a small charge. In addition, shopkeepers may be willing to specially order certain items. (Some stores have a policy requiring customers to accept and pay for items they order, so enquire before placing an order.) If you don't want to go out shopping, you can try shopping on line. In 2000, **MalaysiaDirectory.com** launched an on-line shopping mall service selling flowers, mobile phones, sports equipment and other products.

Bargaining is an integral part of daily life in Malaysia and most of Southeast Asia. Unless you are shopping in a large department store where prices are fixed, you probably can make your purchase for less than the written or quoted price. It is wise to do research before purchasing expensive items so that you will be able to distinguish the quality of merchandise and recognise a fair price.

References to guide you in your shopping include the brochure *Shopping Around Kuala Lumpur* (published by Tourism Malaysia); the books *Selamat Datang: Kuala Lumpur from A to Z*, (published by the American Association of Malaysia); and *Welcome to Kuala Lumpur* (published by the Association of British Women in Malaysia), and the magazines *The Finder* and *The Expat*, which advertise many up-scale local businesses.

SHOPPING IN KUALA LUMPUR

Shopping in K.L. can be an adventure. Browsing in Chinatown, Little India, Malay markets, specialty shops, department stores, hypermarket warehouse clubs and colourful day and evening markets is a pastime many people enjoy. Below is a list of the shopping areas most popular among expatriates. For a list of the locations of night markets, consult the "Star Metro" section of *The Star* newspaper.

Golden Triangle Area

The busiest shopping area is the "Golden Triangle," located in the southeast quadrant of the city and bordered by Jalan Imbi, Jalan Bukit Bintang and Jalan Sultan Ismail. Located within walking distance are the malls described below:

- *Bukit Bintang Plaza* (Jalan Bukit Bintang; connected to Sungei Wang Plaza). Features jewellery, gifts, shoes, clothing and computer ware, pharmacies, **MPH Bookstore**, **Marks & Spencer** and **Metrojaya** Department Store.
- *Sungei Wang Plaza* (Jalan Sultan Ismail). Houses **Parkson Grand** Department Store, Tops Supermarket and more than 500 specialty shops.
- *Low Yat Plaza* (behind Sungei Wang Plaza). A new complex with several restaurants and shops specialising in jewellery, clothes and computers.
- *Lot 10* (Jalan Sultan Ismail). An up-market complex with an **Isetan** Department Store and Supermarket, **Kinokuniya Books,** designer boutiques, the **Body Shop, Sports Station,** several cafés and a snazzy food court.
- *K.L. Plaza* (179 Jalan Bukit Bintang). Has numerous small specialty shops, **Tower Records** (the city's largest music outlet), and a post office.
- *Star Hill Plaza* (Jalan Bukit Bintang, adjacent to the Marriott Hotel). An elegant, marble and glass mall with designer boutiques, children's clothing shops, **Sports Station, Times the Bookshop**, the upscale **CK Tangs** Department Store, and the elegant **Phillip Wain Health and Beauty Club.**
- *The Weld* (Corner of Jalan Raja Chulan and Jalan P. Ramlee). Features designer shoes, handbags, optical goods, jewellery,

cosmetics, art and handicrafts, and golf and sports equipment. There is also **Reject Shop, Guardian Pharmacy, Sports Station Mega, Phillip Wain Health and Beauty Club** and a supermarket.

- *Shopping Concourses* (Jalan Sultan Ismail). For a selection of designer shops, visit the shopping concourses in hotels such as the **Concorde, Hilton** and **Shangri-La.**

Ampang

Northeast of town centre on Jalan Ampang are the following malls:

- *Suria KLCC* (K.L. City Centre, Jalan Ampang). This is the most up-scale mall in Malaysia. It features **Isetan** Department Store and Supermarket, **Marks & Spencer** (a British clothing store), **Parkson Grand** Department Store, over 280 specialty shops, fast food and fancy restaurants, a post office, a Kedai Tenaga Nasional (for paying utility bills), banks, a cineplex and Parent's Rooms. Call ahead to arrange use of a baby stroller, wheelchair or "power shopper" electric cart (Tel: 03-382-2828).

- *City Square* (Jalan Ampang, adjacent to the Crown Princess Hotel). Features a **Metrojaya, Body Shop, Reject Shop** and **Toys 'R' Us,** as well as shops selling antiques, handicrafts, oriental carpets, furniture and home décor. In the small **Tuck Sang Herbal Food** shop you can feast on special curative soups made of precious ingredients including ginseng, shark's fin, bird's nest, deer's tail and antelope's antler.

- *Ampang Point* (Jalan Memanda, Ampang). A great place to shop for Asian and Middle Eastern handicrafts, including exquisite hand-made carpets from Iran, Afghanistan and Turkey. Visit the **Handicraft Centre** (Lot 02-13, 2nd Floor) and **Mashad Carpets** (Lot F17, 1st Floor).

Chinatown and City Hall Area

To the south of town centre on Jalan Petaling is Chinatown featuring a unique blend of sights, sounds, smells and merchandise.

- *Central Market* (Jalan Hang Kasturi). Offers nearly 100 shops selling handicrafts and jewellery, and holds periodic exhibitions of local artists.
- *Chinatown* (In the area between Jalan Bandar and Jalan Petaling). This is the place to go to find specialty items. Be sure to explore the shops selling Chinese medicine and those selling colourful cars, clothes and other objects made of paper that are used in funerals and other ceremonies. "Genuine copies" of designer watches and handbags can be found at the **Jalan Petaling Night Market**. Near Chinatown, on Jalan Tun Perak, is **Metrojaya Sinar Kota** Department Store.

Photo by Lynn Witham

Fortune Telling

216

Jalan Putra

Northwest of town centre, across from the Putra World Trade Centre, there is a large mall.

- *The Mall* (100 Jalan Putra just opposite the Pan Pacific Hotel). Has six levels of shopping, including **Yaohan** department store, an amusement area and a clean, air-conditioned food court on the top floor.

Jalan Tuanku Abdul Rahman/Jalan Masjid India

Another busy section in the centre of town extends along Jalan Melaka, Jalan Tun Perak and Jalan Tuanku Abdul Rahman (TAR).

- *Globe Silk Store* (Jalan Tuanku Abdul Rahman). The oldest store in the city, this K.L. landmark carries fabric and lower-priced clothes. The street in front of the store is the site of a Saturday evening market.
- *Hankyu Jaya Department Store and Supermarket* (Jalan Raja Laut). Carries housewares and a variety of shoes and clothes for adults, infants and children.
- *Jalan Masjid India,* as well as Leboh Ampang and surrounding streets, displays all sorts of Indian treasures from colourful saris to shiny gold bangles. **Semua House** carries more of the same.
- *Sogo Pernas Department Store* (Jalan Tuanku Abdul Rahman and Jalan Raja Laut). An up-scale department store with Kinokuniya Bookstore, a large supermarket, food court, restaurants and an amusement/video arcade.

Miscellaneous Locations

- *Chow Kit Market* (Jalan Haji Hussein). A colourful market selling baskets, batik fabric, sewing supplies and Malay wedding paraphernalia. Go in the morning for shopping and in the evening for eating. Take your camera, secure your wallet and inspect the quality of goods before you buy.

- *Pasar Minggu* or Sunday Market, is actually held every Saturday night in Kampung Bahru between Jalan Sungei Bharu and Jalan Raja Abdullah. It is a popular spot for shoppers seeking batik, baskets, antiques, shadow puppets and a variety of other items. Be sure to bargain.
- *K.L. Sentral*, the new city transportation hub in Brickfields, will have a large commercial complex. It will open in phases over the next several years.

SHOPPING IN THE SUBURBS

Nearly everything available in K.L. can also be found in Bangsar, Damansara, Petaling Jaya and Subang Jaya, and sometimes for a better price. The most popular shopping malls in these suburbs are listed below.

Bandar Sunway
- *Sunway Pyramid Shopping Mall* (Bandar Sunway). A large, modern shopping mall and entertainment centre with an ice skating rink. The anchor tenant is **Yaohan** Department Store and Supermarket.

Bangsar
- *Bangsar Shopping Centre* (285 Jalan Maarof, Bukit Bandaraya). Has many small up-scale specialty shops and services such as tailoring, beauty care and hair care. There is a large bowling alley, cineplex, nice restaurants, **Kidsport** centre and **Cold Storage** supermarket.
- *Hankyu Jaya Bangsar* (Bangsar Baru). A department store with a small selection of clothes and household goods and a supermarket, computer store and electronics store.
- *Mid Valley Megamall* (Between the Federal Highway and Jalan Bangsar). An up-scale, five-level mall with three anchor tenants

218

(**Carrefour**, **Metrojaya** and **Parkson Grand**), a huge **MPH Bookstore** and a cineplex that features many foreign films.

Petaling Jaya, Bandar Utama and Damansara

- *One Utama* (Jaya Jusco) 1 Leboh Bandar Utama in Bandar Utama. A huge modern complex with a cineplex and anchor tenant **Jaya Jusco** as well as **Reject Shop, Body Shop, Watson's, Nature's Farm, Toys 'R' Us, Mothercare, The Sleep Shop, Laura Ashley, Marks & Spencer, Ikea** (Scandinavian home furnishings) and small shops for clothing, sports equipment, jewellery and most everything else.
- *Atria Damansara* (Jalan SS 22/23, Damansara Jaya). Has a large **Parkson Grand Department Store and Supermarket**, as well as an electrical superstore and many small shops.
- *Jaya Shopping Centre* (Section 14, Jalan 14/17, Petaling Jaya). Has **Sports Station, Guardian**, **St. Michael's**, **Reject Shop, Cold Storage Supermarket** and small shops.
- *Metrojaya Petaling Jaya* (Menara Bakti, Section 14, Petaling Jaya). A department store offering clothing, accessories, cosmetics and housewares.

Putrajaya

- *The Mines Shopping Fair* (in the hub of the southern corridor near the new administrative township of Putrajaya, about 30 minutes from the KLIA). Features a large mall, cineplex, bowling alley, and a family entertainment and amusement centre. Shoppers can travel by water taxi through part of the township.

Subang Jaya

- *Carrefour* (next door to Subang Parade and across the street from the KTM Commuter Train Station). A discount supermarket and department store.

- *Giant Warehouse* (Lot 672 & 673, US J Subang Jaya). A large department store and supermarket featuring among many other items, clothes, stationery and gardening supplies.
- *Subang Parade* (5 Jalan SS16/1). A large mall housing a **Body Shop, Reject Shop, Esprit, Benetton, Toys 'R' Us, Parkson Grand** Department Store and **Tops** Supermarket, boutiques, a health food store, home furnishings stores, fast food restaurants, an amusement park and a cineplex.

GOODS AND SERVICES

Most of the specialised goods and services that you will need are available in K.L. The best sources of reliable service providers are your friends and the books *Selamat Datang: Kuala Lumpur from A to Z* (published by the American Association) and *Welcome to Kuala Lumpur* (published by the Association of British Women in Malaysia). Some notes on these services follow.

Barbers and Hairdressers

Barbers and hairdressers are abundant and most are reasonably priced. Shops in international-class hotels and up-scale malls are the most likely to have up-to-date equipment and to employ hairdressers skilled in creating current styles, but other shops may provide the same quality of service at lower cost. For best results when you visit a hairdresser, take along a picture and describe in detail the hair style you want. If you request colouring or a perm, take along directions from your hair stylist at home. If you prefer to use your own products for hair care, facials and manicures, beauticians will willingly comply.

Caterers

Caterers will provide you with several sample menus and price lists. Generally efficient and reliable, they will do everything for you, from set-up to clean-up, for a reasonable charge.

Clothes

Much of the clothing sold in Malaysia is too small for many expatriates. If you are searching for larger sizes, try stores such as **Marks & Spencer** (Bukit Bintang Plaza, Bandar Utama, Suria KLCC), **British India** (several branches), and the **Reject Shop** (several outlets which offer brand name stock overruns and "seconds" clothes for men, women and children). Also visit the boutiques in Suria KLCC, Mid Valley Megamall, One Utama and Bangsar Shopping Centre, and large department stores such as Tangs (Star Hill), Isetan, Sogo and Parkson Grand. Finally, check *The Finder* and *The Expat* for advertisements. Some expatriates shop their favourite stores at home on-line through the Internet.

Clothing Tailors and Shoemakers

Experienced tailors and dressmakers are prevalent and reasonably priced. They can make clothes, drapes and bedspreads; some will upholster furniture. A few stores (such as Tangs) will do alterations to clothes you buy and even offer fashion consultancy by appointment. Before you select a tailor, ask your friends for their recommendations and ask each tailor to show you a sample of his or her work. To improve the chances for your satisfaction, take along pictures or samples, give detailed written instructions about how you want everything done, start off with a simple item, and ask for an estimate of the cost. If you are not happy with the result, most tailors will rework the item.

When you purchase **fabric**, check the manufacturer's label on the bolt of fabric to make sure that the fabric really is what the merchant's sign says it is. Merchants in fabric and clothing shops often describe viscose or synthetic blends as "rayon," "cotton" or "silk". Buyer beware!

You can even have your **shoes** made in K.L. As the quality of results vary, begin with having the shoemaker copy one pair of your favourite shoes.

Computer Hardware and Software

Imbi Plaza in K.L. is a one-stop shopping centre for all your computer needs. Here you can find international brands of computers, printers, software and supplies, as well as computer wizards who can figure out a way to do most anything you have in mind. In Petaling Jaya, visit **CompAsia: The Computer Superstore** (67C Jalan SS22/23 Damansara Jaya) and the computer centre in the **Mid Valley Megamall**. Also contact **Sapura Service Centre** (Tel: 03-758-8802), a service centre for PC and Macintosh that also sells PC and Apple equipment. In Subang Jaya, visit the computer centre in **Subang Parade**. Three good sources of advertisements are *PC Magazine Malaysia, Computer Shopper Malaysia* and the *Computer* section in the *New Straits Times* newspaper.

Some models of computer equipment and peripherals sold in Asia are suitable for use only with 220-volt electricity. Clones are prevalent and cheaper than name brands, but check the Customs laws of your country before you buy if you intend to take the equipment back home. Be sure to bargain for any equipment you buy.

Computer Repair

K.L. has authorised service centres for all major computer brands. Some centres will send technicians to your home or office to diagnose problems and make repairs. The authorised sales and service centre for Apple Macintosh and Compaq computer is Sapura Service Centre (116 Jalan Semangat, Section 14, Petaling Jaya; Tel: 03-758-8802; Fax: 03-758-8990). They have a Home User Priority Programme. Other computer repair services are advertised periodically in *The Expat* and *The Finder* magazines and in the computer sections of the *New Straits Times* and *The Star* newspapers.

Cosmetics

All major department stores and a shop named **Sasa** (branches in Suria KLCC, Sungai Wang Plaza, Ampang Point and Bangsar Shopping Centre) carry a wide selection of Western and Japanese cosmetics and skin care products. (A tip: storing cosmetics in the refrigerator will keep them fresh longer.)

Dry Cleaners

Dry cleaning service is available through shops in large shopping malls and also in some department stores (such as **Isetan** at Suria KLCC, **Lot 10** on Jalan Bukit Bintang and **Tangs** at Star Hill Centre) that make arrangements with large hotels to provide the service to customers. Some shops offer express service and delivery in Klang Valley.

Electrical Products and Household Goods

Most electrical products and some computer and camera equipment carry a one-year warranty that is valid only in Asia. Be sure to request a warranty card and enquire about after-sales service. If you take equipment for repair, provide the repair person with the operating instructions booklet and technical diagrams for the equipment. When you purchase any electrical products (including cameras and televisions) or household goods, be sure to bargain.

Furniture

Many large stores sell furniture in Asian and Western styles in a variety of price ranges. For a unique selection of contemporary home furnishings and decorative items, visit **Peter Hoe Beyond** (139 Jalan Tun H.S. Lee) and **Rain Forest** (several branches).

Furniture Makers

An alternative to buying ready-made furniture is to have furniture hand crafted to suit your tastes and budget. Many expatriates choose this option and some are so pleased with the results that they ship the furniture back home.

Having furniture made is a task that demands your full attention. Before the work begins, write down every detail of how you want each item constructed and finished. Specify the size and shape of the piece, the type and quality of wood, type and colour of finish, shape of corners, type of hinges, etc. You probably will get the best results if you can show the furniture maker a picture or sample of what you want.

Before you complete the deal, ask for a written estimate of the cost and a written copy of the details of the design and construction. If the furniture will be made of wood, ascertain that the wood has been seasoned (otherwise it may warp or crack) and ask for a guarantee. To protect your investment, stop by the shop frequently to see how the construction is progressing and to answer questions that may arise.

If you plan to export any wood, wicker or bamboo items, check with the embassy of the country to which you will send the items to enquire if it is necessary to have them fumigated. Items shipped to Australia, New Zealand or the United States must be accompanied by a fumigation certificate.

Gold

Gold jewellery is sold by weight in most Asian countries. Daily prices for 22-karat and 24-karat gold are set by the Government and posted in most shops. The first price you are quoted for an item is always negotiable as it includes the price of the gold, a variable amount for the workmanship, plus a surcharge based on the assumption that the purchase will be made by credit card. To ascertain how much bargaining room you have, enquire about the weight of the gold and multiply that by the daily price. If you buy gold jewellery, obtain a certificate stating the weight and gold content of the item, as well as the per-gram and workmanship charges. If you buy jewellery containing gems, buy from a reputable dealer. Some shops will buy high quality, used gold from customers.

Photo by Lynn Witham

Searching for Gold

Handicrafts and Decorative Items

Asian handicrafts and decorative items are featured at the **Central Market** (Jalan Hang Kasturi), **Peter Hoe Evolution** (2 Jalan Hang Lekir, just across from the entrance to the Central Market), **Kompleks Budaya Kraf** and **Karyaneka** (Jalan Conlay, off Jalan Raja Chulan) and **Asli Craft Adventure** (La Gong Resort near Batu Caves).

Unique household items are featured at **Aseana** (Suria KLCC, 1st Floor) and **Claycraft** (Lot 304, Suria KLCC). **Claycraft** also has a large shop in Sri Hartamas (20 Jalan 25/70A, Desa Sri Hartamas) that carries clothes, furniture, food and pottery that is modern in style but inspired by the multi-cultural heritage of Malaysia. (It also has pottery making classes.)

225

To watch pewter being made and to purchase it at a savings, visit the **Royal Selangor Pewter Factory** in Setapak. To observe the process of batik making, visit the **Batik Malaysia Berhad** factory at No. 15, Jalan Cahaya 1, Taman Cahaya, Ampang.

For a special cultural experience, visit **Pucuk Rebung Malaysian Heritage and Style** (Suria KLCC, Level 3, Lot 305; Tel: 03-382-0769). The shop is small, but it has some breathtaking examples of museum-quality Malaysian arts, crafts and fashions. Some items are for sale and others form part of a permanent collection. The curator has been collecting Malaysiana for over twenty years and knows the history of each piece in the shop. His vision is to help define a clear pan-Malaysian culture that takes in the entire ethnic mix that makes up modern Malaysia, and to raise the public's awareness of the country's rich tradition of arts and crafts. In addition to selling and collecting artifacts, Pucuk Rebung offers other services such as sourcing for specific pieces, educational seminars on Malaysian artifacts, and interior design for private and corporate clients.

Photo by Puah Chin Kok, courtesy of Pucuk Rebung.

Silver fruit bowl, inspired by antique tepak sireh set, silver repoussé and cut-out hand work, contemporary, Malay, Kelantan.

Chapter Fifteen

ACCOMMODATING CHILDREN

K.L. FOR KIDS

K.L. is a great place to raise children. Malaysians are friendly, food choices are endless, activities are plentiful and the standards of education in most schools for expatriate children are quite high. This chapter gives an overview of the Malaysian educational system, a discussion of some issues related to education for expatriate children, and descriptions of schools open to expatriate children. It also offers some suggestions on recreation for and travelling with children.

Photo by Lynn Witham

Malaysian Schoolgirls

EDUCATION FOR EXPATRIATE CHILDREN

Nearly all expatriate children in K.L attend private, non-governmental schools that use a language other than Malay as the primary medium of instruction and that prepare students for further education in their own country. K.L. hosts several English-medium schools as well as schools with other mediums of instruction including French, German, Japanese, Chinese, Indonesian and Persian (Farsi). More than 7000 children attend international schools in the K.L. area.

Standards of education in most schools for expatriate children are quite high. Parents generally are satisfied with the education their children receive, and the majority of students find that transition into educational institutions back home is smooth. In recent years some expatriate high school graduates have begun to enrol in the **twinning programmes** established between Malaysian educational institutions and foreign colleges and universities. This allows them to stay in Malaysia for a couple extra years before transferring abroad to complete their degree programmes. Normally all credits for courses taken in Malaysia are transferrable.

No free public education is available for expatriate children in Malaysia and the costs of private education are high. In addition to tuition, most schools charge fees for application, assessment, enrolment, tuition deposit, commitment deposit, school development and building funds, insurance, activities, uniforms, meals and late payment. Many employers pay all or part of tuition fees, and costs of books and uniforms for dependants of their employees.

Registration

International schools in K.L. normally are filled to capacity. Before going to Malaysia, parents are strongly urged to call or write for information about schools that are of interest, and to enquire about advance registration. Even if application for admission is made in advance of arrival in Malaysia, your child may have to be put on a waiting list. Some expatriate children have missed a term or more of school because the schools of their choice were so crowded they were not able to enrol when they arrived. In most schools, space is especially limited for children who need special tutoring in English as a second language.

Some schools require that expatriate students possess a valid Student Pass when applying for admission. Most schools issue an

229

Offer of Place Letter when an application has been approved. Once your child receives notification of admission, confirm your acceptance in writing immediately and notify the school of the date your child will begin to attend. If your child cannot begin on the date you have indicated, again notify the school by phone and in writing, as most schools reserve the right to give away your child's reserved place if he or she does not attend as expected and if no communication is received. Records from schools your children have attended may have to be presented to school authorities upon enrolment.

School Calendar
Dates of the school year vary from school to school. **American** curriculum schools usually begin in the third week of August and end in the second week of June. The year is divided into two semesters with a six-week break at Christmas, a ten-week break in the summer and shorter breaks in spring and fall. Most **British** schools run from late August to late July. There are three terms with four-week holidays at Christmas and Easter and an eight-week holiday in the summer. The **German** school year runs from mid-August to mid-June. The **French** school year runs from mid-September to the end of June. The **Japanese** school year begins in April and consists of three four-month terms. Students transferring from **Southern Hemisphere** countries in which the school year begins in January may need to consult with school officials to set up a special programme.

Special Education Facilities
If you have a child with special educational needs, you are advised to discuss the situation with school officials before you go to Malaysia. Information can be obtained from school principals.

The **International School of Kuala Lumpur** (ISKL) has a special programme for children with mild to moderate learning disabilities. Assistance is offered only for students who do not require attendance in the learning skills centre for more than 25% of their academic day. ISKL is not equipped to offer assistance to students who need speech therapy or physical therapy, nor to students who have severe learning disabilities or emotional disturbances. Two schools that accommodate children with more serious disabilities are the **ELC School** and the **Future Minds Centre**. In addition, some schools, such as ISKL and Kolej Tuanku Ja'afar, have special courses for **advanced students.**

KINDERGARTENS AND NURSERY SCHOOLS

The majority of pre-schools included in the list below are affiliated with primary schools. Numerous other independent pre-schools operate in K.L. If you prefer a pre-school that is located close to your home, ask your friends and neighbours where they send their children. Instruction in all the schools listed below is in English unless otherwise noted.

- *Alice Smith School Kindergarten:* 2 Jalan Bellamy, 50460 K.L. (Tel: 60-3-248-3674, 244-9248, 241-7185; Fax: 60-3-248-3418). Accepts children 4 to 7 years old. The majority of children are from Britain, Ireland, Australia or New Zealand.

- *Country Heights Kindergarten:* 1 Jalan Senyum Matahari, Country Heights, Kajang (Tel: 60-3-8736-8277; Fax: 60-3-8736-8278). The curriculum is 80% Montessori and 20% designed to fit the local environment. The programme includes three languages (English, Malay and Mandarin), mathematics, physical education, moral studies, arts and crafts, music and movement, and creative activities. About 90 students aged 2+ through 6 attend the kindergarten; 60% are local and 40% are expatriates.

- ***Deutche Schule Kuala Lumpur Kindergarten:*** No. 11, Jalan 14/55, 46100 Petaling Jaya, Selangor (Tel: 60-3-755-8524). Accepts children aged 3 through 6. Has about 30 students. All instruction is in German.
- ***Ecole Française de Kuala Lumpur Kindergarten:*** 8-A Jalan Tun Ismail, 50480 K.L. (Tel: 60-3-291-3850, 294-8995; Fax: 60-3-293-6450). Accepts all French-speaking students from age 2. All instruction is in French and all teachers are trained in France.
- ***ELC International School:*** Lot 3664, Sierramas, Sg. Buloh, 4700 Selangor (Tel: 60-3-656-5001/2; Fax: 60-3-656-5003; E-mail: Kaloos@pc.jaring.my). (Mailing address: P.O. Box 64, Sg. Buloh, 47000 Selangor.) The curriculum includes reading, mathematics, practical life skills, nature study, art, music and physical exercise and supports total development of the child. The environment for children aged 3-4 is relaxed and informal; for children aged 5-6, it is more structured.
- ***Fairview International School Pre-School:*** 270 Jalan Ampang, 50450 K.L. (Tel: 60-3-457-7266). Accepts all English-speaking children from age 4. Teachers are Montessori trained and Montessori materials are used. The curriculum includes English, mathematics and Malay. Students are expatriates and Malaysians.
- ***Garden International School Kindergarten:*** 12 & 14 Persiaran (Tel: 60-3-456-9030); 6 Jalan Tinggi, Road 6/12, 46000 Petaling Jaya, Selangor (Tel: 60-3-7783-5200); and 16 Jalan 1/61A, Off Jalan Bukit Kiara, K.L. (Tel: 60-3-651-8988, 7783-5200). Has three locations in the K.L. area. Accepts children from age 3+. The programme is structured to make learning enjoyable and to instil in children a love for books. The curriculum includes social training, nature science, music, games, cookery, arts and crafts.

- *Good Shepherd Kindergarten:* Maryvale, 8 km., Jalan Ulu Kelang, Ampang P.O., 68000 Selangor (Tel: 60-3-456-5205; Fax: 60-3-453-2976). Has 250 students of many races aged 4 through 6. Classes are fully Montessori. Teaching is individualised, focusing on numbers, language, sensorial activities, art, crafts, singing, rhythm and movement. Transportation can be arranged from some locations.
- *International School of Kuala Lumpur Pre-School:* PT 3350 Jalan Melawati 3, Taman Melawati, 53100 K.L. (Tel: 60-3-408-3566; Fax: 60-3-408-4166). Accepts children from age 4. Based on the premise that young children learn through action and interaction, the programme aims to promote cognitive, social, emotional and physical development. Bus transportation is provided.
- *Kidsport Malaysia—Family Fun and Fitness:* 2nd Fl., Lot 131, New Wing, Bangsar Shopping Centre, 285 Jalan Maarof, 59000 K.L. (Tel: 60-3-253-7723). (Also a branch in Subang Jaya; Tel: 03-724-2390). An educational and fitness centre with a structured programme for children aged 3 through early teens. Activities include gym sessions, reading and writing, science and art lessons, cognitive and social skills, story-telling, computer, homework tutoring and games. Special programmes include: **Weesports**, **Kidsclub**, **Magical Movement**, **Games**, **Fun To Be Fit** and **CompTrek.** The centres also offer **FasTracKids**, an enrichment programme for potentially gifted children aged 3 to 7, a **Pay-for-Play** programme where parents can supervise their children during play, and a convenient **"Drop and Shop"** programme where parents can leave children off for supervised play for an hourly fee.
- *Mont Kiara International School Kindergarten:* 22 Jalan 1/70C Jalan Mont Kiara, Off Bukit Kiara, 50480 K.L. (Tel: 03-253-8604; Fax: 253-6245). Accepts children from age 3.

- *Mutiara International Pre-School:* Lot 707, Jalan Kerja Air Lama, Ampang Jaya, 6800 Ampang, Selangor (Tel: 60-3-452-1452, 457-8678; Fax: 60-3-452-3452; E-mail: MIGSTM.net.my). Accepts students aged 3+ for a relaxed, play group, exploration- and discovery-oriented programme that includes some basic instruction in reading and math.
- *Sunshine Playgroup:* American Association of Malaysia, 15-A Jalan Wickham, (near the Raintree Club), 55000 K.L. (Tel: 60-3-451-9625). A mother-and-child-oriented playgroup for children up to age 3. Goals are to give mothers the opportunity to meet other mothers and to work with their children in a group setting. Sessions consist of free play, snacks, singing and structured activities.
- *Tadika Sri Montessori:* (formerly London Montessori Centre), 80 Jalan Balau, Damansara Heights, 50490 K.L. (Tel: 60-3-253-2267). Accepts children aged 2+ to 5. Students of all ages study together in half-day (morning or afternoon) or full-day sessions, five days a week. Children usually move into the full-day programme at age 5. All teachers at the school are trained in the Montessori method. The curriculum covers practical life skills, sensorial skills, language skills, mathematics skills and cultural skills as well as singing, dancing and outdoor activities. Lessons in playing musical instruments are available.
- *Tinkerbell Kindergarten:* 328 Jalan Tun Razak, K.L. (Tel: 60-3-2164-3743). Accepts children ages 3 to 6. Older students are given instruction in arts, crafts, movement and mathematics.

PRIMARY AND SECONDARY SCHOOLS

Probably the best way to choose schools for your children is to call or write the schools before you go to Malaysia and then to visit them once you arrive. It is important to enquire about the curriculum, services and educational philosophy of each school, and to discuss these issues with your children. Some of the schools in K.L. are religiously oriented and have rather stringent behaviour and dress codes. To avoid problems, children should be made aware of the rules in advance of their attendance at such schools. Most schools offer modern facilities and a full programme of after-school special interest groups, co-curricular activities and sports.

- *Alice Smith Primary School:* 2 Jalan Bellamy, 50460 K.L. (Tel: 60-3-248-3674, 244-9248; Fax: 60-3-248-3418; E-mail: klass@po.jaring.my). Founded in 1946, this private, not-for-profit school has a reputation for providing children with a high standard of education combined with an emphasis on good conduct and respect for others. It accommodates children ages 4 to 9 and offers a curriculum that builds on the **National Curriculum for England and Wales**. The campus is located in a beautiful wooded area adjacent to the Royal Palace (Istana Negara).

- *Alice Smith Middle and High School:* Equine Park, 50460 K.L. (Tel: 60-3-583-3688; Fax: 60-3-583-3788; E-mail: klass@po.jaring.my). The school is located on a new campus in the Multimedia Super Corridor, just 12 minutes from Cyberjaya, and is easily accessible from other well-established suburbs. Approximately 900 students from the EU and other European countries, Southeast Asia, Australasia, America and Africa attend the Primary, Middle and High Schools.

  The school offers a curriculum that builds on the **General Certificate of Secondary Education (GCSE)** in Years 10 and 11 and **Advanced ('A') Level** in Years 12 and 13. Children are exposed to a wide range of learning experiences and teaching styles. Field trips are offered to places such as the Outward Bound Schools in Penang, Melaka and Sabah. The extra-curricular and expeditioning programme includes the Duke of Edinburgh Award Scheme.

- *Chinese Taipei School:* Good Year Court 6, Persiaran Kewajipan, 47610 Subang Jaya, Selangor (Tel: 60-3-731-0189;

Fax: 60-3-731-0190). The school offers classes for students from Primary 1 through Form 6, and follows the **Taiwan school curriculum**.

- *Deutsche Schule Kuala Lumpur:* 5 Lorong Utara B, Off Jalan Utara, 46200 Petaling Jaya, Selangor (Tel: 60-3-756-6557; Fax: 60-3-756-7557). Established in 1979, the **Grundschule** (Primary School) has about 70 students aged 7 to 11 and the **Gymnasium** (Secondary School) has about 50 students aged 11 to 16. Teachers are German-trained and all instruction is in German. For further German education, older students can attend the **German School of Singapore** (72 Bukit Tinggi Road, Singapore 289760) which offers classes through the Baccalaureate.

- *Ecole Française de Kuala Lumpur:* 8-A Jalan Tun Ismail, 50480 K.L. (Tel: 60-3-291-3850, 294-8995; Fax: 60-3-293-6450). The French School, which follows a **French curriculum**, is open to all French-speaking students aged 2 to 18. All instruction is in French and all teachers are trained in France.

- *ELC International School:* Lot 3664, Sierramas, Sungai Buloh, 4700 Selangor (Tel: 60-3-656-5001/2; Fax: 60-3-656-5003; E-mail: Kaloos@pc.jaring.my). (Mailing address: P.O. Box 64, Sg. Buloh, 47000 Selangor.) Established in 1987, ELC International School is a private school with the objective of encouraging and enabling a multi-racial group of children to seek high levels of achievement. ELC stands for Excellence, Loyalty and Commitment. ELC Primary and Secondary Divisions follow the **National Curriculum from the United Kingdom**. Enrolment is open to children of expatriate parents residing in Malaysia and to Malaysian children who have received permission from the Ministry of Education.

- *Fairview International School:* 29 Jalan U Thant, 55000 K.L. (Tel: 60-3-451-8863; Fax: 60-3-451-8401). Founded in 1978, this is a private primary and secondary school following the **British curriculum.** Students are accepted from age 6+ through age 16, number about 500 and represent 35 countries. The curriculum from Junior I to Form VI is designed to allow smooth transition from one level to another and to prepare students for the **London GCE 'O'** and **'A' Levels.** Students are expected to adhere to the school's strict code of behaviour and discipline.

- *Garden International School:* 16 Jalan 1/61A, Off Jalan Bukit Kiara (P.O. Box 13056, 50480 K.L.); (Tel: 60-3-651-8988; Fax: 60-3-651-2468; E-mail: admissions@gardenschool.edu.my; Homepage: www.gardenschool.edu.my). Founded in 1951, GIS is a private, co-educational, international school offering instruction on both **primary and secondary** levels. The school's **mission** is to provide a thorough, balanced and integrated education in a broad range of areas and to prepare students for higher education. In addition to the main campus, which moved to a six-acre site in Bukit Kiara in 1996, the school operates two other branches in K.L.

  The Primary School follows the guidelines of the **British National Curriculum**, enhanced and adapted to meet local requirements. The Secondary School offers a broad-based course of study, culminating in the University of Cambridge **International General Certificate of Secondary Education (IGCSE)** examinations. To account for differing abilities, students can take Core or Extended levels of the curriculum, or a mixture of the two. **English as a Second Language** assistance and **Special Needs Assistance** are available for children up to age 14. Private bus service is available from most areas of K.L. and Petaling Jaya. Early application is recommended as demand for places is heavy.

- *Indonesian School:* 1 Lorong Tun Ismail, 50480 K.L. (Tel: 60-3-292-7505/7682). The school offers the **Indonesian curriculum** on both elementary and secondary levels. All instruction is in the Indonesian language.

- *International School of Kuala Lumpur Elementary School:* PT 3350, Jalan Melawati 3. Taman Melawati, 53100 K.L. (Tel: 60-3-408-3566; Fax: 60-3-408-4166; E-mail: iskl@iskl.edu.my; Homepage: www.iskl.edu.my; Mailing address: P.O. Box 12645, 50784 K.L.) The Elementary Programme follows the American curriculum. Bus transportation is available. (Please also see the following description of ISKL.)
- *The International School of Kuala Lumpur Middle/High School:* Jalan Kerja Ayer Lama, 68000 Ampang, Selangor (Tel: 60-3-456-0522/0735; Fax: 60-3-457-9044; E-mail: iskl@iskl.edu.my; Homepage: www.iskl.edu.my; Mailing address: P.O. Box 12645, 50784 K.L.) Founded in 1965, ISKL is a private, co-educational day school for students in **Kindergarten through Grade Twelve** (with an optional Grade 13). ISKL is the largest international school in Malaysia, with over 1,700 students representing more than 50 nationalities. The largest groups are Americans (about 25%), Koreans, Australians, Japanese and Malaysians. Faculty members represent about 10 countries.

     ISKL is accredited by the Western Association of Secondary Schools and Colleges in the United States and is a member of the National Honor Society. It follows an **American-oriented college preparatory curriculum** and almost all graduates go on to tertiary education. Entering students who are not fluent in English must take the **English as a Second Language** classes offered by the school on a space-available basis. Apply early as vacancies are limited.

     ISKL accepts students with mild or moderate **reading difficulties** or **learning disabilities** whose needs can be met with minor changes to the regular curriculum. For students with **above average intelligence**, the school offers an **International Baccalaureate (IB) Diploma Programme**, a two-year, academically challenging pre-university course designed to facilitate the mobility of students and to promote international understanding. Students who are not part of the IB Programme can take individual IB courses.

Students can take field trips in Malaysia and the region and can go on homestays with Malaysian families during vacations. The school operates buses to the suburbs of Subang, Damansara and Petaling Jaya.

- ***Japanese School of Kuala Lumpur:*** Saujana Resort, Lingkungan Golf, Section U12, Off Jalan Lapangan Terbung, Shah Alam, Selangor (Tel: 60-3-746-5939; Fax: 60-3-746-5949; E-mail: jskl@jskl.edu.my; Homepage: www.jskl.edu.my; Mailing address: P.O. Box 6579, Kampung Tunku, 47307 Petaling Jaya, Selangor). Established in 1966, it caters only to Japanese expatriate children temporarily staying in Malaysia. With a population of 1200, the school provides education for children through Grade 9 based on the curricula and practices set by the Japanese Ministry of Education. The medium of instruction is Japanese and 90% of the teachers are Japanese nationals.

- ***Kolej Tuanku Ja'afar:*** 71700 Mantin, Negeri Sembilan (Tel: 60-6-758-2561/2953; Fax: 60-6-758-1139; Website: www.jaring.my/ktj). Founded by the royal family of Negeri Sembilan in 1991, Kolej Tuanku Ja'afar is an elite, co-educational, **secondary boarding school** located on a rural campus less than one hour south of K.L.

Some 480 Malaysian and expatriate students (primarily from Korea, Australia, the U.K., Japan, the USA, China, Singapore and Indonesia) attend the school. The highly qualified **teaching staff** is approximately 75% Malaysian and 25% British.

The school follows a balanced, broadly based approach to education and subscribes to the philosophy that everyone is good at something, and from this base attempts to foster self-confidence and self-discipline in its students. Small classes and individual **tutoring** enable students to reach high levels of academic performance and to gain places in prestigious universities throughout the world.

239

The school runs two parallel curriculum streams up to Form 5: the **Malaysian Stream** leading to the PRM examination at the end of Form 3, the SPM examination at the end of Form 5, and the **International Stream** leading to the Cambridge 'O' Levels in Form 5 and the 'A' Levels after Form 6.

Photo courtesy of Kolej Tuanku Ja'afar

Kolej Tuanku Ja'afar

The International Stream begins with Form 1 in August; new students are also accepted in January. On weekends students participate in Saturday morning classes and in a wide range of activities.

- *MAZ International School:* 1 Maz House, Jalan 20/19 5, Paramount Gardens, 46300 Petaling Jaya (Tel: 60-3-7874-2930; Fax: 60-3-7725-0286). MAZ is a private, international school based on the **British curriculum** and serving students from Primary One to Sixth Form ('A' Levels).

- *Mont Kiara International School:* 22 Jalan 1/70C Jalan Mont Kiara, Off Bukit Kiara, 50480 K.L. (Tel: 03-253-8604; Fax: 253-6245). The school accepts students ages 3 to 18 and follows on a **North American curriculum.**
- *Mutiara International School:* Lot 707, Jalan Kerja Air Lama, Ampang Jaya, 6800 Ampang, Selangor (Tel: 60-3-452-1452, 457-8678; Fax: 60-3-452-3452; E-mail: MIGSTM.net.my). This private, international school based on the **British curriculum** attempts to foster the academic, moral and social development of its students. Enrolment is open to children of expatriate parents residing in Malaysia and to Malaysian children who have received permission from the Ministry of Education. The medium of instruction is English; Malay is a language of importance. Form V and VI students sit for the **General Certificate of Education (GCE) 'O' and 'A' Level** examinations or the University of Cambridge **International General Certificate of Secondary Education (IGCSE) 'O' and 'A' Level** examinations.
- *Sayfol International School:* 261 Jalan Ampang, 50450 K.L. (Tel: 60-3-458-8781/91; Fax: 60-3-457-9464). Opened in 1986, the school follows a **British-based curriculum** and has over 1,000 students from nursery through secondary levels. About 40% of students and teachers are expatriates, representing over 60 nationalities. Final-year (Year 11) students sit for the **General Certificate of Education (GCE) 'O' Level** exam. Form Four (Year 12) students take the **GCE 'A' Level** exam. Both exams are given by the University of London Examination Board. The school maintains high academic standards and encourages students to develop their full potential intellectually, socially, emotionally and physically.
- *Utama International School:* Lot 27, Jalan Usahawan 5, Kawasan Perindustrian Ringan, 53200 Setapak, K.L. (Tel: 60-3-421-2490; Fax: 60-3-421-2527). This private, international school for children ages 5 to 15 is based on the **British curriculum.**

241

Photo by Lynn Witham

Sunway Lagoon—For Kids of All Ages

RECREATION FOR CHILDREN

There are plenty of activities to keep children busy in K.L. In addition to school activities, children can take lessons in sports, music and arts, for example, and become involved in sports teams and youth organisations such as **Welbos, Brownies, Cub Scouts, Boy Scouts, Girl Scouts, Girl Guides**, the **YMCA** or the **YWCA**. During vacations, children can participate in the Malaysian homestays and **domestic and international trips** arranged by many schools. For additional ideas about recreation for children, please see the chapter on *Relaxing and Renewing* and check the magazines *The Finder* and *The Expat*.

Photo by Lynn Witham

Fun in the Sun

Places for Fun

For family fun on weekends, some suggestions are mentioned below:

- **Butterfly Park** (Jalan Cenderasari; Tel: 03-293-4799).
- **Genting Highlands** (located 45 minutes from K.L.) has rides (similar to Sunway Lagoon) and a heated pool. The skyride from the bus terminal to the top is a real treat.
- **Forest Research Institute of Malaysia** (FRIM) (in Kepong) has a tropical rainforest with a wonderful hanging bridge that allows you to walk over the tree tops.

243

- **Kidsport Family Fun and Fitness** (at Bangsar Shopping Centre; Tel: 03-253-7723) has activities for infants, elementary schoolers and young teens.
- **Malaysia Agricultural Park** (Shah Alam) is fun for older children. It has several gardens, a fishing lake and hiking trails. Visitors can rent bicycles and camp or rent chalets for overnight stays.
- **Mines Beach Resort and Wonderland** (Jalan Sungei Besi; Tel: 03-8943-6688) 25 minutes from K.L., is a family beach resort for day or overnight guests. The hotel and spa overlooks a 150-acre lake and features water sports such as waterskiing, jetskiing, speedboating and canoeing. There is also a golf club and a theme park featuring boat and train rides, laser shows, a roller coaster and an astroliner.
- **National Zoo and Aquarium** (located in a large tract of jungle in Ulu Kelang, just ten minutes from the centre of K.L.) has exhibits for kids of all ages. Among the 4500 inhabitants of the zoo are over 1,000 species of Malaysian flora and fauna, and nearly 400 species of exotic birds, animals and reptiles from far corners of the world. Tenants of the aquarium include more than 80 species of marine life. For young visitors the highlight of a trip to the zoo is a ride on a boat, train, camel or elephant.
- **Petrosains** (Level 4, Suria KLCC, Petronas Twin Towers; Tel: 03-581-8181) is an interactive petroleum science discovery centre. Advance booking is recommended.
- **Shah Alam Lake Gardens** (Taman Tasik Shah Alam; Tel: 03-550-2588) is a pleasant place for picnics and boat rides. Features the Wet-World Water Theme Park, with a 222-metre-long watercoaster and other activities for children.
- **Starlight Express** (The Mall shopping complex in K.L.) is an amusement centre that offers many rides and attractions for children.

- **Sunway Lagoon Theme Park** (Jalan PJS 11/11, Bandar Sunway, 46150 P.J.; Tel: 03-735-8000/735-6000) is a favourite of kids. It has a Waterpark featuring an 80-foot high landscaped waterfall, a wave pool, toboggan slide, giant waterslides, numerous thrilling rides and a kid's activity pool. It also has Fort Lagoon Wild Wild West and an Adventure Park, both filled with exciting rides. Nearby Sunway Pyramid has an ice skating rink. The five-star hotel and good restaurants make this a fun weekend retreat for the whole family.
- **Taman Alam** (Kuala Selangor, about an hour from K.L.) is a nature park and bird sanctuary. The 800-acre park has over 150 species of birds and many species of wild animals. Kids also enjoy a visit to nearby Kampung Kuantan where they can see fireflies at dusk.
- **Taman Desa Waterpark** (Taman Desa, off Old Klang Road) is a fun waterpark.
- **Taman Suria KLCC** (Petronas Twin Towers) has a wonderful picnic area and a shallow wading pool for kids.
- **Taman Titiwangsa** (Jalan Kuantan) is a lake and park with boating, jogging and tennis. Other areas are Taman Jaya Pond (on the corner of Jalan Timor and Federal Highway in Petaling Jaya) and Taman Tasek Park (on Jalan Ulu Klang near the corner of Jalan Ampang).
- **Templer's Park** (Rawang, Selangor, 22 kilometres from the city) is an ideal place for a refreshing swim, picnic and nature walk. Located on 4,000 acres of forested hills, the park has a network of well-groomed paths and an abundance of pools, waterfalls and jungle streams. A Bird Park, located on about 200 acres of land, features a walk-in aviary with numerous species of Malaysian and foreign birds (Tel: 03-291-6011). Nearby is the Orchid Garden, with over 800 orchid species from Malaysia alone (Tel: 03-291-6011).

Chapter Sixteen

JOINING THE
WORKFORCE

THE ECONOMIC SCENE

The Federal Territory of Kuala Lumpur serves as the country's bustling hub of business, government and tourism. Its modernising infrastructure and impressive skyline are the proud results of the country's stunning economic growth. That growth should not be taken for granted.

At the time of Independence in 1957, the economy was agriculture-based and dependent on exports of tin and rubber for foreign exchange. Today the agriculture, forestry and fishery sector accounts for less than 10% of the Gross Domestic Product (GDP) and less than 8% of total export earnings. In the 1980s this sector was surpassed by the manufacturing sector which today accounts for nearly 30% of the GDP and about 85% of export earnings.

This transformation was made possible because the Malaysian government, in a concerted effort to build the economy, has implemented successive plans for industrialisation, launched new industries, set up Free Trade Zones, created incentives to encourage foreign investment in the developing economy, initiated an ambitious programme of privatisation, and contributed a large portion of its budget to education. This effort has paid off handsomely. The country's growth has surpassed that of most developing nations. Real GDP growth achieved remarkable 5%-8% annual levels in the 30 years to 1997, suffered a brief drop during the regional economic crisis, and returned to pre-crisis levels in 1999.

FOREIGN INVESTMENT

The area to benefit most from the country's economic growth has been the Federal Territory of Kuala Lumpur. It has been successful in luring foreign investment and is the site of offices, distribution centres, manufacturing facilities and regional headquarters of more than 1,500 foreign companies. That number is increasing as multinationals, deterred by the increasing costs of doing business in Singapore, shift their facilities to K.L. Principal foreign investors are the USA, Japan, Singapore, Pakistan, Switzerland, the Netherlands, Germany, the U.K. and Taiwan.

The Territory and the surrounding State of Selangor continue to actively promote foreign investment, especially in high value-added, capital- and technology-intensive and knowledge-based industries that will support the development of the Multimedia Super Corridor. The numerous incentives offered to foreign investors continue to make investments attractive. Two important incentives are a negotiable level of foreign equity, assuring that projects are mutually beneficial to foreign and Malaysian investors, and permission for foreign personnel to be employed in key managerial and specialised technical posts when there are no Malaysians available or qualified to fill the posts.

247

SOURCES OF INFORMATION

Foreigners wishing to make general inquiries about the possibility of establishing manufacturing operations and other types of business ventures in the Federal Territory should contact the Malaysian Industrial Development Authority (MIDA). MIDA is a Government agency that promotes and co-ordinates industrial development activities and advises the Government in formulating and implementing industrial development policies. MIDA headquarters is located at 6th Fl., Wisma Damansara, Jalan Semantan, Damansara Heights, 50490 K.L. (Tel: 60-3-255-3633; Fax: 60-3-255-7970/0697; Website: **www.mida.gov.my**; E-mail: promotion@mida.gov.my); the agency has many offices abroad. IT investors interested in the activities of the MSC can contact Multimedia Development Corporation (Tel: 60-3-818-8477; E-mail: info@mdc.com.my). For details on the regulations regarding employment of foreigners, visit the Website: www.mida.gov.my/policy/chapter5.html#5_.

Business Organisations

International and local business organisations in Malaysia are a valuable source of contacts and information for foreign business people. Local organisations may not function in the way some foreigners expect, however, as many businesses in Malaysia are family owned, and the owners tend to be quite private about the details of their business affairs. Foreigners hoping to do business with a private company, for example, may have difficulty obtaining specific information about the company until company officials are certain that the foreigners are sincerely interested in collaborating in a business venture. For a list of business associations in Malaysia, visit the **Malaysia Homepage** at: www.mymalaysia.net.my/.

EMPLOYMENT FOR SPOUSES

Spouses of foreigners working in Malaysia often wish to continue working in their chosen career field. However, they face a dilemma, as Employment Passes (work permits) are difficult to obtain. With a little imagination, however, it may be possible to find activities that will enhance one's professional qualifications. Individuals searching for such activities can canvass the community for possible opportunities and consider volunteering their time to keep active in their fields. In rare instances, volunteer work in organisations leads to paying positions.

In schools for expatriate children, employment opportunities may exist for qualified foreign teachers. Information can be obtained by contacting the principals of the schools mentioned in the chapter on *Accommodating Children*. In addition, anyone who has a special skill may be able to teach a course through the YMCA, YWCA or a cultural organisation. Some expatriate spouses have found jobs doing acting, modelling, freelance writing, market research and information technology work. For information about the procedure for obtaining an Employment Pass, please see the chapter on *Complying with Regulations*.

VOLUNTEER OPPORTUNITIES

The tradition of volunteer work is becoming more established in Malaysia and many opportunities for volunteer work for foreigners do exist. To explore the opportunities, contact country organisations (please see the list in the chapter on *Relaxing and Renewing*) and speak with the Community Liaison Officer of various embassies (many embassies maintain lists of organisations that accept volunteers). Alternatively, if you have a particular skill or interest, you could identify related organisations and contact them directly.

Volunteers are often welcomed at hospitals as well as at schools for the blind, deaf, spastic and mentally retarded, and at community service and social welfare organisations such as the Malaysian Red Crescent, the Women's Aid Society and the Centre for Battered Women. Sometimes the National Zoo seeks volunteers, as does the SPCA (Society for the Prevention of Cruelty to Animals).

International schools often need teachers' assistants or tutors, and special interest groups for expatriate children, such as Girl Scouts and Boy Scouts, often need leaders. School authorities can provide more information. The Malaysian-American Commission on Educational Exchange (MACEE), a resource and counselling centre for Malaysian students planning further study in American colleges and universities, can sometimes use volunteer assistants. Finally, many country organisations and women's groups welcome volunteers to help with the crafts bazaars they hold for the purpose of raising money for charity.

BUSINESS ETIQUETTE

Malaysians are accustomed to interacting with people of different cultures and to a great extent are adept at adapting their style of communicating and doing business to accommodate foreign business people. Malaysians will appreciate foreigners who take the time to learn something about Malaysian communication styles and business etiquette, however, and foreigners who do learn will have a competitive edge over those who do not.

Personal Introductions and Networking

When you want to meet particular Malaysian business people or government officials, try to obtain a letter, verbal recommendation or personal introduction from a mutual business associate or another Government official. This is especially useful if you would like to meet with a high-level Federal Government official. Also try to meet and maintain periodic contact with all the people who can influence the progress of your work.

Business Cards

Malaysians generally exchange business cards with new acquaintances. They carry the cards in a small case and offer their cards by holding them in both hands, right-side-up, with the print facing the recipient. They don't write on the front of cards or stuff them into a back pocket, and they often place them on a nearby desk or table for easy reference during conversation. Cards of foreign business people should be in English (or English and Malay) and should include the full name and a clear job title or titles. Spouses of foreign business people may also find it convenient to have name cards.

Names

Malaysian names and titles can be confusing. Ask when in doubt. It is best to address a person by his or her given name only if you are invited to do so or if he or she addresses you by your given name. Malaysians may address you with a polite title (Mr., Mrs., or Miss) plus your first name. To show respect, you can do the same with them verbally and in writing. In formal business interactions and writing, use the appropriate title plus the family name. For more information, please refer to the sections on Names in the chapter on *Meeting the People*.

Modes of Address

When addressing Malays verbally or in writing, the following polite titles are used:
- *Encik* (**Mr.**) Formal and respectful. Similar to the French "Monsieur," *Encik* may be used with or without a surname.
- *Tuan* (**Mr.**) Formerly used with or without a surname for high-ranking male civilians, army officers and Europeans.

251

- *Haji* is used to address a man who has performed the *Haj* (the Muslim pilgrimage to Mecca). It is used alone, with a surname or with the title Tuan to show special respect. (Tuan Haji + surname)
- *Abang* (**older brother**) Used with or without a surname to address close male friends and relatives (including one's husband).
- *Puan* (**Mrs.**) Formal and respectful and may be used with or without a surname. Used for married women and mature unmarried women.
- *Cik* (**Miss** or **Ms.**) May be used with or without a surname. It is sometimes used by a married business woman with her maiden name.
- *Tuan-tuan ∂an Puan-puan* (**Ladies and Gentlemen**)

Religious and Official Titles

As you will discover after reading the newspaper a few times, Malaysia has a complex system of titles. A brief explanation of the most common titles appears below. If you need more information, you will find it in *Malaysian Protocol and Correct Forms of Address* in the list of *Suggested Readings*. Malaysians take titles seriously. Do not joke about titles, and do practise using and pronouncing them correctly, especially when you will be meeting people, introducing people, giving speeches or receiving awards.

A Muslim man who has made the pilgrimage to Mecca is given the honorary title *Haji*. A Muslim woman who has made the pilgrimage to Mecca is given the honorary title *Hajjah*.

Malay Sultans are addressed as *Tuanku* and their male and female children and grandchildren as *Tunku* (in some states spelled *Tengku*). Tunku/Tengku are sometimes translated as "Prince" or "Princess".

Titles of honour are bestowed on Malaysians of all races (and occasionally on foreigners) in recognition of meritorious service. The highest title is *Tun*, which is limited to 50 living men and women (excluding foreigners). Governors of the four states without Sultans are given this title at the first vacancy. The wife of a *Tun* is addressed as *Toh Puan*. The husband of a *Tun* receives no title.

Tan Sri, a title of chivalry, is granted by the *Yang di-Pertuan Agong* (the King of Malaysia) to a maximum of 195 living persons (excluding foreigners). The wife of a Tan Sri is addressed as *Puan Sri*. The husband of a *Tan Sri* receives no title. An ancient Malay title of honour granted by rulers of the various states is *Dato* (in the states with Sultans) or *Datuk* (in the Federal Territory and states without royal rulers). The wife of a *Datuk* is addressed as *Datin*. The husband of a *Datuk* does not automatically receive a title.

Appointments and Greetings

Malaysians generally arrive on time for formal business appointments and they expect foreigners to arrive on time as well. Plan your schedule with downpours and traffic jams in mind.

The normal business greeting between Malaysian and foreign businessmen and Malaysian and foreign businesswomen is a handshake; between Malaysians and foreign business people of opposite genders it is a handshake or simply a cordial nod. Wait for Malaysian men or women to extend their hands and then shake if they do. During greetings and conversations you can show respect for people of higher rank or of the opposite gender by using rather indirect eye contact.

Business meetings often begin with small talk. After a while the host usually offers visitors a beverage. During the meeting, the host may take calls or answer the questions of people who stop by the office. At the end of the meeting the host may accompany visitors to the door or the elevator.

Business Attire

To make the best impression, foreign business people should dress in a manner that is neat, professional and conservative.

Business Attire for Men

For men, the most common work attire is a conservative long-sleeved shirt, a conservative tie, dark slacks, dark socks, dark shoes and fashionable, "branded" accessories such as a briefcase, belt, watch, pen and daily planner. This attire is appropriate for factory visits and informal office visits.

For formal meetings, meals and receptions, a dark-coloured (blue, brown or grey), conservative suit and tie with a white shirt is appropriate. Blazers or sports coats are not commonly worn for business. For very formal occasions, a tuxedo or white dinner jacket may be worn, but a suit and tie are equally acceptable. Batik shirts, especially those made of hand-painted silk, are considered quite formal dress. They are worn without a tie and are appropriate for certain Government functions. Men who attend palace functions or call on high-ranking Government officials commonly wear a morning coat.

Invitations to events often specify that dress should be "casual" (sports shirt and trousers), "lounge suit" (dark business suit), or "batik" (a long-sleeved batik shirt).

Business Attire for Women

For women, appropriate work attire includes lightweight suits and dresses with jackets in natural-fibre fabrics and blends. For women in high-level positions, accessories include a fashionable, "branded" briefcase or tote, belt, watch, pen and daily planner, as well as authentic (not costume) jewellery.

For formal evening wear, a long dress is appropriate. The more conservative Malaysians respect modesty in dress, so unless you want to attract attention, dresses you wear to formal occasions at which Malaysians will be present should not be sleeveless and should not have plunging necklines. If there is a chance that royalty might be present, the royal colour, "Windsor yellow," should not be worn. Women who attend palace functions or call on high-ranking Government officials often wear hats, gloves and stockings. Colours that are not popular among Malaysian women for parties, weddings or royal audiences include solid black, solid white and solid navy-blue, as these colours are commonly worn to funerals. Black is worn to formal evening functions, however.

Business Gifts

It is not appropriate to present expensive gifts to Malaysian Government officials and business executives as the gifts might be interpreted as bribes. Good quality company logo gifts such as appointment books, pocket calculators, paper weights and calendars are appropriate gifts to present at the conclusion of business negotiations. Do not give Chinese associates clocks or items in groups of four, and do not give Malay associates anything made with alcohol (such as perfume) or pig products (such as pigskin). Gifts should be tastefully wrapped. Malaysians generally do not open gifts in front of the giver.

BUSINESS COMMUNICATION

Below are some important points to note when you are communicating with Malaysians, especially in business situations.

Malaysian Terms

It is important to use correct terminology to refer to things Malaysian. The national language is "Malay" in English, *Bahasa Malaysia* (Malaysian Language) or Bahasa Melayu (Malay Language). The Government is the **Malaysian Government**, and the money is **Ringgit Malaysia** (RM) or **Ringgit**.

255

Foreigners sometimes confuse the words "Malaysian" and "Malay". **"Malaysian"** refers to people of all races who are citizens of Malaysia; **"MaLAY"** (emphasis on the second syllable) refers to people of the Malay race and does not include Chinese, Indian, Eurasian and other citizens of Malaysia. *"Bumiputra"* refers to Malays and other indigenous groups, and means, literally, "sons of the soil".

Locally, the racial groups are simply known as the Malays, the Chinese, the Indians and the Eurasians. Malaysians use the term "race" to refer to ethnic background and it is not offensive to ask people what race they are. Chinese and Indian citizens are also referred to as Malaysian Chinese and Malaysian Indians. They are surprised when foreigners, not knowing the history of Malaysia's pluralistic society, assume that they are citizens of China or India.

Topics of Conversation

Safe topics of conversation include food, sports, travel and Malaysian cultural events or traditions. Topics to avoid unless you know your counterpart well include politics, religion, sex and racial relations. Also avoid joking about or making derisive comments about the Prime Minister and the King, government officials, the practices of Islam, the position of the *Bumiputra,* Malaysian infrastructure or business practices, or your Malaysian colleagues. Refrain from using off-colour language (even though Malaysians may) and from telling jokes with racial, sexual, religious or political overtones.

Be discreet when discussing business matters and avoid asking business or personal questions unless Malaysians ask first. Expect to be asked questions that you might regard as rather personal (about salary, rent, cost of possessions, etc.) and find a way to answer that is comfortable to both you and the questioner.

Malaysian English

"Manglish," as the English spoken in Malaysia is sometimes called, is based on British English but contains variations in vocabulary and pronunciation with which you may not be familiar. Don't hesitate to ask Malaysians for clarification. A few examples are listed below. For more examples, refer to the book *Manglish: Malaysian English at its Wackiest!*, by Lee Su Kim.

- bring: often used instead of "take," as in "I'll bring you to the Post Office".
- bungalow: refers to a large, two-storey house.
- can/cannot: In the Malay and Chinese languages it is common to answer a question that contains certain verbs by repeating the verb in the answer; this often carries over into English. Consequently, the answer to the question, "Can you help me?" is often "Can" or "Cannot, *lah*". Similarly, "Have you got any papayas?" could be answered "Got" or "Not got".
- clarify: sometimes means "to retract one's statement" rather than "to make clear".
- follow: as in "Siti followed us to the cinema" means "Siti came with us to the cinema". (Translation from Malay "*ikut*.")
- go back: means "go home," as in "Are you going back now?"
- *lah:* an emphatic particle added after a word or phrase to show a range of emotions including anger ("How dare you, lah!"), resignation ("I get by, lah."), polite disagreement ("No, lah."), or polite suggestion ("You should do it, lah.").
- last time: means "before" or "in the past" (not "the last time"), as in "Last time, when I lived in K.L., I ate here every day".
- over: means "more than," as in "It costs twenty over dollars".
- send: sometimes means "to take," as in "Can you send me home after work? My car is in the garage".
- sleep late: means "to go to bed late," as in "I slept late last night".

- stay back: means "did not leave the place or area right away," as in "After the conference my friend and I stayed back and chatted about work".

Misunderstandings

When you communicate with Malaysians, keep in mind that few of them speak English as a first language. You can reduce the chances of misunderstandings by making slight adjustments in your speech and manner. Avoid using idioms, slang and business jargon. Speak slowly and clearly. Repeat and/or write down numbers. Repeat and clarify important information, especially during telephone conversations. When **misunderstandings** do occur, clarify them tactfully and gracefully so that people will not feel inadequate or offended.

Misunderstandings often occur due to confusion of first, middle and last (family) names, especially when foreigners register as hotel guests. (Hotel clerks sometimes take the middle name from the passport and assume that it is the family name.) As a safeguard, suggest that people who call you ask for you under your first, middle and family names if the operator informs them that you are not registered, and notify the appropriate hotel personnel if you are expecting an important visitor call, fax or visit.

Giving and Receiving Information

When you make business presentations, do not assume that you have been understood or that listeners agree with what you have said if they do not ask you questions or raise objections. Reinforce your points with concrete examples and allow time for people to approach you individually during breaks.

Similarly, when you ask a question, you may not always receive a direct response. To get the information you desire, you may need to strengthen your relationship with the person you are asking, revisit the issue at another time and in another context, or seek the information from a different source.

Finally, Malaysians may respond with hesitation when asked to do something that they have never done. Take the time to explain and give examples or show models.

Men and Women in the Workplace

Malaysian women are an important force behind the country's development and are involved in a wide variety of professions including education, management, banking, medicine, small business and information technology. Women are also active in politics and hold influential positions in state and federal government, as well as in the diplomatic service corps. Be careful not to underestimate a Malaysian woman's status, education, or competence. Condescension is quickly noticed and resented.

Malaysian women must keep their personal reputations above question if they are to remain respected in business and in the community. Foreign males should avoid suggesting familiarity by teasing or making casual comments to women in public settings.

If you have a Malaysian female secretary, you can put her at ease and enhance her productivity by giving clear direction and by showing respect. Be aware that actions such as tossing documents on her desk, criticising her in public, leaning over her desk or shoulder to check a document, or meeting with her in her work area (rather than having her come to your office) might feel intimidating to her. If you are male and meet with your secretary alone in a room, leaving the door slightly ajar can avert any suspicions of impropriety.

Working with Malaysians

In addition to observing Malaysian business etiquette, some important keys to working successfully with Malaysians are: to take a personal approach; to show that you are competent and trustworthy; to show trust and respect for Malaysian colleagues; to be patient but persistent; to adjust your communication style to the people with whom you are doing business; and to remember that culture can make a difference. The last point is the most important. It is not uncommon for expatriates to spend several months working in Malaysia, thinking that their relationships with their Malaysian colleagues are progressing smoothly, and then find that serious problems have been brewing under the surface. The keys to avoiding such a situation are to gain insight into the culture from the onset, to learn how to read the subtle signals that Malaysians send, and to learn how to send the signals that you intend to send. Business people can benefit from predeparture or post-arrival business-focused intercultural training and follow-up consulting, and from reading books on Malaysian management such as *Understanding the Malaysian Workforce: Guidelines for Managers* and *Going Glocal: Cultural Dimensions in Malaysian Management*.

CHAPTER SEVENTEEN

RELAXING AND RENEWING

RELAXING AND RENEWING

Leisure activities are plentiful in Malaysia. You will have no trouble filling your spare time, especially if you are adventurous and willing to try new activities as well as to continue familiar ones. You can follow the arts scene, engage in sports, take lessons, join professional, social and special interest organisations, and do volunteer work. Information on all of these activities is included in this chapter. Other sources of information are the local newspapers, the magazines *Day & Night*, *Vision Kuala Lumpur* and *Kuala Lumpur Now!* Also check the Yellow Pages of the Telephone Directory, consult the Cultural Liaison Officers of foreign embassies or contact a representative of Tourism Malaysia.

ENTERTAINMENT AND CULTURE

Nightlife in Malaysia revolves around activities in restaurants, clubs and cultural organisations, and is supplemented by visits to cultural shows, concerts, the theatre and the cinema. For information about weekly cultural events, consult Tourism Malaysia, local newspapers and the following websites:

- Kulture: The Arts of Kuala Lumpur: **www.kulture.com.my**
- K.L. Homepage: **www.mnet.com.my/klonline/www/ klomain.htm**
- Malaysia Homepage: **www.mymalaysia.net.my/**

Restaurants

Even the most demanding gourmets will enjoy Kuala Lumpur's many fine restaurants serving Malay, Chinese, Indian, Thai, Japanese, Korean, European, fusion and a variety of other cuisine. To find recommended restaurants, check the newspapers, monthly tourist publications and the book *Malaysia's Best Restaurants*.

Photo courtesy of Mines Beach Resort and Wonderland

Time to Relax

Night Spots

In K.L there are several night clubs with international floor shows; many are in the first-class hotels. Most larger hotels have cocktail lounges and discotheques, or restaurants that offer dining and dancing to the music of local or foreign bands and vocalists. Many discotheques are open only to members and hotel guests, and some have strict dress codes. A popular haunt for classical music lovers is **No Black Tie** (No 27 Jalan Mesui, Off Jalan Nagasari, Bukit Bintang; 03-241-7073) which features live music to accompany food and drinks.

Cultural Shows

Cultural presentations and folk art festivals are hosted by international hotels and held at other venues such as the following:

- **Central Market** (Jalan Hang Kasturi; Tel: 03-2274-6542). Has events including traditional Malaysian martial arts, comedy performances and traditional Indian dancing.
- **Malaysian Tourist Information Centre (MATIC)** (Jalan Ampang; Tel: 03-264-3929). Holds traditional dance performances several times a week.
- **Neleyan Titiwangsa (Seafood Village)** (Taman Tasik Titiwangsa, Jalan Temerloh). Dance performances every evening except Wednesday.
- **Restauran Sri Melayu** (1 Jalan Conlay, Tel: 03-245-1833). Traditional shows and mock Malay weddings every evening.
- **Restauran Sri Putra** (Putra Plaza, Merdeka Square; Tel: 03-294-3411). Holds a buffet dinner and cultural show every evening.

Theatre, Concerts and Art Exhibits

The arts scene in K.L. is growing rapidly. Frequent performances are staged by local and foreign musicians, orchestras, ballet troupes and theatrical groups. The **Malaysian Philharmonic Orchestra** and visiting orchestras perform regularly at the **Dewan Filharmonik Petronas** (Petronas Twin Towers; Tel: 03-207-7088). Musical and theatrical performances are held at **National Theatre** (Jalan Tun Razak; Tel: 03-4025-1030), **Actors' Studio Theatre** (Lot 19 Plaza Putra, Dataran Merdeka, Jalan Raja; Tel: 03-294-5400), **Five Arts Centre** (27 Lorong Datuk Sulaiman 7, Taman Tun Dr Ismail; Tel: 03-715-48-58), the **Akademi Seni Kebangsaan** (139 Jalan Ampang; Tel: 03-264-9180), **Experimental Theatre** (Jalan Tun Ismail: Tel: 03–294-0271) and **Sutra Dance Theatre** (12 Persiaran Titiwangsa 3; Tel: 03-421-1092). Art exhibits are held at **Galerie Petronas** (Petronas Twin Towers; Tel: 03-207-7770; 1-800-88-2222) as well as at hotels and shopping malls.

Cinema

Cinemas regularly feature American, Hong Kong, Indian and Indonesian films and less frequently show Japanese, Australian, British and Malaysian films. Most films are sub-titled. Local daily newspapers list the screening times of feature films. Some films are screened for only a few days. To avoid the crowds, call ahead for tickets and pick them up in the afternoon prior to show time.

In addition to the public cinemas, the following organisations show films periodically: Alliance Française, British Council, Goethe Institut, Japanese Cultural Centre, Lincoln Cultural Centre in the U.S. Embassy and the Russian Cultural Centre. Regular screenings of international film classics are offered at the **Citron Filmnet Café** (Lorong Stoner, behind the Bombay Palace Restaurant; Tel: 03-241-5323; 241-9562; E-mail: filmnet@tm.net.my). Dinner is available at the café prior to screenings. Members can also rent videos and register for film appreciation courses. **Kelab Seni Filem Malaysia** screens international classics, and the **University of Malaya** has a yearly week-long international film festival. The cineplex at the **Mid Valley Megamall** (03-9368-3366) regularly shows international films and hosts periodic week-long film festivals from various countries including Iran and China.

Video Rentals

Video cassettes of foreign films can be rented (and purchased) in K.L.. Your friends will be able to tell you which shops carry the widest selections. Many films are subtitled in Malay and some are altered during censoring. The quality of the videos often leaves much to be desired; many are taped in theatres, so extraneous sounds often override the film soundtracks.

Television and Radio

K.L. is currently served by two Government-operated stations and two commercial stations that broadcast primarily in Malay, Mandarin, English and Tamil. Programming is about 60% local content and 40% foreign content (primarily from the U.S., Hong Kong, China and India). All channels must conform to strict Government guidelines concerning national security, national aspirations and Islam as the official religion. Some foreign programmes are dubbed in Malay, but most are subtitled. Daily **programme listings** for all channels can be found in the national newspapers. News in English is broadcast at 8:00 p.m. daily on TV2, 11:00 p.m. daily on NTV7, 11:00 p.m. and 12:00 a.m. daily on TV1 and 12:00 a.m. daily on TV3.

Astro, a cable subscription service, offers numerous television and radio channels. English-language stations include CNN International (news), Bloomberg (financial), CNBC (financial), Discovery (documentary), ESPN (sports), HBO (movies) and TNT (cartoons). For more information, call Astro at 1-800-827-333 or visit the website at www.astro.com.my.

Several FM and AM stations broadcast in K.L. **Radio 3 KL** and **Radio 4** broadcast in English, and **Radio 2 broadcasts music**. International programming in English is available through

265

the **Voice of America** (Website: www.voa.gov/)and the **British Broadcasting Corporation** (BBC) English World Service (Frequencies: SW-15.310MHz, 11.750MHz, 9.740MHz and 6.195MHz; Website: www.bbc.co.uk/worldservice).

Newspapers and Magazines

Four English language daily newspapers provide limited coverage of international news and extensive coverage of local news and sensational topics. *The New Straits Times* tends to take a pro-government stance and to avoid mention of the more sensational stories that are covered in depth by *The Star* and *The Sun*. The *Malay Mail* is the most sensational and leans towards coverage of human interest and entertainment items. All papers give lists of happenings in K.L. and other cities and all can be delivered to your home.

Foreign newspapers such as *Asian Wall Street Journal, International Herald Tribune, USA Today, Guardian, London Times, Financial Times, The Australian* and *Bangkok Post* as well as numerous international English-language business and special interest magazines can be subscribed to or purchased at newsstands and hotel bookshops. To subscribe to newspapers and magazines, contact the following:

- *Foreign magazines & newspapers:* Most can be ordered through Magazine Services Sdn Bhd (Tel: 60-3-7785-0489; Fax: 60-3-7784-0854).
- *Asian Wall Street Journal:* (Tel: 60-3-206-4061; Fax: 60-3-206-4132).
- *International Herald Tribune:* (Tel: 60-3-242-8418; Fax: 60-3-242-9418; E-mail: subshk@ihthk.com).

Books and Bookshops

British, Australian, American and Southeast Asian books on diverse subjects can be found in bookstores and hotel newsstands. If you cannot find the books you are looking for, you can order them from an Internet mail order book service such as **Amazon.com.**

Several bookshops have branches throughout the KL area. Among the largest are **Times, MPH, Popular** and **Kinokuniya**. For business books, also try the **Malaysian Institute of Management (MIM)** (227 Jalan Ampang, K.L), the **University Book Store** (United Overseas Bank Bldg., 2 Jalan Tengah, 46200 Petaling Jaya), and the **University of Malaya Co-op Bookstore** (Jalan Pantai Baru, K.L.). K.L.'s largest English-language bookstore is the **MPH Bookstore** branch in the Mid Valley Megamall (Tel: 03–9368-3818). The store features a café, CDs and cassette tapes, magazines, children's books, business and professional books, and large collections of books on self-help, health, hobby, sports, architecture, home repair, local interest, and computer and information technology. MPH will special order titles not in stock and will send them to your home.

Libraries

Books, newspapers, reference materials and films in various languages are available in libraries of cultural organisations, embassies and foreign schools. For a list of opening hours for libraries, consult *The Star* newspaper.

- **Arabic:** Arab Libya Cultural Centre
- **French:** Alliance Française and Canadian Education Centre
- **English:** Australian Information Library, British Council Centre, British High Commission, Canadian Education Centre, New Zealand Education Centre, U.S. Embassy Lincoln Resource Centre, K.L. International School and Children's Library/Play Centre Association

- **Malay:** Malaysian Culture Group, University of Malaya Pantai Valley (Tel: 03-757-5887) and National Library (Perpustakaan Negara) 232 Jalan Tun Razak (Tel: 03-292-3491/3144). Dewan Bahasa dan Pustaka has a collection of material on Malay language and culture. The Malaysian Industrial Development Authority maintains a library of business references. Children's Library/Play Centre Association has books for children.
- **German:** Goethe Institut and German School
- **Indonesian:** Indonesian Library
- **Japanese:** Japan Cultural Centre, Japanese School, Japanese Club, Japan Information Service

Photo courtesy of Kolej Tuanku Ja'afar

A Game of Golf

SPORTS

Sports generate much enthusiasm among many Malaysians and are a common topic of conversation. The country is represented internationally in most sporting events. Popular sports include golf, soccer (known as football), squash, cricket, rugby, tennis, badminton and field hockey. Cycle racing, motor racing, horse racing and amateur boxing are also gaining in popularity. Local sports such as kite-flying, giant top-spinning and *sepak takraw* (a rattan ball game) require great skill and are fascinating to watch.

Foreigners can become involved in sports in Malaysia quite easily, as language is no barrier. There are numerous sports and recreation clubs that welcome expatriate members; many allow corporate membership. The most popular clubs, however, may have long waiting lists or require payment of high fees.

In the Klang Valley, there are venues and associations for numerous sports including the following: abseiling (descending mountains by rope), aerobics, archery, athletics (track and field), badminton, backpacking, bamboo rafting, beach volleyball, bird watching, blowpipe, boating, bowling, camping, caving, cricket, cycling, fencing, field hockey, fishing, flying, football (soccer and street soccer), golf, gymnastics, go-karts, horseback riding, judo, kayaking, lawn bowling, life saving, motorcycling, mountain biking, mountain climbing, nature exploration, Outward Bound, orienteering, parachuting, rock climbing, rowing, running, sailing and yachting, scuba diving, softball, squash, sports for the handicapped, taekwondo, triathlon and waterskiing.

A few unexpected sports are also available. One is **ice skating**. There are rinks at Mines Resort and Sunway Pyramid. Another is **game hunting**. To apply for a licence, contact the Department of Wildlife and National Parks, Block K-19, Government Offices Complex, Jalan Duta, K.L. Still another is **flying**. To enquire about lessons, contact the Royal Selangor Flying Club (Old Airport Road, P.O. Box 11769, 50756 K.L.; Tel: 03-241-1934).

269

Photo courtesy of Mines Beach Resort and Wonderland

Lakeview

For lists of addresses and contact numbers for sports venues and associations, check the daily newspapers and refer to the following books: *Leisure Guide Malaysia*; *Selamat Datang: Kuala Lumpur from A to Z* (published by the American Association); and *Welcome to Kuala Lumpur* (published by the Association of British Women in Malaysia).

Physical Fitness and Spas

Below are just a few of the many spas and fitness centres in the Klang Valley that are popular among expatriates:

- **Phillip Wain Health and Beauty:** (The Weld, Level 3, 76 Jalan Raja Chulan, 50200 K.L.; Tel: 03-2163-2200; and Starhill Centre). Personalised exercise programmes, sauna, facials in a luxurious environment.

270

- **Mandarin Oriental Vitality Club**: (Mandarin Oriental Hotel at KLCC; Tel: 03-380-8888). Has a state-of-the-art gymnasium with personalised training and fitness assessments, an aerobic studio, swimming pool, jacuzzi, sauna, steam room, massage, beauty treatments, tennis courts and squash courts.
- **Renaissance/New World Hotel Sweat Club**: (3rd Fl., 128 Jalan Ampang, K.L.; Tel: 03-261-3323). Personalised exercise programmes; excellent work-out equipment; tennis and squash courts; aerobic and aquarobic dance; steam, sauna and jacuzzi; massage and facial grooming services.
- **Clark Hatch Fitness Centre:** (11th Fl., Crown Princess Hotel, City Square Centre, K.L.; Tel: 03-262-3379/264-9989). Excellent work-out equipment.
- **Fitness International:** (5th Fl., Park Royal Hotel, Jalan Sultan Ismail, K.L.; Tel: 03-242-5588).
- **Pan Pacific Recreation Club:** (Pan Pacific Hotel, Jalan Putra, K.L.; Tel: 03-442-5555).
- **Shangri-La Health Club:** (Shangri-La Hotel, 11 Jalan Sultan Ismail, K.L.; Tel: 03-232-2388).

Photo courtesy of Mines Beach Resort and Wonderland

A Relaxing Ride

LESSONS

Whether you wish to learn a new art or craft, or continue to develop a skill that you have already acquired, you may be able to take lessons in Malaysia. Lessons are available in a wide variety of activities including art, crafts, bridge, cooking, computers, curtain making, drama, dressmaking, flower arranging (*ikebana*), music and languages. For lists of organisations that offer these and other kinds of lessons, ask school officials, check the Telephone Directory Yellow Pages, watch for advertisements in *The Star* and the *New Straits Times*, and consult the books *Selamat Datang: Kuala Lumpur from A to Z* and *Welcome to Kuala Lumpur*.

LANGUAGE CLASSES

Lessons in several languages are available in K.L. Check the Telephone Directory Yellow Pages under the heading "Language Schools" and watch for advertisements in *The Star* and the *New Straits Times*. A few venues are listed below:

- **Alliance Française:** (15 Lorong Gurney, 54100 K.L.; Tel: 03-294-7880). French.
- **Applied Language Systems:** (Tel: 03-704-4915). Bahasa Malaysia for expatriates.
- **Berlitz:** (Unit No 50, G 01 Ground Floor, Wisma UOA Damansara, 50 Jalan Dungun, Damansara Heights, 50490 K.L.; Tel: 03-253-1619; Fax: 03-253-1477). Private instruction and classes in many languages.
- **British Council Language Centre:** (3rd & 4th Fl., Wisma Hangsan, Box 20, Jalan Hang Lekir, 50000 K.L.; Tel: 03-230-6304/5/7/9; Fax: 03-232-9448). Various courses in English language.
- **ELS International Language Centres:** (14A, Lorong Utara A, off Jalan Utara, 46200 P.J.; Tel: 03-758-8530; E-mail: info@els.po.my; Website: www.els.edu.my). Various courses in English language. Branch in K.L.

- **Goethe Institute:** (1 Jalan Langgak Golf, off Jalan Tun Razak; P.O. Box 178, 55000 K.L.; Tel: 03-242-2011). German, Business German and Technical German.
- **Inter-cultural Language School (ICLS):** (Lot D-3, Block D, 2nd Fl., KL Plaza; Tel: 03-244-2060; Fax: 03-244-1850). Japanese, English, Mandarin and Malay. Several branches.
- **International Islamic University Malaysia:** (Centre for Languages, Jalan Gombak, K.L.; Tel: 03-2056-4918). Arabic.
- **Japan Cultural Centre:** (Suite 30-01, Level 30, Menara Lion, Jalan Ampang, 50450 K.L.; Tel: 2161-2104). Intermediate and advanced classes in Japanese.
- **Language House:** (40 Jalan 19/3, 46300 P.J.; Tel: 03-755-0412; Fax: 03-757-4015). Bahasa Malaysia, English, Mandarin, Cantonese, Japanese, French, German, Spanish and Arabic.
- **Malaysian National Institute of Translation:** (Menara Pengkalen, 2nd Fl., 2 Jalan Cangkat Ceylon, 50200 K.L.; Tel: 03-4149-7210; Fax: 03-4149-7215). Courses in translation (French, Spanish, German, Japanese, Arabic and Mandarin) and translation services.
- **Mandarin Kids Language Centre:** (69-1, Jalan Bangkung, Bukit Bandaraya, 59100 K.L.; Tel/Fax: 03-253-0069). Mandarin lessons for children.
- **Russian Cultural Centre:** (205 Lorong Ampang 2, K.L.; Tel: 03-244-4001). Russian.
- **Universiti Kebangsaan Malaysia (UKM):** (Faculty of Languages, K.L.; Tel: 03-292-306). Intensive courses for the public in Thai, French, English, German, Japanese, Korean, Mandarin, Myanmar, Vietnamese and Bahasa Malaysia.
- **Universiti Malaya:** (Faculty of Languages and Linguistics, K.L.; Tel: 03-759-3002). Bahasa Malaysia, English, Mandarin, Cantonese, Tamil, Burmese, Tagalog, Thai, Vietnamese, Korean, Japanese, French, German, Italian, Spanish, Dutch, Portuguese, Russian, Arabic, Urdu and Persian (Farsi).

- **YMCA:** (95 Jalan Padang Belia, 50470 K.L.; Tel: 03-22274-1439; Fax: 03-2274-0559). Various languages (including Sign Language). Has a Japanese Language and Culture Club.

RELIGIOUS WORSHIP

Religious worship is an important aspect of life for many Malaysians. Many religious organisations are active in social welfare projects. While Islam is the official religion, members of other faiths are allowed to practise freely. K.L. and the Klang Valley have places of worship for followers of Islam, Buddhism, Hinduism, Christianity (of several denominations) and the Ba'hai faith. Members of other faiths sometimes gather in homes. For listings, consult the Yellow Pages of the Telephone Directory or ask your embassy.

SERVICE ORGANISATIONS

Many international organisations have chapters in K.L. Among them are **Apex, Hash House Harriers, Jaycees, Kiwanis Club, Lions Club, Lions Host Club, Oasis, Rotary Club** and **Toastmaster's International**. These and other service organisations are described below. For names and telephone numbers of the current Chairpersons, please contact your embassy or check the daily activities columns in the local newspapers.

- **American Association of Malaysia:** (15-A Jalan Wickham, near the Raintree Club, 55000 K.L.; Tel: 03-451-9625/9610; Website: www.americanassoc-malaysia.org.my /aam; E-mail: aam1776@po.jaring.my). (For a description, please see the following section.)
- **Jaycees:** An international organisation that provides service to the community and business skills training to its members. Non-racial, non-political, non-religious and open to all men aged 18 to 40. Women can join the Pearl Jaycees.

274

- **Kiwanis Club:** Brought to Malaysia in 1976; has 20 branches in the country.
- **Lions Club:** Largest service club in the world, with over 70 branches in Malaysia. Following the meaning of its Lions name (Liberty, Intelligence, Our Nations Serve), the club is active in community service projects. Membership is open to men. The affiliated Lioness Club admits women and the Leos Club admits youths.
- **Malaysian-American Commission on Educational Exchange (MACEE):** (8th Fl., Menara John Hancock, 6 Jalan Gelenggang, Damansara Heights; Tel: 03-253-8107). A bi-national commission that provides information and counselling to Malaysian students wishing to further their education in the United States.
- **Rotary Club:** (P.O. Box 581, 2 Jalan Ceylon, K.L.; Tel: 03-232-8893). A worldwide service organisation focusing on vocational, community and international service. Active in Malaysia since 1930. Membership is open to business and professional men. Wives of Rotarians can join the Inner Wheels Club; young adults aged 18 to 30 can join the Roteract Club.
- **Toastmasters Club:** Founded in the United States in 1924 for the purpose of teaching members effective techniques of leadership and public speaking. Open to men and women. Sponsors numerous activities and a Youth Leadership Programme.
- **YMCA:** (95 Jalan Padang Belia, 50470 K.L.; Tel: 03-2274-1439). Offers lodging, language classes and sports activities. Both men and women may become members.
- **YWCA:** (12 Jalan Hang Jebat, 50150 K.L.; Tel: 03-201-7753, 238-3225). Offers lodging and classes. Organises a Writers' Club, a Sing-Along group, a Wednesday Morning Club and a Summer Day Camp for Children.

- **YWCA Women's Development and Concerns Club:** (12 Jalan Pedang Belia, K.L.; Tel: 03-238-3225, 201-7753).

CULTURAL AND SOCIAL ORGANISATIONS

Numerous cultural and social organisations exist in K.L. A few are listed below. Others not listed below include the **International Women's Group, Netherlands Association, Scandinavian Society, Association of Pakistani Women, African Ladies Group** and **South African/Malaysian Group**. Check the following website for a longer list: **www.mol.com**.

- **Alliance Française:** (15 Lorong Gurney, 54100 K.L.; Tel: 03-292-5929). A non-profit cultural organisation with branches worldwide. Screens French films, offers instruction in French language for children and adults, loans French books, records and periodicals and sponsors a variety of cultural activities including concerts, stage shows and exhibitions. There is also an **Association Francais de Malaysia** (Tel: 03-294-2117).

- **American Association of Malaysia:** (15-A Jalan Wickham, near the Raintree Club, 55000 K.L.; Tel: 03-451-9625/9610). A social and service organisation open to foreigners of any nationality. Has a community centre, a pre-school playgroup and an active teen centre programme. Sponsors activities such as craft workshops, handicraft bazaars, family B-B-Q's, country-western dances, bridge and mahjong lessons, local and overseas tours, aerobic exercise classes and video showings of American sports events. Also sponsors a helpful *Amah Workshop* and a worthwhile course for newcomers called *Living in KL*.

- **American Women's Association:** Contact the American Embassy, K.L. (Tel: 03-248-9011).

276

- **Association of British Women in Malaysia:** (c/o British High Commission, P. O. Box 11583, 50750 K.L.; Tel: 03-248-2122). A non-political and non-profit making social organisation open to women who are citizens of the United Kingdom and women who have connections to the United Kingdom by birth, marriage or descent. A major part of its effort is charitable in nature, benefiting the local community. Welcomes newcomers to a wide range of regular and special activities.
- **British Council:** (Jalan Bukit Aman, K.L.; Tel: 03-298-7555 and 66 Jalan SS15/4 47500 Subang Jaya, Selangor; Tel: 03-732-4885/6/7). A global network, established in 1934 to promote understanding between Britain and other nations through cultural, educational and technical cooperation. Centres have libraries, offer educational counselling for Malaysians wishing to study in the U.K., and provide instruction in the English language and training courses leading to the internationally recognised RSA/Cambridge Certificate in TEFLA (Teaching English as a Foreign Language to Adults).
- **Canadian Women's Association:** (c/o Canadian High Commission, P.O. Box 10990, 50732 K.L.; Tel: 03-2161-2000). A social and charitable organisation open to women who are citizens of Canada, wives of Canadian citizens and wives of foreign employees of Canadian firms. There is also a **Canadian Association** (Tel: 03-254-3270).
- **Deutsche Women in Kuala Lumpur–Kuala Lumpur Post:** (c/o German Embassy; Tel: 03-242-9666). The purpose of the group is to provide an opportunity for the German community to meet and to obtain information about Malaysia. Organises the Kuala Lumpur Post, a monthly gathering of German-speaking people in K.L., and publishes a newsletter containing cultural events, addresses for garage sales and other news.

- **Goethe Institut (German Cultural Centre):** (1 Jalan Langgak Golf, off Jalan Tun Razak, P.O. Box 1, 55000 K.L.; Tel: 03-242-2011). Part of a worldwide German cultural organisation. Screens German films, offers German language lessons and maintains a library of German books and records.
- **International Cultural Society:** (P.O. Box 2257, K.L.). A public organisation established for the purpose of studying various cultures of the world. Foreign members are welcome.
- **International Women's Association of K.L.:** Meets periodically and welcomes women of all cultures. Please contact your embassy for the name and telephone number of a current Chairperson.
- **Japan Club of Kuala Lumpur:** (258 Jalan Ampang, 50450 K.L.; Tel. 03-2274-2274). Supports Japanese residents of Malaysia by providing social and educational activities, and by building friendship between Japanese residents in Malaysia and their Malaysian hosts. Two unaffiliated groups with many Japanese members are the **Malaysian Japanese Association**, an organisation for Japanese who are married to Malaysians, and **Majaka**, an informal support group of Japanese women who are married to Malaysian men. The Japan Club may be able to provide the name and telephone number of the current Chairpersons of these groups.
- **Japan Cultural Centre:** (Suite 30-01, Level 30, Menara Lion, 105 Jalan Ampang; Tel: 03-2161-2104). Promotes cultural exchange through the performing arts, education and sports between Japan and other countries. Sponsors performances of Japanese cultural troupes, offers intermediate and advanced classes in Japanese, screens Japanese films, maintains a library.
- **Malaysian American Society:** (P.O. Box 789, K.L.; Tel: 03-451-9625 for information). A private non-profit society for the promotion of cultural exchange between Malaysia and America.

- **Malaysian Australian New Zealand Association (MANZA):** (P.O. Box 10873, 50728 K.L.; Tel: 03-238-1754, 232-8766). A social and charitable organisation open to Malaysian citizens and to people who have ties to Australia or New Zealand by birth, marriage, education, domicile or military service. Objectives are to serve as a channel for cultural exchange and to raise funds for local charities.
- **Malaysian Culture Group:** (c/o American Association; Tel: 03-451-9625). Has a multi-cultural membership interested in Malaysian and Southeast Asian art, culture, history and religion. Holds lectures, sponsors excursions, coordinates a study group and maintains a library.
- **Scandinavian Society Malaysia (SSM):** (171 Angkasaraya Building, 123 Jalan Ampang, 50450 K.L.; Tel: 03-252-1471; Fax: 03-252-3196). Supports the Scandinavian community and new Scandinavian expatriates by organizing activities. Anyone interested in keeping in touch with the Scandinavian community is welcomed to join.
- **Russian Cultural Centre:** (205 Lorong Ampang 2, K.L.; Tel: 03-244-4001). Offers activities and courses in Russian. Has a selection of Russian books and magazines.

PROFESSIONAL ORGANISATIONS

If establishing intellectual contacts with Malaysians is your goal, consider contacting some of the country's universities and professional organisations. Please note that some organisations require prospective members to complete an application form and present written documentation of credentials (such as copies of university degrees). A few organisations are listed below. Check the following website for a longer list: **www.mol.com**.

- **Asia Foundation:** (197-7 Jalan Ampang, 50450 K.L.). A branch of an American-based foundation that assists local institutions involved in educational and socio-economic development.

- **Malaysian Historical Society:** (958 Jalan Hose, 50460 K.L.; Tel: 03-248-1469). Is involved in the restoration and preservation of historical sites.
- **Malaysian Institute of Management (MIM):** (227 Jalan Ampang, 50450 K.L.; Tel: 03-2614-5255, 2165-4671; Fax: 03-2164-3220; Homepage: www.mim.edu.my). Sponsors a variety of intensive business-related courses conducted by local and foreign professionals. Offers part-time MBA programmes in Finance, International Management, Human Resource Development and Information Technology in collaboration with foreign universities. Has a business bookstore and library.
- **Malaysian Institute of Training and Development (MITD):** (Level 3, Block D, Plaza Mont Kiara, Jalan Bukit Kiara, 50480 K.L.; Tel: 03-653-3880; E-mail: mitdkl@po.jaring.my). Runs a two-year distance learning master's degree programme called the Master of Science in Training and Human Resource Management offered by Leicester University in England.
- **Malaysian Nature Society:** (JKR 641, Jalan Kelantan, 50480, K.L.; P.O. Box 10750, 50724 K.L.; Tel: 03-287-9422; Website: www.exto/.com.my/mns). An independent society for the study of Malayan and regional natural history; maintains a small library; sponsors lectures, field trips and exhibits; and publishes nature books and the *Malayan Nature Journal*. Open to all interested.
- **Malaysian Society of Marine Sciences:** (P.O. Box 250, Jalan Sultan Post Office, Petaling Jaya, Selangor). Sponsors annual seminars and underwater photography competitions, and works toward the preservation of Malaysia's marine environment.

- **Malaysian Zoological Society:** (Zoo Negara Malaysia, Hulu Kelang, 68000 Ampang, Selangor; Tel: 03-408-3422/24/27/28). Oversees the 65-acre National Zoo and is active in the fields of conservation, research and education. The Zoo coordinates a volunteer programme, animal sponsorships, educational tours and special events open to the public.
- **National Language and Literary Agency:** (P.O. Box 803, K.L.; Tel: 03-248-1011). Dewan Bahasa dan Pustaka, as it is called in Malay, is dedicated to the development and enrichment of the Malay language.
- **Royal Asiatic Society, Malaysian Branch:** (130-M, Jalan Thamby Abdullah, off Jalan Sambanthan, 50470 K.L.; Tel: 03-274-8345). Dedicated to the study of Malaysia, Singapore and Brunei.
- **Women's Institute of Management:** (No 7, Jalan Abang Hj Openg, Taman Tun Dr Ismail, K.L.; Tel: 03–7725-0288; Fax: 03–7725-0286). Offers management courses, including a two-year Masters in International Management, through the University of East London.
- **World Wide Fund for Nature Malaysia:** (49 Jalan SS 23/15, Taman SEA, 47301 P.J; Mailing address: Locked Bag 911, Jalan Sultan Post Office, 46990 P.J.; Tel: 03-703-3771; Website: wwfmal.cjb.net). Engages in scientific research, wildlife and parks management and environmental education. Offers lectures, screens wildlife films and publishes a newsletter.

SPECIAL INTEREST GROUPS

There are many special interest groups in K.L. Some are organised by Malaysians and others by foreign cultural organisations. Watch the papers and contact cultural organisations for information about specific groups.

EDUCATION FOR ADULTS

Some expatriates choose to further their education while they are in Malaysia. In addition to taking courses offered by professional organisations, expatriates also take the **correspondence courses** in a variety of subjects that are offered by a number of American, British and Australian universities. Many courses are fully accredited, and it is possible to obtain British 'A' Levels by completing correspondence courses. If you are interested in taking such courses, you may find it easier to make arrangements before you leave for Malaysia. For listings of universities offering correspondence courses, check libraries and advertisements in newspapers such as the *International Herald Tribune.*

Some expatriates take the degree programmes or evening and weekend courses in business and other subjects that are offered by **representatives of foreign universities** in Malaysia. The standardised tests necessary for admission to universities in various countries are offered periodically in Malaysia. Embassies may be able to tell you the dates of the tests.

Finally, some expatriates arrange to audit courses or take external degree courses offered by **Malaysian colleges and universities**. As permission of the Registrar and the professor of the class generally are required, having a personal introduction and being able to speak some Malay will be of assistance.

TRAVELLING OUTSIDE OF K.L.

For assistance in planning excursions in Malaysia and beyond, you may wish to use the services of a travel agent. Many experienced agents have offices in K.L. They can often arrange flights and hotel stays at rates lower than you can obtain directly from airlines, hotels or Internet bookings.

Excursions in Malaysia

No matter what your pleasure, you will not have to travel far from K.L. to find a change of pace. The country's **beach and island resorts** offer fun in the sun and the sea. The beautiful **hill resorts** offer respite from the heat and humidity of the lowlands. And the **national parks** offer endless opportunities for adventure and exploration of nature. For more information, speak with your travel agent and request the following Tourism Malaysia publications: *Malaysia Islands and Beaches, Malaysia Underwater Havens, Malaysia Hill Resorts, Malaysia National Parks* and *Malaysia Fascinating Adventures.*

Tourism Malaysia, in conjunction with Malaysia Airlines and the private sector, has designed a Domestic Tour Package Programme featuring numerous holiday tour packages to various spots in Malaysia. These tour packages, most of which include airfare and hotel, offer an economical way to travel in comfort. Any office of Tourism Malaysia or MAS can provide details.

Various community and special interest groups also arrange tours to places of interest in Malaysia and surrounding countries. In many cases, membership in the group is not a prerequisite for participation in the tours.

Finally, numerous tour operators (listed in the Telephone Directory Yellow Pages under "Travel Bureaus" offer domestic as well as international tours. One recommended agent, **Heritage Travel and Tours** (03-2273-3973), has a large expatriate clientele and specialises in designing individual and group itineraries to sites on and off the beaten track in Malaysia and beyond.

Excursions beyond Malaysia

Popular destinations for short "get-aways" and longer vacations are Singapore, Thailand (Bangkok, Phuket, Koh Samui, Chiangmai), Indonesia (Bali), Vietnam, Maldives, Hong Kong, Korea, India and China. Reasonably priced tours are available to all of these destinations.

HOLIDAYS IN SELANGOR

Malaysia's multi-cultural population celebrates numerous festivals and observes many religious occasions. Below is a list of holidays celebrated in the State of Selangor. Twelve of them (all but Thaipusam) are national holidays. No dates are mentioned for those that fall on different days each year. For more information, please contact Tourism Malaysia (Tel: 03- 441-1295).

- *Hari Kebangsaan (National Day)*–(31 August) Malaysia's Independence Day, celebrated throughout the country with colourful parades and processions.
- *Workers' Day (Labour Day)*–A national holiday celebrated on 1 May.
- *Yang di-Pertuan's Birthday (King's Birthday)*–A national holiday celebrated on 3 June.
- *Hari Raya Puasa*–(*Hari Raya Aidilfitri*) Muslims mark the end of the fasting month of Ramadhan with prayers and open houses.
- *Hari Raya Haji*–(*Hari Raya Aidilada*) Muslims mark the end of the Haj, or pilgrimage to Mecca, with prayer and feasting. This is an especially important day for Muslims who have made the Haj.
- *Awal Muharram*–Muslims commemorate the *Hegira*, Prophet Muhammad's migration from Mecca to Medina in 622 A.D. (the year from which the Islamic calendar begins), with religious lectures and discussions. This is the first day of the Muslim New Year.
- *Prophet Muhammad's Birthday*–Muslims celebrate the birthday of the Prophet Muhammad with prayers and processions.

- *Chinese New Year*–Chinese celebrate their most important holiday with family gatherings, religious ceremonies, ancestral observances and the giving of *ang pow* (red packets containing money). A one-day holiday in Kelantan and Terengganu; a two-day holiday in other states.
- *Wesak Day*–Buddhists commemorate the birthday of Lord Buddha with the liberation of captive birds at Buddhist temples and street processions of decorated floats and statues of Buddha. A public holiday in all states except Sabah and the Federal Territory of Labuan.
- *Deepavali*–In this "Festival of Lights", Hindus commemorate the slaying of the tyrannical King Naragesuaran by Lord Krishna and symbolises the victory of light over darkness. Celebrated in all states except Sabah, Sarawak and Labuan Federal Territory.
- *Thaipusam*–Hindus mark the victory of Lord Subramaniam over demons with a day of penance and thanksgiving. A public holiday in Johor, Negeri Sembilan, Perak, Penang and Selangor, the states with the largest Indian populations.
- *Christmas Day*–(25 December) Christians celebrate the day when Christ was born with carolling, church services and gatherings with family and friends. Non-Christians often join the festivities.
- *New Year's Day*–(1 January)–Christians celebrate the new year with parties on New Year's Eve and New Year's Day. A holiday except in the states of Johor, Kedah, Kelantan, Perlis and Terengganu.

CONVERSATIONAL PHRASES IN MALAY

How are you? (*What news?*)	*Apa khabar?*
All is well. (*The news is good.*)	*Khabar baik.*
Peace be with you. (*Muslim greeting*)	*As-salaamu-alaikum.*
And with you also be peace. (*Response*)	*Wa'alaikum u'salaam.*
Have you eaten yet? (*Common greeting*)	*Sudah makan?*
Not yet. (*Common response*)	*Belum*
Yes, already. (*Common response*)	*Ya, sudah*
Welcome	*Selamat datang*
Good morning	*Selamat pagi*
Good "mid-day" (*12 p.m.-2 p.m.*)	*Selamat tenga hari*
Good afternoon (*2 p.m.-5 p.m.*)	*Selamat petang*
Good evening/night (*after 5 p.m.*)	*Selamat malam*
Goodbye (*said to person leaving*)	*Selamat jalan* (Safe trip)
Goodbye (*said to person staying*)	*Selamat tinggal* (Safe life)
See you later	*Jumpa lagi*
Please (*offering something*)	*Silakan*
Please (*asking a favour*)	*Tolong*
Thank you	*Terima kasih*
Thank you very much	*Terima kasih banyak*
You're welcome	*Sama sama*
Please forgive me/Excuse me	*Ma'afkan saya*
It doesn't matter	*Tidak apa*
Please come in	*Silakan masuk*
Yes/No	*Ya/Betul–Tidak/Bukan*
Can/Cannot	*Boleh/Tidak boleh*
Good! Fine! Great!	*Bagus! Hebat!*
Really?	*Ya, ke? Betulkah?*
Wow!/Goodness!	*Amboi!/Alamak!*
Be careful!/Watch out!	*Hati-hati!/Awas!*

COMMON ACRONYMS AND ABBREVIATIONS

air-con	air conditioning
DAP	Democratic Action Party
J.B.	Johor Bahru, Johor
IC	Identity Card
K.B.	Kota Bharu, Kelantan
K.K.	Kota Kinabalu, Sabah and Kuala Kangsar, Perak
K.L.	Kuala Lumpur
KLCC	Suria Kuala Lumpur City Centre at Petronas Twin Towers
KLIA	Kuala Lumpur International Airport in Sepang
KLSE	Kuala Lumpur Stock Exchange
KTM	Keretapi Tanah Melayu, the Malaysian Railway System and station in K.L.
LRT	Light Rail Transit system in K.L.
MAS	Malaysia Airlines
MC	Medical Certificate/ medical leave ("I went on MC.")
MCA	Malaysian Chinese Association
MIC	Malaysian Indian Congress
MIDA	Malaysian Industrial Development Authority
MSC	Multimedia Super Corridor
MP	Member of Parliament
NST	New Straits Times (newspaper)
PAS	Parti Islam Sa Malaysia (an opposition party)
Petronas	Petroleum Nasional Berhad (National Oil Company)
P.D.	Port Dickson in the State of Negeri Sembilan
P.J.	Petaling Jaya, Selangor
the PM	the Prime Minister
RM	Ringgit Malaysia or Malaysian ringgit (local currency)
UMNO	United Malays National Organisation

EMERGENCY NUMBERS

Red Crescent Ambulance   Tel: 03-201-0280
St. Johns Ambulance   Tel: 03-985-2008
Emergency Assistance
(Police & Ambulance)   Tel: 999
Fire Brigade   Tel: 994
Tourist Police   Tel: 03-249-6593

TELEPHONE SERVICE NUMBERS

007   International Direct Dial (followed by country code and telephone number)
108   Telephonist-assisted International Calls
100   Telephone, Datel and Telefax Malfunctions
101   Trunk Call (Long Distance) Operator
102   Trunk Call Enquiries and Service (including Home Country Direct Enquiries)
103   Directory Enquiries (Telephone Numbers)
104   Telegrams and Cables
1051   Time Announcement
1052   Weather Forecast for K.L. and Petaling Jaya
1060   Enquiries about changes in phone numbers
1061   Calls to Ships
1062   For Telecard Holders
1091   Telecaj (to charge calls to a third number)

MAKING TELEPHONE CALLS

- **To call Malaysia from overseas** (except from Singapore), dial the country code (60) followed by the one- or two-digit city code (03 in Kuala Lumpur) and the telephone number. There is no need to dial a "0" prior to the city code when calling Malaysia from overseas.

- **To call a mobile phone number in Malaysia from overseas** (except from Singapore), dial the country code (60) followed by the mobile phone number, but omit the "0" at the beginning of the mobile phone number.
- **To call Singapore,** dial "02" from within Malaysia and "65" from outside of Malaysia, plus the business or residence number.
- **To call other areas of Malaysia from K.L,** dial the city code listed below plus the business or residence number.
- **To make local calls within K.L. or within other cities,** dial the telephone number only; there is no need to dial the city code.

CITY CODE NUMBERS

03   Kuala Lumpur, Shah Alam, Petaling Jaya, Damansara, Rawang, Port Klang, Klang, Kajang

04   Penang, Butterworth, Kangar, Alor Setar

05   Ipoh, Taiping, Cameron Highlands

06   Melaka (Malacca), Seremban, Muar, Port Dickson

07   Johor Bahru, Batu Pahat, Kluang, Mersing

09   Kuantan, Kuala Terengganu, Kota Bharu, Kerteh

082   Kuching (Sarawak)

085   Miri (Sarawak)

086   Bintulu (Sarawak)

087   Labuan (Federal Territory, off the coast of Sabah)

088   Kota Kinabalu (Sabah)

089   Sandakan (Sabah)

02   Singapore (when dialling from Malaysia)

USEFUL WEBSITES
- **BBC World Service:** www.bbc.co.uk/worldservice
- **Bank Negara:** www.bnm.gov.my/
- **Books:** www.amazon.com
- **Cable Television:** www.astro.com.my
- **Groceries:** www.theglobalgrocer.com
- **Immigration:** www.imi.gov.my
- **Internet Service Providers:** www.jaring.my
  www.tm.net.my
- **K.L. Homepage:** www.mnet.com.my/klonline/www/
  klomain.htm
- **Kulture–The Arts of Kuala Lumpur:** www.kulture.com.my
- **Malaysia Homepage:** www.mymalaysia.net.my/
- **Malaysia Airlines:** www.malaysia-airlines.com.my/gst
- **MIDA:** www.mida.gov.my
- **Real Estate:** www.propertyzoom.com/pro_aspsearch.asp
- **Search Engines:**
  www.catcha.com
  www.jaring.my
  www.MalaysiaFocus.com
  www.malaysian-infoweb.com
  www.mol.com.my
  www.myweb.com.my
- **Telekom:** www.telekom.com.my/telecard

USEFUL RESOURCES FOR NEWCOMERS

American Association of Malaysia. **Selamat Datang: Kuala Lumpur from A to Z**. Kuala Lumpur: American Association of Malaysia, 2000. (Tel: 03-451-9610/9625).

American Association of Malaysia. **Selamat Datang: Welcome to Kuala Lumpur**. Kuala Lumpur: American Association of Malaysia, 2000. (Tel: 03-451-9610/9625).

Association of British Women in Malaysia. **Welcome to Kuala Lumpur**. Kuala Lumpur: British Women's Association of Malaysia, 2000. (Tel: 03-248-2122).

Automobile Association of Malaysia (AAM). **Malaysia Motoring Guide**. Kuala Lumpur: Tourism Publications Corporation, updated periodically.

Leisure Guide Malaysia. Kuala Lumpur: Leisure Guide Publishing, updated periodically.

Malaysia Tatler. **Malaysia's Best Restaurants**. Kuala Lumpur: Malaysia Tatler, updated yearly.

Passport to Kuala Lumpur. Kuala Lumpur: Kuala Lumpur Tourist Association, 2000.

Rowthorn, Chris, et al. **Malaysia, Singapore and Brunei**. Hawthorn, Victoria, Australia; Oakland, California, USA: Lonely Planet Publications, updated periodically.

The Expat (Magazine). Kuala Lumpur: Borneo Vision Sdn Bhd, published monthly. (Tel: 03-284 9539; Fax: 03-284-9692.)

The Finder Malaysia (Magazine). Kuala Lumpur: ACP, published monthly. (Tel: 03-7725-9998; Fax: 03-7725-4070)

Vision KL (Magazine). Kuala Lumpur: AsiaReach Media Sdn. Bhd, published monthly. (Tel: 03-284 2788; Fax: 03- 284-5788; Website: www.visionkl.com)

Visitors' Guide to Malaysia. Kuala Lumpur: Tourism Publications Corporation, updated yearly.

CULTURE, SOCIETY AND LANGUAGE

Abdullah Ali. **Malaysian Protocol and Correct Forms of Address.** Singapore: Times Books International, 1986.

Abdullah S. Hadi. **Everyday Stories for You and Me.** Kuala Lumpur: Malaysian Institute of Management, 1999.

Bloomfield, Frena. **The Book of Chinese Beliefs.** London: Arrow Books, 1983.

Hunan, Heidi. **Culture Shock! Malaysia.** Singapore: Times Books International, 1991.

Lee, Kam Hing and Tan, Chee-Beng, eds. **The Chinese in Malaysia.** Kuala Lumpur: Oxford University Press, 2000.

Lee, Su Kim. **Malaysian Flavours.** Subang Jaya, Selangor, Malaysia: Pelanduk Publishers, 1996.

Lee Su Kim. **Manglish: Malaysian English at its Wackiest!** Kuala Lumpur: Times International Books, 1998.

Mohamad Taib Osman, ed. **Malaysian World View.** Singapore: Institute of Southeast Asian Studies, 1985.

Noor, Datin Aini Syed. **Malaysian Customs and Etiquette.** Singapore: Times Books International, 1991.

Rashid, Rehman. **A Malaysian Journey.** Kuala Lumpur: Rehman Rashid, 1993.

Raslan, Karim. **Ceritalah: Malaysia in Transition.** Singapore: Times Books International, 1996.

Tan, Thomas Tsu-wee. **Your Chinese Roots.** Singapore: Times Books International, 1986.

Tong, Cheu Hock. **Chinese Beliefs and Practices in Southeast Asia.** Subang Jaya, Selangor, Malaysia: Pelanduk Publishers, 1993.

Traditional Malaysian Cuisine. Kuala Lumpur: Berita Publishing, 1983.

HISTORY AND POLITICS

Baker, Jim. **Crossroads: A Popular History of Malaysia and Singapore**. Singapore: Times Books International, 1999.

Gullick, J.M. **A History of Kuala Lumpur 1856-1939**. Kuala Lumpur: Malaysian Branch of the Royal Asiatic Society (MBRAS), 2000.

Kaur, Amarjit and Metcalfe, Ian, eds. **The Shaping of Malaysia.** London: Macmillan Press; New York: St. Martins Press, 1999.

Mahathir Mohamad, Dr. **The Malay Dilemma**. Singapore: Federal Publications Ltd., 1970.

BUSINESS AND MANAGEMENT

Abdullah, Asma, ed. **Understanding the Malaysian Workforce: Guidelines for Managers.** Kuala Lumpur: Malaysian Institute of Management, 1992.

Abdullah, Asma. **Going Glocal: Cultural Dimensions in Malaysian Management.** Kuala Lumpur: Malaysian Institute of Management, 2000 (second edition).

Aminuddin, Maimunah. **Malaysian Industrial Relations and Employment Law.** Kuala Lumpur: McGraw-Hill, 1999.

Goh, Chen Chuan. **How to Set Up and Manage a Business in Malaysia.** Kuala Lumpur: Leeds Publications, 1999.

Goh, Chen Chuan. **Step-by-Step Guide to Management and Company Formation in Malaysia**. Kuala Lumpur: Leeds Publications, 1999.

Gomez, Edmund Terence and K.S. Jomo. **Malaysia's Political Economy: Politics, Patronage and Profits**. Cambridge, UK: Cambridge University Press, 1999.

Kandasamy, Maheswari. **Malaysian Management Cases**. Subang Jaya, Selangor, Malaysia: Pelanduk Publishers, 1999.

Malaysian Institute of Management. **Management in Malaysia**. Kuala Lumpur: Malaysian Institute of Management, 1999.

Malaysian Institute of Management. **Voice of Management: The Malaysian Challenge.** Kuala Lumpur: Malaysian Institute of Management, 2000.

Mendoza, Gaby. **Management The Asian Way.** Kuala Lumpur: Asian Institute of Management, 1991.

Pang, Johnson. **Banking and Finance in Malaysia.** Shah Alam, Selangor, Malaysia: Times/Federal Publications, 1995.

Tan, Jing Hee and You Poh Seng with Emily Ding, eds. **Developing Managers in Asia.** Singapore: Addison-Wesley, 1986.

Yong, Alex K.B. Malaysian Human Resources Management. **Kuala Lumpur: Malaysian Institute of Management, 1996.**

THE AUTHOR

Lynn Witham is an intercultural business consultant and trainer, and is President of Witham & Associates, a group of intercultural specialists who provide services to multinational companies and other organisations working across international borders. She and her Associates work with clients on intercultural issues related to global teamwork, technology transfer and OJT, human resources management and development, adaptation of training programmes for delivery abroad, and selection, preparation and support of expatriates.

Active in the field of intercultural communication for 25 years, Lynn Witham has worked in Asia, Europe, the Middle East and North America, and speaks several languages including Malay/Indonesian, Farsi, Italian, French and Spanish.

In 1985, she began working in Malaysia, and subsequently wrote *Malaysia–A Foreigners' Guide*, a handbook for expatriates living in Malaysia. She continues to travel to Malaysia frequently to work with clients and visit friends. For her, being in Malaysia feels in many ways like *"balik kampung"* (going back home).

Her e-mail address is: WithamAssociates@aol.com.

INDEX